THE ONLINE STUDENT

MAKING THE GRADE ON THE INTERNET

D1508982

THE ONLINE STUDENT
MAKING THE GRADE ON THE INTERNET

RANDY REDDICK
Texas Tech University

ELLIOT KING
Loyola College

HARCOURT BRACE COLLEGE PUBLISHERS

Fort Worth Philadelphia San Diego New York Orlando Austin San Antonio
Toronto Montreal London Sydney Tokyo

Publisher	Ted Buchholz
Editor in Chief	Christopher P. Klein
Senior Acquisitions Editor	Stephen T. Jordan
Senior Project Editor	Steve Welch
Production Manager	Serena Manning
Art Director	Melinda Welch

ISBN: 0-15-503189-9

Copyright © 1996 Harcourt Brace & Company

All rights reserved. No part of this publication may be reproduced or transmitted in any form or by any means, electronic or mechanical, including photocopy, recording or any information storage and retrieval system, without permission in writing from the publisher.

Requests for permission to make copies of any part of the work should be mailed to: Permissions Department, Harcourt Brace & Company, 6277 Sea Harbor Drive, Orlando, Florida 32887-6777.

Address for Editorial Correspondence: Harcourt Brace College Publishers, 301 Commerce Street, Suite 3700, Fort Worth, TX 76102.

Address for Orders: Harcourt Brace & Company, 6277 Sea Harbor Drive, Orlando, FL 32887-6777. 1-800-782-4479, or 1-800-433-0001 (in Florida).

Printed in the United States of America
6 7 8 9 0 1 2 3 4   066   9 8 7 6 5 4 3 2

Preface

In the mid-nineteenth century, John Henry Cardinal Newman envisioned a university as a place of the world, where the masters of human thought would gather with students to study, to learn, to explore, and to understand the world. Knowledge would be pursued for its own sake.

Newman held a profound, romantic vision of the university and one that still informs much of higher education, particularly at the undergraduate level. Colleges and universities reflect the coming together of teachers and students in the pursuit and sharing of knowledge.

Gathering together is at the center of the idea of the university—teachers and learners from many disciplines interacting in one place. With the emergence of the Internet, however, the "gathering together" of teachers and learners is no longer bound by space or time. The Internet as an international networking of computer networks allows students and teachers around the world to communicate, to share information, to pursue knowledge in ways that were not possible before—to come together in cyberspace.

The Online Student is intended to facilitate that process for both students and their professors. It systematically explores new possibilities for study, for learning, for exploration, and for understanding enabled by this new channel of communication called the Internet. Aimed primarily at students and their faculty in the first two years of their higher education, its goal is to allow students and professors to expand their reach, to find the resources they need to enhance their classroom experience wherever those resources may be located around the world.

The Online Student carefully explains the different applications available via the Internet, from simple e-mail to Multi User Dungeons. It describes the practical uses of those applications in higher education. And it catalogs sources of information of potential interest to students and professors across the academic disciplines from the fine arts to the sciences.

Nearly jargon-free, *The Online Student* is for faculty, students and other learners from all academic backgrounds pursuing the full range of academic interests. It is specifically tailored to the needs of people who access the Internet through their campuses. Our desire is to ensure that everybody on campus can take advantage of this dynamic new resource to help them meet their goals.

Like the Internet itself, this book is still a work in progress. Links to many of the sources listed in the final five chapters can be found at the Web site http://gordonpub.loyola.edu/olstudent/. That site will provide an easy vehicle for people who wish to "surf" these resources. We will add additional links as we identify more valuable resources.

We feel deep gratitude to many people. First, we want to thank our families—our wives Nancy and Anita; and our children Laura, Ben,

Roxanne, Jennifer, Heather, and Jacob; and Aliza and Marcie. This book represents a lot of late nights and lost weekends and we thank you for your love, patience and support.

We would also like to acknowledge Terry McCoy Jr., Jack Martin and Calvin Carr of Gordon Publications, who have encouraged and supported King's exploration of the Internet. It was in his role as editor of *Scientific Computing & Automation Magazine* that King began extensively using the Internet to explore the resources available to scientists.

Loyola College in Maryland provided Internet access and other resources. The links to this book will be posted on the Web server of The Center for the Advanced Study of Online Communication, a research center at Loyola under King's direction.

At Texas Tech University, faculty and administration of the School of Mass Communications provided encouragement for this project. Special thanks to Roger Saathoff, Jerry Hudson, John Fryman, Hershel Womack, and Liz Watts for their interest, encouragement and helpful questions.

Many students at colleges and universities throughout the United States helped to create *The Online Student*. They agreed to have their own stories told and their names used. Special thanks are due to students at Loyola College in Baltimore and Texas Tech University in Lubbock.

While many were involved, some deserve special recognition: Brenna McBride, Maureen Keller, Dominick Russo, Krista DiConstanza, Monica Munoz-Tiumalu, Dominic Cortez, and Sandra Pulley. These students freely gave of their time to test material in this book and to teach it to other students. They helped to find other students on the Net who had informative network stories to tell (not all were used), and they helped to locate places in cyberspace that would be instructive or entertaining for other students.

At Harcourt Brace, Stephen T. Jordan has been both a patient and encouraging editor on the one hand and a forceful taskmaster when necessary, on the other. Steve Welch, Serena Manning and Melinda Welch have continued to work miracles in the production end of things with this book.

Finally, we want to thank the thousands of people who have taken the time to create e-mail discussion lists, build Web sites, and in other ways provide the technology and content that has made the Internet revolution in higher education possible. In a few instances we have named such individuals, but by-and-large they remain anonymous, selfless contributers.

Randy Reddick   Texas Tech University (r.reddick@ttu.edu)

Elliot King   Loyola College, Baltimore (king@loyola.edu)

Contents

Chapter 3   Electronic mail   33

Chapter 4   Surfing the World Wide Web   53

Chapter 7   Sharing through Usenet   125

Chapter 8   MUDs, IRC, other connections   145

Chapter 12   The social sciences grade

Chapter 13   Making the business grade

Chapter 14   Making the sciences grade

THE ONLINE STUDENT
MAKING THE GRADE ON THE INTERNET

Chapter 1

Introduction: Students online

The graduate student was baffled. Conducting research into the commercial aspects of early journalism, he constantly came across the term *square*. He had no idea what the term meant so he asked his faculty advisor. She didn't know either, so she queried an online discussion list for journalism historians. Within hours the term had been defined by several experts.

When Leslie Hunovice's daughter left for college, he knew that he would miss her terribly. They had always been very close, talking every night about the events of the day. Loath to lose the steady interaction, he signed up for CompuServe and soon was exchanging electronic mail messages with his daughter daily. At night they would talk on the telephone as well. The two drew even closer than they had been before.

The syllabus for Dr. Tim Allen's Geology 100 class at Keene State College in Keene, New Hampshire, runs six pages long. It is illustrated with a picture of a globe and a geologic time line. If students misplace their syllabus, however, Allen does not replace it. Instead, they can download another one from Allen's pages on the World Wide Web. He also requires his students to get e-mail accounts so that he can send them messages directly about arrangements for field trips and other issues.

A professor based at a school on the East Coast teaches summer school every year on the West Coast. But his research does not suffer. Every day he uses the computer network at the West Coast school to log onto his computer account in the East. Although he is 3,000 miles away, it as if he is working in his regular office.

Rutgers University's Barbara Straus Reed had a student interested in computer-mediated communication and she wanted a bibliography of relevant sources of information. A colleague of hers was able to retrieve a file stored on a computer in Australia with more than 270 books, articles and papers on the subject.

Heather Finlayson was a 24-year-old graduate student in Ontario, Canada, when she encountered a man who called himself Blade in cyberspace. They struck up a real-time conversation online. Before long she took a trip to the United States to meet this person who had intrigued her so much. Not long afterward, she knew she was in love.

What do these stories have in common? The Internet. The prototype of what is being called the Information Superhighway, the Internet is a dynamic new medium made up of the internetworking of computers around the globe. Through the Internet people can communicate and exchange information with colleagues, teachers, friends, relatives and strangers across campus, across states, across oceans, and across the world.

Because of the Internet's roots in research and education, almost all universities and colleges in the United States and in many other parts of the world are connected to the Internet. Consequently, the Internet is providing an entirely new dimension to the academic experience in every academic discipline and in every aspect of campus life. Students and teachers can interact more intensely, professors and students can work with experts, and information once reserved for specialists can now be used by first-year students in introductory courses.

The mission of this book

This book is about empowerment:

- Empowerment of students to learn, to be independent, and to slip the constraints imposed by the conditions at their particular college or university.
- Empowerment of professors to ask more of their students, to interact with both students and colleagues in new and dynamic ways, to circulate their research and insights in new ways, and to expand the scope of their activities.

The mission of this book is to help students and teachers work better, to engage in new and novel learning experiences and relationships, to draw the world to the campus, and to project the campus into the world.

And the mission of this book is to help students and teachers have fun exploring their new possibilities. Yes, the Internet and Internet resources are useful. Yes, they can help you locate and retrieve information to which you would otherwise have no access. Yes, they can be used to communicate with people with whom you normally would not interact. But most importantly, the Internet, as trite as it might sound, makes learning and teaching more fun.

It is fun for art history students to peruse the paintings in museums from Paris to Melbourne. It is fun for political science students to debate with politicians and political operators from the two major and many minor political parties. It is fun for astronomy students to view images from the latest NASA satellite and ask questions of the scientists involved. And it is fun to interact with students around the world after hours.

In addition to being a tremendous resource, the Internet can also be fun for faculty. The Internet accelerates the pace of discovery. It can automate many of the most tedious aspects of research; it can put you in contact with new communities of scholars; and it will open new opportunities in every aspect of academic life. Just as important, the Internet enhances the teaching experience as students produce more comprehensive and more interesting work.

The virtual classroom and the world library

The communication tools available via the Internet can be directly applied to two of the central functions of all colleges and universities. First, using the Internet, students and teachers no longer have to be physically in the same space to interact. Nor do they necessarily have to meet at a specific time. Instead, students and teachers can easily work together no matter where they are and what their schedule.

At the same time students and teachers are no longer limited by the library on their own campuses for scholarly information, collections of data, and other research-related material. Through the Internet students and scholars have access to information stored on every continent. And increasingly sophisticated Internet tools have generally made it easy to locate and retrieve that information.

For whom this book is and is not written

You do not have to be a Macintosh maven, a Windows whiz or a Unix virtuoso to use this book. Nor do you have to be a computer science student, computer guru, or have any interest in computer programming at all. You do not have to be a graduate student or technical genius.

This book is for the entire academic community, from first-semester freshmen to graduate students to professors emeriti, from music majors to medieval scholars to molecular biologists. It will tell you in plain English how you can take advantage of the access your campus provides to the Internet to enrich your life on campus inside and outside the classroom.

Its particular focus, however, is on first- and second-year students across the disciplines and their teachers. Many first- and second-year students will have robust, low-cost Internet access for the first time. With guidance from their instructors, these students will be able to incorporate the benefits of the Internet into their entire academic experience.

Given its audience, the book rests on certain assumptions. In most cases, first- and second-year students—and students and professors in disciplines not typically associated with computing skills—are generally interested in their own fields of study. They are presumably not too interested in computing. So it is the aim of this book to make the Internet an easy tool for them to apply to their interests in the same way that they might now write research papers using a computer and word-processing software. The focus of the book is on applying the Internet to specific tasks.

Second, students need to accomplish specific tasks. This book has been written with the responsibilities of students and professors regarding research, teaching, and learning in mind. On the other hand, one of the strengths of the Internet is that it allows those activities to take place outside traditional settings. So *The Online Student* also takes into account the broader interests of students in college as well.

Third, this book is for students who access the Internet through their campuses. It does not describe alternative routes such as commercial database services like CompuServe and America Online, except in passing. Nor does it explore the offerings of independent Internet providers now available. Accessing the Internet through a campus network has its own set of advantages and disadvantages, which are fully explored.

Finally, although the book is not aimed at computer fanatics, it does assume that students are familiar with personal computers and use computers in some way, probably for word processing. It assumes you know how to turn a computer on and off, save files, and perform other elementary tasks.

What this book is and is not

Although this book describes how to make use of computer-based Internet tools to do better research and to enhance the classroom experience, this book is NOT a computer book. It is written in English, generally speaking, the academic variety of English, toned down a little.

There is no attempt in this book to be all-inclusive or encyclopedic. Instead, we have focused on a limited selection of network tools that are
  • Easily and commonly accessible through the Internet.
  • Either indispensable (like e-mail) or provide a high rate of
    return for the time invested in learning them.
We have thus intentionally avoided some network facilities altogether. And we have intentionally refrained from providing exhaustive discussions of those tools we do describe.

Instead, *The Online Student* teaches how to use online tools and how to get further help for each tool. This is especially important when we are describing a moving target like the Internet, which changes shape from week to week. Each tool is described in a setting that illustrates how the tool may be (or has been) used by students or professors.

As with tools of the non-computer variety, users become more proficient and skilled with frequent use. *The Online Student* describes the tools and provides electronic addresses of computer sites housing information or providing services of particular value to academics. It is hoped that you will test the tools and hone your skills by employing them at as many sites as you wish. To facilitate that process, the second section of the book contains an extensive list of electronic addresses for online resources. Those chapters are organized according to the major schools and disciplines associated with universities.

Because most campuses have complex computing infrastructures, *The Online Student* occasionally describes commands unique to VMS or Unix systems. But it generally assumes most readers will be accessing online resources from a personal computer of the Macintosh or DOS/Windows variety.

It has been the studied intent of this book to describe the online world as it is seen by people using the lowest common denominator in terms of equipment, software, and access. That means it describes ways to get connected to distant computers and talk to those computers through a program with a plain, text-based, command-line interface. However, software with graphical user interfaces is clearly coming to dominate the campus environment, at least at the user level. Consequently, the book also describes services and network tools (like the World Wide Web) that thrive on graphical user interfaces demanding more powerful personal computers, more sophisticated software, and special kinds of network connections.

The campus computing environment

Not long ago when students first arrived on campus they might have heard about the football team, fraternities or fantastic courses. Nobody bothered to talk much about the computer infrastructure. Administrators, advisors and faculty assumed that students who needed to use computers on campus would be introduced to them through specific classes. But most students, especially those not in the sciences, would have little need for campus computing. Their own personal computers would suffice, should they need computers at all.

The growth of the Internet has changed that scenario. The Internet has transformed the campus computer network into a general-purpose tool for all students and faculty in virtually every discipline.

Unfortunately, not every college and university has responded to this change in a timely fashion. Many of you will find that you will have to uncover the computing facilities on your campus on your own. It will be up to you to decide what you need, locate where it is, and determine what you have to do to get access to it.

Keep in mind that two factors govern the availability and the sophistication of computing facilities at every campus. On the one hand, colleges and universities realize they need up-to-date technology to attract students and faculty. On the other hand, most institutions of higher education work within serious budget constraints. So the investment in technology varies greatly from campus to campus. The facilities you have at your liberal arts college will not be the same as the resources your high school buddy who attends the state university will have. Fortunately, a lot of software for the Internet is provided free to educational institutions. If your school doesn't have something, you may still be able to get it for free.

Most campuses do have a wide variety of different types of computers, including mainframe or minicomputers, which dominated computing through the early 1980s; Unix workstations, which became popular in the mid-1980s and are generally less powerful than mini- and mainframe computers but more versatile than PCs; and personal computers, including Macintosh and DOS and Windows-based PCs, which are the kinds of computers most people use. Once you begin your exploration, you will find that you probably can arrange to use all three types of computing. Moreover, it is very likely that some of the tasks you need to perform will require one kind of computer, while other tasks are best performed elsewhere.

For example, most schools maintain electronic mail (e-mail) accounts for students on a minicomputer or a Unix workstation, which serve as host computers. (The term *host computer* will be explained later in this chapter.) To use these computers, which are shared by many people and often store confidential information (like e-mail), you will have to establish an account and receive a user name and a password. By setting up an account, you reserve storage space on a hard disk. The password means that not just anybody can access your information.

On the other hand, many schools now have large laboratories filled with personal computers that anybody can use. Many students use the computers in these laboratories for word processing, graphics, and other general computer applications. While you can store information on these computers, for the most part, and in most cases, the information will not be private. The next user will be able to look at your files.

To make the situation more confusing, during the first five years of the 1990s, colleges and universities have connected many of the different computers available on campus together into what is called a local area network. When computers are connected to a local area network, a user sitting at one computer can access information or applications residing on a different computer. Generally, a school will have several local area networks connected to each other in one campus-wide network.

And there is still one more twist. Many schools will allow what is called dial-in access to their computers or computer networks. That means that if you have a password and a PC with a modem, your computer can phone into a specific computer or network from your home. There are different types of dial-in access. Some only provide access to a single, central computer. Others provide access to several computers on campus. A third type allows for access to the Internet.

The Internet, which will be fully explained in the next chapter, is a network of networks at campuses, businesses, the government, and nonprofit organizations in countries on every continent. In the same way that the local area network in your school allows you to access information and applications software running on different computers on campus, the Internet allows you to access information and applications on computers around the world.

Understanding client-server computing

As local area networks developed, connecting more powerful computers with less powerful ones, a specific kind of computing evolved. This is called client-server computing and is the basis of many Internet applications. With client-server computing, one computer does not do everything that is needed to perform a given task. Instead, different computers on the network perform different parts of the task. In this way, the task can be completed more efficiently and computer resources used more economically.

Most client-server computing—particularly Internet applications—consists of a two-part operation. In the first part, you request a specific piece of information or a specific job to be completed. In part two, your request is fulfilled and the results are returned to you for display.

The software that makes the request or issues the instructions as to what is to be done is called the client. The software that fulfills the request and returns the results is called the server. To put it in more familiar terms, think about a client and an accountant. The client asks the accountant to prepare her income tax return. The accountant performs the work and returns the results.

With the Internet, you use the client software to make requests to a server. For example, a World Wide Web client, called a browser (Chapter 4), makes requests to a Web server for information. So for you to surf the Web, you need access to a Web client.

This client-server relationship is crucial to understanding the Internet and what happens among computers on the Internet. If you understand this client-server relationship and two other network concepts, you will be able to understand much of the workings of the Internet. You will understand why some things work on the network under one set of circumstances and not under others. When the unexpected occurs on the Net, you will have at your disposal the principles to explain the event. You will better understand whether the problem is with the client, which is under your control, or the server, which usually is not.

The network-host relationship

Beyond the client-server relationship, the other two critical concepts are those of the network host and the types of network connections. In simple terms, a computer is performing host duties when it controls computer terminals or other computers emulating terminals that are attached to it via a network.

As pointed out earlier in this chapter, in a university computing environment, students and faculty members typically apply for accounts with some sort of central computing facility. When you get the account, you are given a user name and a password. With your account comes an e-mail address. You are allocated a certain amount of disk storage space on the central computer. That computer, which is a host, runs all day and all night. It receives mail for you and stores it until you read the mail and dispose of it. You interact with the host computer through the use of a terminal or a computer that is acting like a terminal. However, all the action—all the computing—takes place on the host.

Typically your host computer also provides you with a number of software programs that it will run on your behalf. On a college computing system, these programs include word processors, statistical packages, and other software. The *other* software in which we are interested includes Internet client software: Telnet, mail, and FTP certainly, and often client software for browsing GopherSpace and the World Wide Web. You may find other Internet clients and utilities such as WAIS, IRC, Finger, and so on.

To connect to your campus host computer, you might use a computer and modem at home and access the university computer system through telephone lines. Another host relationship exists when campus-based computers connected directly to a university ethernet (or other network) run software that makes the computer appear to be a *dumb* terminal attached to the university's main computer system. In each case, the university system is providing access for your computer—access to a network that reaches beyond campus and access to the software necessary to navigate that network.

One machine plays many roles

When we use network-navigating software that resides on our host, the host now becomes a network client to some other computer, which is a server. For example, a professor might use her computer at home to dial into her university system, which is host to her e-mail account and provides her with access to the Internet. Once she is connected and logged in, she might type "gopher" to launch Internet Gopher client software (see Chapter 5) that resides on her host. As she makes a menu selection, her host computer then establishes connection with another computer several hundred miles away and asks the distant computer to serve up some files. Thus the host computer has also become a client to the distant computer.

At the same time it is possible that other people are accessing the host, asking it for files. The host then can perform server duties as well. It is easy to see how confusion can result when one computer may be in turn client, server, and host. Indeed, one of the strengths of client-server computing and the Internet is that any computer on the network can be a client or a server, depending on the task it performs.

One way to remember the difference between a server and a host is that a server provides documents (text, program, or data files) while a host computer provides network access, disk space, and/or software access. Although one machine may in turn play all three roles, the functions are distinct.

One parting word about hosts. To this point we have described what is called a local host. This is a host that physically resides on your campus and upon which you have an account giving you limited disk space. But let's say your local host does not offer WAIS database-searching software (see Chapter 9) and you want to conduct a WAIS search. Using Telnet (Chapter 6) you can log into a computer on another campus or at some distant business complex that does have a WAIS client you can use. This distant computer becomes a remote host because it is distant and yet it is providing you access to network facilities.

Client location governs functionality

The distinction between local and remote hosts has an important impact on the functionality of the client software to which you have access. All files and information on the Internet are maintained and communicated in client-server relationships. The server makes files available to other machines (clients) in a format recognized by client software running on the client machine. Where the client software is located and how it is accessed determines what features of the client are available to you as a user and how efficiently the client software operates from the user's point of view.

In terms of where the software resides, a client may be said to be local or remote, just as a host is local or remote. You have a local client if the client software you are using to go out and get information resides either on your host computer where you have disk space or if it resides on a computer at your desk and you have disk space available on it. With remote clients, you sit at a dumb terminal—or an intelligent computer running terminal emulation software—connected to a distant host computer on which you have no disk space allotted.

Because you do not have access to disk space when you are working with a remote client—you may be logged on as a public or anonymous user—you may not be able to use all the client's features. For example, you will not be able to keep *bookmark* or *hot list* files used by Gopher and World Wide Web clients (Chapter 4 and Chapter 5). Nor will you be able to keep the news.rc file Usenet news readers employ to keep track of your subscriptions and what you have read (Chapter 7). If you do a WAIS search (Chapter 9) from a remote client, you may not *save* the results because you do not have disk space. You have the same limitations on files retrieved through remote Gopher or World Wide Web clients.

Network connection type affects functionality

Basically you connect to the rest of the world on the Net in one of two ways. In the first scenario, your computer has a network card and network wires coming into your computer through the card. This is known as a *hard wired* connection or a *direct* connection. Such a connection is desirable because it frees the user from reliance on host computers for access and for client software. Instead, one is free to select one's own client software for Internet access and avoid slowdowns brought on by overworked, bogged-down hosts. Data files move quickly across the network, free from slow modem bottlenecks.

In the second scenario, you use telephone lines and a modem to reach a host computer that then gives you Internet access. This is known as a *dial-up* connection. Normally this arrangement forces you to rely on the software provided by the host computer. Some schools have dial-up services that offer SLIP (Serial Line Internet Protocol) or PPP (Point-to-Point Protocol) access. Such access permits the network navigator to use local clients specially configured for such access. Although you still must go through a modem to access the network, SLIP and PPP connections provide many of the benefits of direct connections. If you must go through a dial-up connection, try to get one with SLIP or PPP access.

Getting started

The campus computer infrastructure and the concept of client-server computing are both complex. You will probably need guidance to help you locate the resources you will need. Consequently, when you are ready to begin to use the Internet, you should first check with your office of academic computing services or office of information services or a similarly named office. You will then want to ask a series of questions:

- Where and how can you get a computer account with e-mail?
- What Internet client software is running on the host to which you are assigned?
- Where on campus are there Internet clients running on publicly accessible computers, preferably Apple Macintosh or IBM PC-compatible personal computers running Windows?
- Does the school provide dial-in PPP or SLIP access?

The answers to those questions will tell you which Internet applications are available, where the appropriate computers are located, and what you have to do to access them.

Professors and staff should ask computer service support personnel to come to their offices to make sure their office computers are part of the campus network and running TCP/IP (which will be explained in Chapter 2). They should request either Windows on their PCs or a Macintosh computer so that they can make use of client software using point-and-click graphical user interfaces.

In many cases you will use different computers for different types of Internet applications. For example, for e-mail, variations of e-mail such as Internet discussion lists and Usenet Newsgroups, FTP (Chapter 6), and Gopher, it is often most convenient to run the client software on your host computer. For Telnet (Chapter 6) and the World Wide Web, using client software running on a Mac or Windows machine with their graphical user interfaces is often more convenient. If you have a computer with a direct link to the network (which should be the case for faculty members), it may be easier to run all the client software from your desktop.

How to use this book

The best advice about how to use this book depends largely on what you know already, how comfortable you are with computers, how interested you are in the Internet generally, and most importantly, what you want to achieve. The Internet is a dynamic tool. It may become very important to you and your work. Or it may be mainly recreational. The decision is yours.

Chapter 2 provides a broad overview to the Internet itself, a short introduction to available Internet applications, and insight into some key concepts. We suggest that beginners start with Chapter 2. After all, although you do not have to know how gasoline fuels an internal combustion engine in order to drive a car, it is useful to know that a car is powered by an internal combustion engine using gasoline. If you understand fundamental concepts about the Internet, it will be easier to master the specific applications.

Chapter 3 explains e-mail and the different ways in which it can be used. E-mail, of course, is used to communicate with other people. Communication has always been the most important and widespread activity on the Net.

Chapter 4 and Chapter 5 look at the World Wide Web and Gopher, which are Internet applications designed to locate and retrieve information from around the world. In the past two years, the World Wide Web has become the most efficient, practical and dynamic method to locate and retrieve information. Use of the Web has been growing geometrically since 1993 and many people believe it is the prototype of the Information Superhighway. Gopher is an older application that performs largely the same job. Although in some ways it has been eclipsed by the Web—which provides access to Gopher servers as well as Web servers—Gopher is still a valuable application in many circumstances. Moreover, newer Gopher clients also provide some of the advantages commonly associated with the World Wide Web.

Chapter 6 explores Telnet and FTP. Both Telnet and FTP are basic applications that have been a part of the Internet since it was first established in the late 1960s. Both provide important functions for serious Internet users.

Chapter 7 and Chapter 8 describe other ways for people to communicate with each other via the Net. Usenet Newsgroups are the sites of some of the most controversial discussion and information online. Internet Relay Chat, MUDs and MOOs, which provide real-time interaction online, are fun to use and have been effectively employed in specific educational settings.

Chapter 9 and Chapter 10 offer a strategy for effectively using the Internet for research, teaching and learning as well as outline the rules of behavior appropriate in cyberspace and the legal responsibilities of those using the Internet.

The second part of the book directs you to specific Net resources organized by academic discipline. The final section in this part of the book contains resources that could be useful or interesting to students outside their academic responsibilities, including how to use the Internet to look for a job.

The book was written to be used sequentially. Once you are comfortable with e-mail and have access to the World Wide Web, you can take advantage of a lot of what the Internet has to offer. The more you know, however, the more you may want to know. And then you can move through the applications described in the other chapters.

A few conventions used in this book

Throughout *The Online Student*, directions are given on how to access various network sites and to issue certain network commands or special software commands. Most of those instructions are self-explanatory. However, for those less comfortable with computer manuals a couple of screen and text conventions are worth noting.

<CR>, when it appears in text, stands for *carriage return* and means you should hit the Return or Enter key on your computer keyboard.

The caret (^), on screen or in command summaries in *The Online Student*, is shorthand for the Ctrl key on the keyboard. It is generally used in combination with other characters to indicate that you should hold down the key while you are typing the indicated character. For example, ^C means Ctrl-C, or hold down the Ctrl key while you hit the C key.

When something doesn't work

The Internet is not yet the Information Superhighway. Instead, it should be thought of as a highway system under perpetual construction. As you use the Internet, you will encounter traffic jams; information that you can access today will be closed off to you tomorrow, and possibilities will open every day.

When you try to use some of the resources described in this book, you may not be able to get through. Some may have moved. Some will be shut down.

Guaranteed.

When that happens, move on to new resources. Cyberspace is already a rich cornucopia of information and people interacting with each other. If you show patience, understanding and a little diligence, you will be richly rewarded. Now let's take a look at what the Internet is all about for the academic community.

Chapter 2

Learning the lay of cyberspace

A senior at Texas Tech University, Sandy Price was doing a report on archeological excavations of Native American settlements. She was particularly interested in gaining information about Native American activity in West Texas near where she was living. Veronica searches of Gopher resources did not prove very helpful. A WAIS search identified a database in Finland that led to some files on a server in Italy. Those in turn led to computer resources first in Japan and finally in Australia. On a computer in Australia she found reports of two separate digs in rural West Texas within an hour's drive of where she lived.

In a matter of just a few minutes, Sandy had used the Internet to track down the information she needed. Because she understood basic Internet software tools, she was able to effectively use the network to complete her assignment. At the end of this chapter, the reader will

- Have a grasp of what the Internet is, how it is organized, and how it works.
- Be able to explain how information is organized and stored in files on computer networks.
- Know the difference between ASCII and binary files and what each is used for.
- Be able to discern the format of many files from their names.
- Understand the shorthand called Uniform Resource Locator (URL) used for describing any computer file on the global Internet.
- Be introduced to the six primary methods of organizing and distributing computer files on the global Internet.

What the Internet is (not)

Some veteran users of the Internet like to argue that the Internet defies definition. In a well-known story, one old-timer once defined the Internet by describing what it wasn't. Quickly, others shortened his definition to "The Internet—not."

While complex, the structure of the Internet is understandable. The Internet is a term used to describe the interconnection of many computer networks in a way that allows them to communicate with each other. Although the popular term Information Superhighway is misleading, the Internet is like the nation's road and highway system and conceptually functions in much the same way.

Consider this extended metaphor: In the United States, you can drive a car from Los Angeles to New York. You can do this for two reasons. First, there are physical links called roads. These roads take many different forms. In front of your house, the road may be a single lane. You then may turn onto a slightly larger road with two lanes and a line down the middle. The next street may have traffic lights to control the flow of traffic. Eventually you will reach an interstate highway that has several lanes of traffic moving at high speeds in the same direction. To arrive at your final destination, you must go through the same process but in reverse. You exit from the interstate highway and then travel on a series of successively smaller streets until you arrive at a specific location.

Rules to govern traffic

In addition to the physical links, however, to make the trip from Los Angeles to New York safely, you need to have a set of rules that govern the way all the travelers use the roads. You must know that you cannot cross a double line in the middle of a road, that you must stop at red lights, and that you must travel within certain speed limits, depending on the type of road and weather conditions.

The Internet can be thought of as a road and highway system, not for moving people and goods, but for moving packets filled with information. The Internet is made up of physical links, but in the same sense that no one road connects a home in Los Angeles directly to a home in New York, no one single link connects all the computers on the Internet. Like streets, computers are linked in successive levels. As we mentioned in Chapter 1, your university or college may have a local area network to provide a direct link for computers in a single department, and the departmental networks may, in turn, be connected campus-wide. Departmental and even campus-wide networks are like neighborhood streets. They are under the control of the campus system administrators of the facilities.

In the automotive world different neighborhoods are linked by larger streets. In the Internet world these larger streets make up what are called regional networks. Regional networks, often called midlevel networks, connect the computers at different universities, businesses and other institutions. Like larger streets, these midlevel networks enable data to travel faster than it does on local area networks. These midlevel or regional networks have names like SURAnet, NYSERnet and NorthWestNet. Even if you don't have a supercomputer center on campus, your school is probably linked to a regional network that does.

National backbones

The specialized computers that control the flow of information on the mid-level networks are also physically linked to what are called *national back-bones*. The national backbones use lines that transmit data at yet higher speeds and use higher capacity computers to handle information traffic. In the United States there are several national backbones for the Internet, in-cluding networks run by the Department of Defense, the Department of Energy and NASA. The largest and most influential backbone, and the one that has enabled the Internet to be used by a wider community of people, has been the high-speed network initiated by the National Science Foundation. It is now run by a consortium formed by AT&T and MCI.

In addition to being linked to regional networks, the national backbones are connected to each other. They are also connected to computer networks on every other continent in the world. The Internet itself then is the word used to describe the interconnection of these successive levels of networks. As such, the Internet is the series of physical links that serves as the road system for computer-based information. It encompasses the local networks within organizations through which information moves slowly but only for short distances; the midlevel networks linking universities, large com-panies and other organizations; the national backbones, which allow a lot of information to travel long distances at very high speeds; and the com-puter networks in other countries that enable the sharing of information internationally.

TCP/IP packaging rules define Internet

It is important to understand that the Internet is not any single network. It is not even any single national backbone network. Instead, it is the intercon-nection of thousands of networks around the world. But the physical links are only one part of the Internet. The sets of rules or protocols that allow the information to travel from computer to computer on the Internet are equally important. If a computer or computer network does not operate according to that set of rules, it is not part of the Internet.

Think of it this way. Motor vehicles and airplanes are both forms of trans-portation but airplanes cannot use the road system. There are many types of networks and ways to send information between computers. But only com-puters that follow the specific rules associated with the Internet can use the Internet.

The dominant protocol or set of rules used on the Internet is called the Transmission Control Protocol/Internet Protocol (TCP/IP). The IP part of the protocol is the address for every computer that is physically linked to the Internet. Each computer has a unique address. The IP part of the protocol identifies the sender and destination of information and also serves as the foundation for locating information throughout the Internet.

The TCP part of the protocol controls the way information is sent through the network. It is according to the TCP protocol requirements that the ability to log onto remote computers, transfer files, and perform other applications on the Internet have been developed. At one level, TCP serves as a quasi-operating system for Internet applications, allowing Internet applications to interact on computers that, themselves, have different operating systems such as Windows, DOS, Macintosh OS, Unix or VMS.

In summary, the growth of the Internet has stemmed from two factors. Physical links consisting of high-speed data lines have been established connecting the computer networks—or internetworking, as the jargon sometimes has it—of universities, governments, businesses and other organizations. These links have created a de facto national network. Second, the widespread acceptance of TCP/IP protocols allows information to travel transparently through the linked networks, which make up the Internet even though different computers have different hardware architectures and operating systems.

Network control

Understanding of the structure of the Internet sheds light on several important questions. First, who controls the Internet? The answer is that at this time no one entity controls the entire Internet. After all, it is an international network. Instead, there is a layer of control at every network level.

For you, the most important layer of control will be the system administrators at your campus. The system administrators decide who gets an Internet account and the rules governing that account. The system administrators will select Internet tools to which you have access. For example, they may choose not to develop a complete link to the Internet but only to support electronic mail. The system administrators can decide how much information you can store in your account and how much information on the central computers at your site will be available to other people on the Internet. Similarly, if you access the Internet through a commercial provider or a company for which you may work, the system administrators for those networks will make the key decisions.

In turn, the midlevel networks have network operation centers and network information centers that provide database, registration and directory services. Individual universities, organizations and businesses negotiate their connection with the Internet through these regional bodies.

Finally, the national backbone networks have their own governing organizations. As the Internet has grown, however, the rules governing its use have come under scrutiny, and there are frequent proposals to change the usage policy. As the Internet has grown to include commercial ventures, it is increasingly being used for business as well as educational and research activities. As access to and use of the Internet has grown, the federal government has increasingly considered ways in which it should be regulated. It is important to remember that you have no inherent right to access to the Internet and you will be expected to follow the rules.

Cost structure

The lack of a centralized management organization has also had an impact on the cost of using the Internet. Building, maintaining and developing the Internet is an ambitious and costly undertaking. The national backbones were initially subsidized by the federal government, and some of the regional networks have received state funding. Currently, universities, business enterprises and organizations generally pay a flat monthly or annual fee to connect to either a regional network or a national backbone. Once connected, however, organizations are usually not charged on a usage basis. Consequently, most colleges and universities do not charge individual users for using the Internet.

Looked at another way, the cost of the Internet is like the cost of cable television. With cable, you pay a monthly fee and then you can watch as many programs on as many different channels as you like. With the Internet, once the monthly charge is paid, users can generally employ as many services as often as they like without additional charges.

This current pricing structure is significant for students. It means that you can search through the Internet as diligently as you want for relevant information and can communicate with as many people as you can identify via e-mail without worrying about receiving a huge bill at the end of the month. Moreover, it means the Internet can open sources of information— both archival and human—that would be too expensive or difficult to access in any other way.

For example, an editor of a specialized science magazine was looking for someone to write articles about new developments in laboratory automation. Working through the Internet, he came in contact with scientists in St. Petersburg, Russia, who were active in that area. Over the course of several months, the editor and the scientists collaborated to develop two articles. At one point in the editing process, the editor was exchanging information with the scientists on an almost daily basis. He did not have to worry about accruing huge costs. Also, the time differential between the United States and Russia was not a problem.

Some people would like to change the pricing mechanism for the Internet. They would like to see users charged for the time they are actually online or for the specific services they use. If the pricing mechanism is changed, it could have a dramatic impact on the functionality of the Internet for students.

The growth of the Internet

The growth of the Internet can be measured in three ways: the number of host computers connected to the Internet, the number of users connected to those host computers, and the amount of information or traffic carried on the Internet. Because of its decentralized structure, precise usage figures are hard to determine. But by all measures the Internet is rapidly growing. By some estimates the number of users is growing by 50 percent per year and the amount of traffic is growing at a rate of 20 percent per month. At least one analyst anticipates the number of host computers connected to the Internet may jump tenfold from nearly one million in 1993 to 10 million by the turn of the century.

One of the few objective measures of the growth of the Internet is the host domain name survey. That survey counts what amounts to the number of networks on the Internet. From January 1993 to January 1994, the number of host domains climbed 69 percent from 1.3 million to 2.2 million. During the first six months of 1994 a new computer network connected to the Internet every 30 minutes as the number grew from 2.2 million to 3.2 million. During the last quarter of 1994, the Net grew by 26 percent, and a count in January of 1995 listed 4.85 million host domains.

To give some sense of how many users that translates into, most universities are seen on the Internet primarily as one host domain. The main host domain at Texas Tech University, for example, is ttu.edu. On just one computer host at that domain (the ttacs host) there were 7,887 individual accounts in the spring semester of 1995. Large commercial network access providers like Netcom, PSI, and Onramp likewise have thousands of users. Large high-tech corporations like Texas Instruments, IBM, and MCI have thousands of individual users covered under their domains. Online services such as CompuServe and America Online count their users in the millions, yet they are seen in the host domain name survey as one host domain.

It is impossible to know how many people have accounts on more than one host, but if each host domain averaged only 100 users, we would be talking in the 500 million user range. Some people project that by the late 1990s more than 100 million people will have access to the Internet. If those projections prove accurate, and it is impossible to say with certainty that they will, the Internet will eventually represent a communications network that will rival the telephone system in its importance. In any case, by the time you graduate and enter the work world it will be very important for you to be comfortable with using the Internet.

A history of the Internet

Ironically, the Internet was not originally conceived as a global communications system. Like some other useful technologies, the Internet has its roots in the need for military preparedness. In the late 1960s the Advanced Research Projects Agency of the United States Department of Defense began funding projects to develop an experimental computer network to support military research by allowing people spread across the country to more easily share their computer files and send messages to each other.

The Department of Defense had specific requirements for the way it wanted to link host computers. It wanted the network to be able to function even if parts of it had been disrupted, presumably in a war. The researchers decided that by using an addressing system, which they called the Internet Protocol (IP), the communicating computers themselves could ensure that the information was successfully transmitted or received and every computer on the network would be able to communicate with every other computer on the network. This kind of arrangement, in which every computer on the network can fulfill all the communication tasks among computers on the network, is called peer-to-peer networking.

In 1969 an experimental network called ARPAnet was launched with four nodes. The participants included two University of California campuses (Santa Barbara and Los Angeles), the Stanford Research Institute, and the University of Utah. Developing ARPAnet was complicated because different sites used different types of computers, and the protocols that were developed had to work on many different computer architectures and operating systems. The challenge was to develop rules of communication that would allow information to be sent over many different kinds of networks without regard to the underlying network technology. These protocols began to appear in the mid-1970s and were known as the Transmission Control Protocol, or TCP. By the early 1980s all the systems associated with ARPAnet standardized on TCP/IP.

Supercomputing centers established

The next impetus for the Internet came in 1987 when the National Science Foundation decided to establish five supercomputing centers around the country and link them through its own high-speed network known as the NSFnet. Because the cost to connect researchers directly to the supercomputing centers with dedicated high-speed data lines would have been prohibitive, NSF encouraged research institutions to form regional networks, which, in turn, were linked to the supercomputing centers. That strategy has led to the basic structure of the Internet, with its multiple layers of networks.

In 1990 an effort was undertaken to include commercial and nonprofit organizations as well. By the middle of 1993, by some estimates there were more than three million commercial Internet users and that number was growing at a rate of 10 to 20 percent a month. Commercial organizations have the fastest rate of connection to the Internet of any single type of user community. In 1994 the number of sites with commercial domain addresses (.com) surpassed the number of sites with educational domain addresses (.edu).

Files are the basic unit

All of the Internet was set up with the idea that computers at distant locations—no matter what kinds of computers they were—could pass messages in the form of files to one another. It is helpful to understand files and file structures.

When you become adept at cruising the Internet you may view great works of art in the Louvre's online exhibits one moment, check job listings in California, and search the catalog at the Library of Congress a moment later. Next you may send e-mail to a friend on a junior-year-abroad program, check the weather back home, listen to a new band on Virtual Radio, download some new software, and finally play an interactive game.

All these network objects—the music, the e-mail message, the museum artwork, book reviews, the computer software, and the weather map—reside in files stored on networked computers. At the request of one computer on the network a second computer *serves* (or sends out) onto the network a digital copy of the desired object. Computer files stored and sent out onto a network come in two basic types, based on the kind of information they contain.

The difference between ASCII (text) files and binary files

ASCII files are purely text; they are often called simply *text files*. They are files generally meant to be read by people, much as you would read any other text you might find in a newspaper, a magazine or a book. ASCII files have in them strings of text containing letters, numbers, spaces, and some punctuation—the kinds of things you would find on the keyboard of a manual typewriter. Text files—ASCII files—have as their mission in life to simply pass along the bare words and numbers that communicate meaning to human beings through spoken and written language.

Binary files, on the other hand, are meant to be read by computers and computer peripherals. They contain code important to and understood by such electronic devices as laser printers, computer processors and CD players. In an ASCII file, there is no provision for defining italics, underlining, bold characters, or different styles or sizes of type. All of those distinctions require special codes unique to certain printers, computer monitors, and even software. If you've spent a good deal of time formatting a term paper with different typefaces, underlining, boldfacing, and italicizing, the only way to save all that effort is in a binary file, named for the binary coding scheme employed by computers. Most word processors save their files by using binary coding. *Simple* word processors that work only in ASCII are often called *text editors*. Windows Notepad, Macintosh TeachText, and the DOS Edit programs are all text editors that routinely save files in ASCII (text-only) format.

If you use graphics (including lines, boxes, circles, drawings and photographs) in your reports, your reports must be stored in binary files. Likewise, files containing music or movies are binary. The e-mail message you sent at 7:30 p.m. was an ASCII file, and so too (most likely) were the book reviews you captured a few minutes earlier. The computer software you downloaded was binary because it contained computer code.

While ASCII files may seem rather boring from a design point of view—containing nothing but plain text—they have the advantage of being readable on any kind of computer by just about any word processor. That is why so much information available on the Internet is stored in ASCII files. The chief limitation here is that simple text editors like Notepad and TeachText have limits on the size of file they can read, generally about 40,000–60,000 bytes of information (about 12–25 typewritten pages). So if you want to read a large file, you'll have to use a serious word processor.

File names suggest format (file nature)

To be stored, files have to be named. Happily, file naming conventions often give clues to the nature of a file's contents. Plain, ASCII text files, for example, commonly have file names ending in .txt to denote a text file. A file formatted for a PostScript printer commonly has a name ending in .ps. These special endings of file names are called file name extensions.

An understanding of file naming conventions is helpful whether you have occasion to retrieve files interactively or not. If you are accustomed to using a Macintosh and naming files with several words separated by spaces, that practice is not tolerated for the vast majority of files you find on the Internet. Instead of spaces, multiple word file names generally separate words with underscores (_) or dashes (-). Many file names have extensions added onto them following a period at the end of the main part of the name. For example, the file mos20a8.zip is the name for the compressed Windows version of NCSA's Mosaic software, version 2.0, alpha 8. The .zip extension to the file name tells us that the file has been compressed and archived using the zip compression scheme.

How directories describe paths to files

So far, we have been speaking of individual files and how file names provide clues to the nature of file contents. All this assumes you know where—in the world—the file resides in the first place. In reality, a number of individual computer files will be grouped together in directories on a fixed disk (hard drive). Disk directories are the virtual equivalent to file folders. Macintosh and Windows operating systems represent directories with folder icons on your computer screen. Folders may be stored inside folders. On a computer disk, directories that reside within (or underneath) other directories are called *subdirectories*.

Think of it this way: Your mailing address includes your name, a street number, a city, a state or province, and a postal code. So, too, the complete address (precise location) of a file on a fixed computer disk includes not only the file name, but a listing of all the directories and subdirectories on the disk leading to the file. On DOS and Windows machines as well as on larger minicomputers and mainframes that one finds at colleges and universities, this is known as the file's *path*.

For example, the original computer file containing the text, tables, formatting instructions and graphics links for this chapter was called Chapt02.ws and it resides in a directory (folder) called student that in turn is inside a folder (directory) called online inside a folder called ws on my computer's hard drive. In traditional notation the full file specification would be

   \ws\online\student\CHAPT02.WS

The URL: A global, cross-platform standard

This path system of notation, with some minor adjustments, applies to the naming of files on the Internet. A notation system known as *Uniform Resource Locator,* or URL for short, identifies a file by providing the name of the machine on which the file resides, the machine's Internet address, path to the file, and the program protocol or kind of Internet software by which the file may be retrieved (See Fig. 2-1).

For example, a file known as the International Student Government home page is described by the URL

   http://www.umr.edu/~stuco/national.html

The URL tells us the file document is called national.html and that it may be retrieved using HyperText Transfer Protocol (http). Furthermore, the URL tells us the document is on a machine answering to the name or alias www at the domain umr.edu in a folder one level down from the top, called ~stuco. In URL notation, the folders or directories are set apart by forward slash marks and the URL starts by naming the protocol used to access the file. The protocol is followed by a colon and a double slash mark. The name of the machine that is host to the document and the machine's Internet domain follow the double slash. Following the machine address the sequence of directories necessary to get to the file is given, each directory or folder set off by slash marks.

"Geography" of the Internet

The first portion of an URL (commonly pronounced like the boy's name, Earl) is the program protocol used to *serve up* the document or to provide access to a file in question. Basically there are only a half-dozen such protocols. Those half-dozen protocols permit tens of millions of persons connected to millions of computer networks worldwide to exchange mail with each other; to post and read messages; to view and retrieve artwork, music, video files, news and weather reports, great literature, software, and scholarly papers; to access libraries, share research, and so on.

Knowing that the overwhelming majority of global Internet resources available to the public may be accessed in one of six ways should help to cut the vastness of the Internet down to size—at least from the vantage point of understanding "what's out there." The six protocols that define access to Internet resources are mail (or e-mail), File Transfer Protocol (FTP), Telnet, Gopher, Usenet (news), and HyperText Transfer Protocol (http). The first three of these protocols are native to TCP/IP (the networking protocol that makes the Internet work). The others are add-on programs. In addition to these primary programs, there is also a small handful of helping programs designed to aid in locating resources controlled by that protocol. Additionally, there is a small group of miscellaneous network programs used for entertainment, communications and other purposes.

Fig. 2-1: The Universal Resource Locator (URL) provides information adequate to locate a file wherever it may be in the world. In this case, the document crim-justice resides on a machine called view at the domain ubc.ca. The document is accessible using Gopher protocol at port 70 of the server.

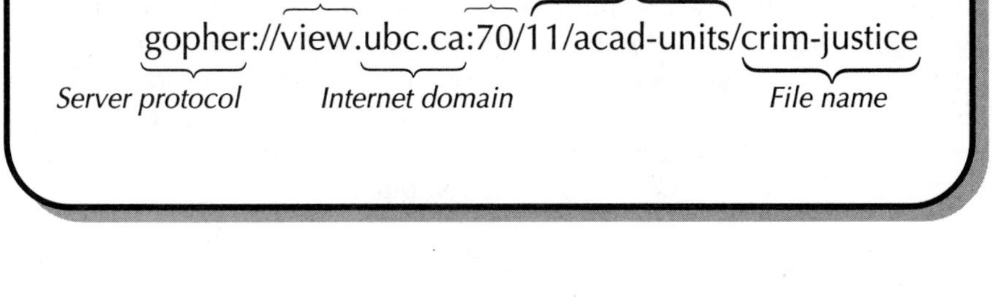

Machine name   Port Num.   Directory path

gopher://view.ubc.ca:70/11/acad-units/crim-justice

Server protocol   Internet domain   File name

One way of coming to understand the whole scope of the Internet is to think of the Internet as a worldwide theme park, a sort of global Disneyland. At Disneyland, attractions built around high-technology visions of the future will be found in Tomorrowland. For example, Space Mountain is there. If you're interested in the Keystone Kops or an old-fashioned nickelodeon, you go to Main Street U.S.A. Pirates of the Caribbean and the Haunted Mansion are in New Orleans Square. And there are services like the Disneyland Railroad to help you move around the different areas.

While Disneyland has 10 zones, the Internet is home to six basic protocols (mail, Telnet, FTP, http, Gopher, and news), each of which has a few specialty clients for getting around. Following is a brief description of cyberspace defined by each of the major protocols.

Electronic mail (e-mail)

E-mail is the electronic equivalent of what the post office does (commonly called snail mail on the network). On the network, mail is a messaging system that handles routing and delivery of messages. Using an addressing system that is uniform worldwide, e-mail makes it just as easy to send a note to your friend studying in India or France as it is to send a question to your professor in the English department. The length of time it takes to get to either destination (generally a few seconds to a few minutes) is about the same too.

The Internet supports mass mail as well. You can sign up for a mail list and receive all the messages sent to one central computer. These mail lists are usually organized around specific subject matter.

Although mail is built into the Internet TCP/IP protocol, most people rely on add-on *mailers* to manage their electronic mail. These go by such names as Pine, Elm, VMS Mail, Pathworks Mail and Eudora. These are powerful client programs that give the savvy user the ability to do lots of things with the Internet's mail capability. E-mail is not necessarily the easiest or simplest of the Internet protocols to master, but it does put one in touch with other people on a network made up largely of machines. E-mail is described in Chapter 3.

Telnet enables remote log-in, provides bulletin boards

Telnet is a program that permits network travelers to log into distant computers as if they were part of that computer. Once you are connected, you are on your own; but many network sites provide welcome screens that give at least some instruction for navigating the remote site. If you are on the road, you can use Telnet to access your home computer and read your mail and do whatever you normally do on the home computer.

Beyond offering a mechanism for remote log-in, Telnet provides a simple bulletin board type of interface. Libraries worldwide have made use of the Telnet protocol. The Hytelnet program puts a browsing/menuing interface onto Telnet-accessible resources, which otherwise have no uniform rules of procedure. Telnet is described in Chapter 6.

File Transfer Protocol (FTP) moves program files

File Transfer Protocol, or FTP, is a program allowing different kinds of computers to pass files along to each other. FTP is generally accessed by anonymous log-in, a process whereby you give "anonymous" as your username when you log into another computer and you give your e-mail address as your password. An FTP help program called Archie is a search utility that locates files available by using the FTP program. FTP is the most common way you can download free software from the Internet. Recently a small group of add-on client programs has appeared, designed to put a friendly face on FTP. These go by such names as Fetch and WS FTP. FTP is described in Chapter 6.

World Wide Web uses HyperText Transfer Protocol

The World Wide Web is a rapidly expanding area of the Internet where information is organized by linking words, graphics, sounds and/or video. The World Wide Web is also called WWW, W3, WebSpace or the Web. This area of the Internet is governed by HyperText Transfer Protocol, or HTTP. Documents posted to (or published on) the Web are written in what is known as HyperText Markup Language, or HTML for short.

HTML describes what a page on the network looks like. It also defines links between network documents. The linking process is generally referred to as *hypertext* when it involves word (text) linking and *hypermedia* when it involves linking graphics, audio and video. The World Wide Web has been described as a *meta* protocol. In addition to HTTP, it can understand and use the other Internet program protocols such as Gopher, mail, news and Telnet. Consequently, it currently represents the most dynamic information space on the Internet.

WebSpace is traversed with programs called browsers. Many browsers, such as Cello, Mosaic or Netscape, have graphical user interfaces (GUI) similar in feel to Windows' and Macintosh's. You make selections by clicking your mouse on highlighted words, icons or graphics rather than typing in menu item numbers. For people without graphics—for example, if you must work directly on a VAX or a Unix machine—there are text-based *browsers* such as Lynx.

The World Wide Web is described in Chapter 4. Tools used to search the World Wide Web are discussed in Chapter 9.

Gopher tunnels through the Internet

Gopher is an Internet add-on program written at the University of Minnesota where the school mascot is the Golden Gopher. Gopher provides access to information through a uniform system of menus, allowing users to navigate quickly through computer systems after learning a few simple keyboard commands.

GopherSpace is a term often used to encompass all the computers, files and other network resources available through Gopher. The Gopher program itself is classified as a browser because it moves you through network resources very much as one simply browsing through a library. You pick a general topic and pull things off the shelf, so to speak, as they interest you. After you wind your way through a series of menus, you come at last to a document containing the information you want. Just as the library has a card catalog that allows you to search for a specific author or title or topic, GopherSpace is home to two keyword-searching programs: Veronica and Jughead. Gopher is also capable of retrieving some files through FTP and of handing off a network session to other network programs such as Telnet or Lynx. Gopher is described in Chapter 5. Veronica and Jughead are described in Chapter 9.

Usenet is the home of network news

Usenet is a network of several thousand bulletin board systems organized into topic-oriented news groups. Within these news groups, people read and post (as if to a bulletin board) messages related to the purpose of the group. There are nearly ten thousand news groups on topics ranging from Elvis Presley fan clubs to biology students, from computer enthusiasts to music composers. Usenet is one of many networks connected to and accessible by the Internet. Usenet news is described in Chapter 7.

Some other Internet programs

WAIS—WAIS (pronounced wayz) is an acronym for Wide Area Information Server. WAIS is a specialty program used for locating network documents containing certain phrases and then retrieving those documents. WAIS is described in Chapter 9.

Internet Relay Chat—A specialty program that permits real-time discussion among people on the network. Sometimes called the Citizens' Band Radio of the Internet. IRC territory is organized into channels based on topics of interest, and chat sessions or discussions are carried on under assumed nicknames. IRC is described in Chapter 10.

MUDs and MOOs—Designed as entertainment, these specialty programs house role-playing games acted out on a global scale. Because MUDs and MOOs provide for real-time interaction across networks, they also offer potential in distance-education settings and other situations where conferencing is valuable. MUDs and MOOs are described in Chapter 10.

Your network connection

As you recall from Chapter 1, your campus probably has a client/server network. For you to use Internet protocols, you must log onto a machine that has client software—the software that will send requests for information to the server. For example, if you want to surf the World Wide Web, you have to log onto a machine that has Web client software, which, as you recall, is called a browser.

At most colleges and universities, there are several ways to log onto an appropriate machine. For example, most campuses have computer labs that are open for students to use. The computers in these labs often run client software for Telnet and the World Wide Web.

Students also can establish accounts on centralized computers, which they access through the campus network. E-mail and Gopher clients are usually accessible through these more centralized computers. Usenet also usually operates on a centralized computer.

If you are not regularly on campus, many schools will allow you to dial into the network using your home computer and your modem. In general, if you dial into the network, you will be able to use only the client software running on the computer you specifically called. However, some universities offer what is called PPP or SLIP access. If your campus does, you will be able to use Internet client software operating on your home computer. If you can, you will want to have a modem that operates at a minimum of 14,400 bits per second (bps).

Finally, if your campus does not provide many Internet clients, in Chapter 6 you will learn how to telnet to other computers and use the clients running there. Students attending smaller schools may find that to use Internet Relay Chat and even to get Usenet News, they will have to telnet to a computer at a different university. In general that will not be the most convenient way to use the Internet. But it does work.

With all these possibilities, it is important to remember on which computer the Internet client software is operating. Where the client software is located and how it is accessed have a significant impact on what features of the client are available. Also it will determine where information is saved— if at all—and where it is printed. Your first step should be to talk either with the computer help desk at your university or with your professors about where the client software you need is running.

The campus library—a case of internetworking

In the abstract, the Internet may sound very confusing. In practice it isn't. But before you begin working with the Internet, you may want to get the feel for the way it works by using another network of linked computers. One may be found as close as your library.

The system put together by the Colorado Alliance of Research Libraries, or CARL, functions in much the same way as the Internet. CARL has developed software that allows libraries scattered throughout the nation to be linked with each other. For example, users at Loyola College in Maryland can access the library system through terminals in the library itself, through Loyola's campus local area network server, or by dialing in using a personal computer.

After accessing the system, users can survey the holdings of the Loyola/Notre Dame Library, which are rather limited. But, by selecting Item 3 from the main menu, users can survey the holdings of the University of Maryland, the Montgomery County Public Library, and the Maryland Interlibrary Consortium. Users can also access the public catalogs from colleges from Florida to Hawaii, including the Lane Medical Library at Stanford University, the Los Angeles Public Library, and the Atlanta/Fulton County Public Library (see Fig. 2-2).

Being able to access those additional libraries is only the first step. Let's say you decide to see what is available at Morgan State University, which is just down the street from Loyola. From Morgan State University, you can also access libraries from around the country, including Arizona State University. From Arizona State, you could access yet more colleges and universities that participate in the CARL network.

Each time you select the public access catalog at a different university, your personal computer or terminal functions as if it were a terminal connected directly to the computer on which that information is stored. What is most significant, however, is that the menu or user interface for each system is exactly the same. It is as easy for you to find information on a public access catalog halfway across the world if it is part of the CARL system as it is to access information in the library you use every day.

More importantly, once you get access to a CARL library system, you have access to the information on the catalogs in many parts of the network, depending on the specific arrangements made by your local librarians. Most college and university libraries belong to some kind of consortium that allows them to share library resources with other libraries. Your college library is probably a part of CARL or a similar consortium.

Conclusion

Internetworking has grown from the early days of the military ARPAnet, to more expanded research networks, and finally into the expansive global

Fig. 2-2: A
library system
screen giving
access to other
libraries
internetworked
through CARL.

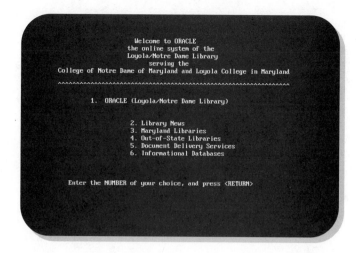

```
                       Welcome to ORACLE
                     the online system of the
                     Loyola/Notre Dame Library
                          serving the
          College of Notre Dame of Maryland and Loyola College in Maryland

~~~~~~~~~~~~~~~~~~~~~~~~~~~~~~~~~~~~~~~~~~~~~~~~~~~~~~~~~~~~~~~~~~~~~~~~

            1.  ORACLE (Loyola/Notre Dame Library)


                    2. Library News
                    3. Maryland Libraries
                    4. Out-of-State Libraries
                    5. Document Delivery Services
                    6. Informational Databases



        Enter the NUMBER of your choice, and press <RETURN>
```

Internet. The possibilities of tens of millions of computers of many different kinds sharing their files is mind boggling in scope. Still, all those millions of computer networks are reached through a relatively limited number of avenues.

Two metaphors can help you tame the network information tide. The first is to think of the Internet as a global amusement park. If the purpose of an amusement part is to have fun, the purpose of the Internet is to share information. Like different rides, different Internet protocols accomplish the objective in different ways.

Another way to think of the Internet is as if it were a global library, which in many ways it is. Books, records, papers, pamphlets and pictures—all in digital format—are stored at various places throughout the world. Because there is no one single owner of the library, there is no one single card catalog. Still, there are browsing and keyword searching devices that take in large gulps of the global library in one swoop.

Generally, the first thing for which people come to the Internet is electronic mail. E-mail allows you to send notes and letters to friends, loved ones, and associates across campus or across the world with equal ease and speed—usually a matter of seconds. We discuss e-mail next.

Chapter **3**

Electronic mail

Keith Thomas had a problem. A graduate student in political science at Brandeis University, Keith was assigned to do a paper about the impact of new communication technology on the political process. Unfortunately, as Keith began his research, he felt that most of the material he found was too dated to form the basis of a strong report.

Then one night he decided to reach out to a professor he knew during his undergraduate days. Although he had taken only one course with this professor, that course had been in political communication. Keith also knew that the professor was deeply interested in new communication technology.

As everybody knows, both professors and graduate students are notoriously hard to reach. So rather than swap endless phone messages in an effort to talk for a few minutes, Keith sent the professor an electronic mail message outlining the project and soliciting advice. The professor promptly answered and the two continued a dialogue for several days fleshing out the issues involved and sharing sources of information. In the end Keith even quoted the professor in his paper.

Since the early 1990s the use of electronic mail, or e-mail as it is generally known, has exploded. As far back as 1992, a survey of corporate management information and telecommunications managers indicated that electronic mail was among the most important technologies in meeting their companies messaging needs. As more and more companies have connected to the Internet, e-mail has become even more important.

Along the same lines, the use of electronic mail among students has steadily increased as well. In addition to communicating with professors, students use electronic mail to communicate with their friends both on and off campus as well as with their parents and others. They can also use e-mail to subscribe to discussion lists in which other like-minded people share ideas on topics of common interest.

In the future students should be able to use e-mail to communicate with administrators as well as prospective employers, friends who have already graduated, and many other people. Indeed, e-mail may soon become as important a means of communication for students as the telephone.

After reading this chapter, the student will

- Understand the anatomy of an e-mail address and the general structure of the e-mail network.
- Be able to construct an e-mail message and manage an e-mail account.
- Comprehend a specific kind of e-mail in which you automatically send to and receive messages from specific groups of people.
- Know some of the rules of etiquette that have emerged in connection with using e-mail.
- Be able to recite some of the legal ramifications of using e-mail.
- Suggest ways to effectively use e-mail.

The basics of e-mail

Conceptually, e-mail is not much different from regular mail, affectionately known as snail mail. You create a message. You address the message to the intended recipient. You deposit the letter into the transmission system, and it is carried to its intended destination.

There are differences, however. First, e-mail arrives at its destination much quicker than regular mail, which aids considerably in communication. For example, Mandy Greenfield was working at the academic help desk at her university on the East Coast when she read about an e-mail discussion list for Jewish students from campuses across the country. She joined the list and read some comments from Robert A. Book at Rice University with which she took issue. So she sent him a personal message via e-mail. For six months they frequently exchanged mail electronically before they met in person. They never had to wait for three, four, or five days for their letters to be delivered. They arrived minutes after they were sent. Not long after their first date they were engaged to be married.

E-mail is also more convenient than regular mail. To answer an e-mail letter, you don't have to find a piece of paper, locate an envelope, remember the person's address, buy a stamp, and remember to put the letter in the mailbox. Instead, you can reply to the message with just a few key strokes. E-mail programs automatically address the reply to the sender of the initial message. Moreover, most e-mail programs allow you to copy all or part of the original message so you can respond point by point. For example, when Mandy objected to Robert's point of view, she could copy the offending passages exactly and then make her point.

Finally, e-mail is still more informal than regular mail. Because some of the software used to create electronic mail messages is fairly crude, many people tolerate spelling mistakes and other errors that would reflect poorly on a person sending traditional snail mail. In many circumstances a formal salutation is unnecessary. And usually you can create a signature that will be automatically attached to all your e-mail correspondence.

But as powerful and convenient as e-mail can be, it is also fairly complicated to master completely. It requires you to have some understanding of the way the computer network at your school works as well as the way the Internet functions. Finally, you will have to master client software as well.

E-mail addresses and getting started

At most colleges and universities, the first step to using e-mail is establishing an account on one of the school computers that is connected in some way to the Internet. This computer, where you set up a mailbox, is host to your e-mail account. An electronic mailbox has two elements. First, it serves as a place in the computer's storage area for the messages you receive. When you access your electronic mailbox, you will see a directory of the messages that have arrived since the last time you checked your mail. You will be able to read through them one by one, responding to and discarding them as appropriate.

An electronic mailbox also gives you an address to which others can send you mail. The address has two parts, consisting of the *username* (in this case the name you use to sign onto the computer on which you have the mailbox) and the full Internet name of the computer. As you learned in Chapter 2, every computer attached to the Internet has a unique identification number. Most system administrators then associate a name with that number to make it easier for people to use and remember. By convention, the two main parts of electronic addresses are separated by the @ symbol.

For example, the e-mail address of Michael Pedone, a junior at Loyola College, is mpedone@loyola.edu. His username, which was assigned by the system administrator when Mike had his mailbox set up, is mpedone. Loyola is the name of the computer on which he has his e-mail account. The .edu reflects that Loyola is an educational institution. In fact, for computers located in the United States, the last three letters of the address indicate the kind of setting, or domain as it is called, in which the computer is located. In addition to the .edu educational domain, there are six other primary top domains as they are called: .gov for governmental computers, .org for computers in nonprofit organizations, .mil for computers associated with military organizations, .com for computers in commercial organizations, .int for international organizations, and .net for computers in companies that provide direct access to the Internet. The e-mail addresses for computers located outside the United States end in a two-letter country code. For example, the addresses for computers in Canada end in .ca; for France, .fr.

Different colleges and universities handle the assignment of electronic mail addresses differently. Some include the exact name of the computer on which you have your account. For example, at Loyola, some people have their e-mail accounts on a computer that the system administrator has named Lust. Their e-mail addresses read: *username*@lust.loyola.edu. Other universities just use the name of the computer that serves as the main gateway between the campus and the Internet for the address. For example, an e-mail address at the University of California, San Diego, reads: *username*@ucsd.edu. Once a message arrives at the computer site ucsd.edu, it is internally routed to the specific computer on which the user has an account.

Knowing how to decipher an electronic mail address will give you some insight into the people with whom you may be corresponding. For example, a person with an e-mail address that includes upenn.edu has an account at the University of Pennsylvania. A person with an account at the University of Baltimore has an e-mail address that includes ubalt.edu. To get an e-mail account and mailbox on your university's computer network, you will have to talk to the academic computer center, system administrator, network operations center, or another office with a name along those lines. Most campuses routinely give e-mail accounts without charge to all students who request them.

When you set up an electronic mailbox, in addition to being assigned a user name, you will receive a password that only you will know. That means that other students or people without authorization will not be able to access your e-mail without your permission. A limited amount of computer storage space will be reserved for your use. Finally, you will be given a procedure describing how to log onto the computer on which your account resides. Usually the machine that you log into for e-mail also is your host for other Internet access.

Finding the right software

Establishing an account is only the first step of the process of getting started. Next, you will have to locate the software you need to read, create, send, delete and manage your mail. As with other Internet applications, e-mail is a client-server application described in Chapter 1. The client software issues requests to the server, which responds by carrying out the task. In addition, with e-mail, the client software may help you manage and manipulate files on the computer on which your account is located as well. You will have to locate where the mail client you can use is running.

In most cases in the academic world, the software you will need for e-mail will be running on the same computer as your e-mail account. That means, if your e-mail account is on, let's say, a Digital Equipment VAX computer, you will probably be using a mail program that runs on the

Fig. 3-1: The e-mail client Eudora (here in the Win version) organizes your mail into three mailboxes: In, Out, and Trash. All new mail comes to your In box. When you delete it, it goes in the Trash box until you empty the trash. Reply messages or others you sent are stored in the Out box until you delete them.

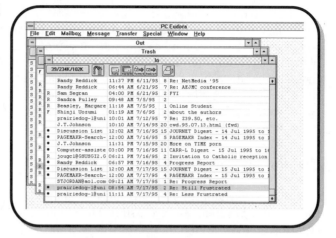

Digital Equipment operating system called VMS. If your account is on a workstation running the operating system Unix, you will use a mail program that runs under Unix.

A common arrangement is for many of the personal computer networks on campus to be running an Internet program called Telnet, which will be fully described in Chapter 6. Students then telnet to the central computer on which they have their mail accounts, log on and then use the mail software there.

Be forewarned. Software that runs under Unix and VMS sometimes is harder to use than software that runs on personal computers under Windows or the Macintosh operating system.

At some universities you may have another option however. Some schools now offer the PPP or SLIP connections described in Chapter 1. If yours does, that means you can have an e-mail client running on your personal computer when you use a telephone line to call the computer on which your electronic mailbox is located. Some schools now allow students living in the dorms to attach their personal computers directly to the university's local area network. Frequently, schools have scattered throughout their campuses labs with computers connected directly to the university network.

If any of these options is open to you—you will have to talk to your academic computing specialists to learn the specific setup in your school—then you can use Internet client software that was specifically designed to operate on a Macintosh, DOS, or Windows machine. This software is much simpler to use than VMS or Unix programs. One of the best-known mail clients for Macs and PCs is called Eudora. Once you feel comfortable with using the Internet, it will be easy to locate copies of Eudora. You will learn how to access software through the Internet in Chapter 6, which covers FTP (file transfer protocol).

Because many students do not have a SLIP or PPP connection and cannot attach their personal computers directly to the university network, we will describe the basic mail commands for composing, sending, reading, replying, deleting and managing mail for those of you who have to log onto the central computer where your e-mail account is located. Moreover, even if you can use Eudora or other personal computer software as your main e-mail client, you will still have to know some basic commands in software running under Unix or VMS to effectively manage your e-mail account.

Creating and sending an e-mail message

Creating and sending short electronic e-mail messages is easy regardless of the computer system you are using. The steps generally will be the same regardless of the system; however, the specific commands needed to complete each step will vary from system to system. Currently, even VMS and Unix have fairly easy-to-use mail programs. You will have to consult with whomever you depend on for e-mail access to learn the exact set of commands to complete the following steps.

To create and send a short mail message, first you log onto the computer on which your electronic mailbox is located and then access the specific mail program running there. For example, when you log onto a VMS system, the first thing you see is a "$," which is called the system prompt. At the system prompt, you type the command "mail." This changes your session prompt to the mail prompt, which looks like "MAIL>."

Once you are into your mail program, you will tell the system that you want to send a message. In VMS Mail, which is an older program, you type the command "send." In other mail programs you can use your mouse to click on the send command.

The computer responds with "To:" and you enter the e-mail address of the person to whom you wish to send mail. After you enter the address, which will be discussed later in this chapter, the computer responds with the line "Subject:" After you enter the subject, you begin composing your message. When you compose a message, you will be using a text editor. The text editor probably will not work exactly like your word processor, so, depending on how user friendly it is, you may want to obtain a list of commands from your computer resource person.

Often, text editing in the mail program is awkward. For example, it may be hard to move between lines to correct mistakes. In those cases, you may want to compose longer messages using your regular word processor and then upload those messages to send them. Once again, the exact process of uploading files from a personal computer to a central computer varies greatly, depending on the exact setup, so you will have to ask somebody for a set of instructions about how to do that.

Fig. 3-2: The mail compose dialog in Pine is typical of the exchange in most e-mail programs. At minimum the program prompts for an address to send the message and for the subject of the message. Then it gives you the opportunity to actually write the message.

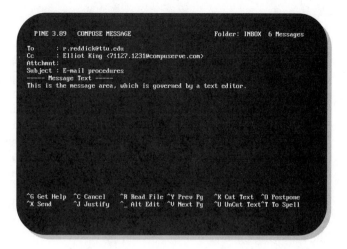

When you finish composing your note, you exit the mail composition utility to send the message to its intended destination. To exit from VMS Mail, you press Ctrl-Z. That is, you hold down the Ctrl key while pressing the Z key. If, after typing your message, you decide that you do not want to send it, you can press Ctrl-C to cancel the message.

If you use a computer running Unix instead of VMS, when you log onto the computer the system prompt may be %. Using Unix Mail, you can send a mail message either from the system prompt or the mail prompt (the prompt you get after you begin running the mail program). From the system prompt %, you type "mail" and the address of the person to whom you wish to send the message. More commonly, you will first call up the mail program to read your mail and then you will want to send messages. To call up the mail program, type "mail" at the system prompt. This will give you the mail prompt, which in Unix Mail is &. You then type "m" and the recipient's address.

In either case, once you have started the send procedure, you will then receive the "Subject:" prompt. After you enter the subject, you hit Return and begin typing the message. If you want to use a text editor to compose the message, you type "~vi" on a blank line. When you are finished composing the message, type <esc>:wq to quit the text editor. To send the message, after you finish writing it hit Return and then type Ctrl-D. If you want to cancel the message before you send it, type "~q" on a separate line.

Sending relatively short e-mail messages is easy, even if you must use software such as the basic Unix and VMS Mail utilities. Programs such as Pine for Unix and VMS make it even more efficient. Instead of forcing you to remember commands, Pine provides menus from which you can select what you want to do.

Making electronic carbons

Most mail programs allow you to send copies of a message to several people at the same time. Let's say you are working on a group project and you want to send the same message to everybody in the group. If you are working with a Unix Mailer, you will see a "Cc:" prompt after you have finished writing your message. Simply type in the addresses of the other people to whom you wish to send the information. To keep a copy for yourself, type in your own address as well.

To get a Cc: prompt in VMS Mail, type "set cc_prompt" and then hit Return. To automatically make yourself a copy of any messages or replies you send, type "set copy_self send, reply" and then hit Return.

When e-mail arrives at its destination, a message will have a header in the following format:

```
TO: Recipient's e-mail address

FROM: Sender's e-mail address

SUBJECT: Subject of the message.
```

There are ways to include your personal name in the "From:" line if you choose. Nevertheless, you should always include your e-mail address as well, either in the "From:" line or in the body of the message, to ensure that the recipient knows how to respond to you via e-mail as well.

Many people like to create what is called a signature file. A signature file is automatically appended to the end of every message you send. The signature usually will include your name; contact information such as address, telephone and fax numbers; and e-mail address, as well as personalizing information like a saying or a graphic. In programs such as Pine and Eudora, signature files are extremely easy to create and edit. In programs such as VMS Mail, they may require three or four lines of programming. A signature file still can be created, but you may have to consult with a veteran user.

Addressing your mail

As you know, the first step in sending e-mail is filling in the recipient's address. As described earlier, e-mail addresses generally adhere to the following structure: *username@computername.domain*. The username is the name of the receiver's e-mailbox. The computername is the name of the computer on which the mailbox is located. The domain describes the kind of network the computer is on.

The exact form of the address you need to use, however, depends on where the receiver's electronic mailbox is located in relationship to your own. If the receiver's electronic mailbox is on the same computer as yours, you generally have to fill in only the username part of the address. If the user is at the same school as you, but has an account on a different machine, you may have to include that information as well. If the receiver's electronic mailbox is not at your school, you will need to know the full Internet address: *username@computername*.edu.

For example, let's say you are a sociology student at the University of California, San Diego. Most sociology students and professors have their electronic mailboxes on a computer called Weber. If you wish to mail to somebody with an account on Weber, you need to enter only the username. If you wish to send a message to somebody in biology, whose mailbox is not on Weber, you will send the mail to *username*@ucsd.

Suppose your parents have joined CompuServe or America Online to be able to correspond with you via e-mail during the school year. CompuServe members have the electronic address *username*@compuserve.com. Subscribers to America Online have the address *username*@aol.com. In the case of CompuServe, the username is usually a number, while at America Online it is generally a nickname. To send mail to them you will have to use their full address.

Some mail programs also require that you signal when you are using full Internet addresses. For example, in VMS Mail, if you wish to send mail through the Internet you must begin the address with IN% and enclose the address in quotation marks. The address for the message to your parents on CompuServe would look like IN%*"username@compuserve.com."*

Finding people

For several reasons, the best way to determine somebody's e-mail address is to ask that person directly. Just because people have e-mail addresses does not mean they actually use e-mail regularly. If you access an address from a directory and send an e-mail message, you have no idea whether the intended recipient actually checks the mailbox.

That rule applies to both students and professors. For example, a sophomore at a liberal arts college sent a note to a professor, who she knew was an active e-mail user, asking for advice about courses she should take the following semester. What she didn't know was that the professor had two electronic addresses and that he periodically looked only at the one to which she sent her message. Indeed, her message was but one of 300 waiting for him at that address. By the time she called on the telephone, he had left town for a conference. She had to register for classes without his guidance.

Nevertheless, many campuses now operate what they call a Campus Wide Information System (CWIS). CWISes frequently run on a Gopher server (Chapter 5), but may run under Telnet (Chapter 6) or http (Chapter 4). The CWIS at your school may have a directory of e-mail addresses for the campus community, and other schools often provide the same service. Once you begin to communicate with people electronically, you will want to save their e-mail addresses. The easiest method is to add e-mail addresses to your standard address/telephone directory entries. Many mail programs support their own electronic directories as well. Often, those directories allow you to associate the e-mail address with the person's name. Once you have made the appropriate entry into the directory, to send mail, you use the person's name at the "To:" prompt.

Getting to the destination

Although widely used, the e-mail network is not as developed as, let's say, the telephone network. As you know, the Internet is actually a network of many different computer networks. Sometimes the individual networks do not communicate with each other as smoothly as possible.

Consequently, when you send electronic mail, you can never be sure exactly how long it will take to arrive. While many messages will be delivered to their destinations within a matter of seconds, others can take a day or more. Furthermore, if the network has problems delivering the message, it may try for some time before returning the message to the sender.

From time to time you will have messages returned to you. When mail is returned, you will also receive a message from what is called the postmaster, which is the software handling your message at different points in the network. If you closely read the message, you should be able to determine the source of your problem—often a mistake you made in the address. If you have made a mistake in the part of the address that follows the @ sign, the message from the postmaster may read "host unknown." If you made a mistake in the part of the address preceding the @ sign, the message will read "user unknown." In that case, you know that the part of the address that follows the @ symbol is, in fact, connected to the Internet.

Receiving and responding to e-mail

Of course, correspondence is a two-way street. When you start writing to people, they will write back. Unfortunately, you generally will not know if you have mail unless you check your electronic mailbox. Consequently, once you start using e-mail, you must make a commitment to check your mailbox regularly. If not, not only are you sure to miss messages, but you give up two of the main advantages of e-mail—the timeliness of the delivery of information and the ability to immediately respond.

A sound strategy is to incorporate checking your e-mailbox into your daily routine. For example, you may want to check your e-mail just before you begin to study each day or between specific classes when you are close to public computers through which you can access your e-mail account. If you check your mailbox regularly, reading, responding to and managing your e-mail is easy.

Fig. 3-3. A directory of your e-mail messages typically looks like this picture from VMS Mail. Messages are numbered and listed with the sender's address (or name), the subject of the message, and the date it was sent.

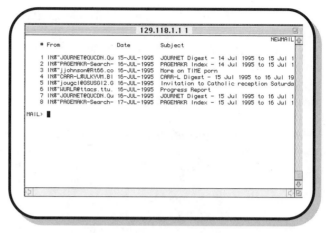

Once you log onto the computer that handles your e-mail, you will receive a notice if you have any mail. If you do have messages, start your mail client program using the procedure described in the previous section. Once the mail software is running, you will receive a list of messages. In some systems you may have to use a directory command (often dir) to view the directory of new mail messages. The directory listing will indicate the e-mail address (or name, if the sender has personalized this line) of the person who sent you the message and the subject line of the message.

At that point you can read the full text of a specific message by entering its number. Once you have read the message, you can delete it, save it electronically, reply to it, or forward it to another person at another address. The commands to perform each of those tasks vary from mail program to mail program, but virtually all programs include each of those functions.

In general, replying to and deleting messages are simple, one-command operations. In VMS Mail, for example, to reply to a message you simply type "reply" at the mail prompt when you are reading the message to which you wish to respond. The address to which the response will be sent and the subject line will be filled in automatically. You type your response, and then follow the same procedures as you did for sending mail. In Unix Mail, to start the reply process you type "r" and the number of the message to which you wish to reply at the mail prompt. In Pine, you type "r" to start the reply dialog, and in Eudora you type Cmd-R (Mac) or Ctrl-R (Windows).

After you read and/or reply to a message you will probably want to delete it. It is extremely important to regularly delete your messages from your mailbox. Remember, your electronic mailbox is actually storage space on a computer. In most cases, you will have only a limited amount of space reserved for your mail. In some systems the amount of space reserved for your use is called your disk quota. If that space or quota is filled, your messages may be automatically returned to the sender (a phenomenon known as bounced mail). If you are using e-mail for personal correspondence, you will miss messages if your mailbox is filled. If you belong to a discussion list, not only will you miss messages, you will create a problem for the person responsible for maintaining the discussion list.

Not all that goes away is deleted

Deleting old mail is important. But deleting mail may be a two- or three-part process. After you have read a message, you can mark it to be deleted by typing "del" in VMS Mail or "d" and the message number in Unix Mail. In Pine, you type "d"—and the message to which you are pointing is marked for deletion. None of these messages, however, will actually be deleted until you exit from the mail program.

If you read a message and do not mark it to be deleted, it will be saved in a special folder automatically set up for old mail. To read the messages in that file, in VMS Mail you type "select mail" at the mail prompt. In Unix Mail you type "mail -f" at the system prompt "%." In Pine you have a main menu choice (L) that lists mail folders for you. To read your old mail, select the one called Mail, as opposed to the Inbox, which contains new, unread mail. Remember, all the messages you do not delete continue to fill up the storage space reserved for you on the computer. In most cases, you should delete messages after you have read them and responded.

Even after you mark messages for deletion and exit your mail program, you may not really have deleted the messages. On many VMS systems, messages so deleted are compacted so that they take up less space. But like so much trash, the trash is still there until it gets hauled off to the dump. On these systems you have to issue the compress command from within the VMS Mail program. VMS Mail then sorts through your mail folders, picks out all the compacted trash (messages you previously deleted) and sends them to a file called something like Mail.old. You then have to exit from Mail. Then, from the system prompt "$," you delete the Mail.old file.

The bottom line of all this discussion about deleting old mail is that, first, you must delete mail to keep your mailbox from jamming up. Second, you need to find out—for your campus and the mail program you use—just exactly what process is necessary for doing that. It may be a simple or a very complicated process, but it has to be done.

Saving your mail messages

Of course, from time to time, you may receive information via e-mail that you wish to save. For example, let's say you are considering taking a course in economics at the University of Florida and you know a friend of yours took a similar course at the University of California, Berkeley. You want to see the reading list to get an idea about what to expect. Your friend obligingly sends you a copy by e-mail. You may want to save the list for future reference.

You have three options for saving information you receive through e-mail. The first is to store files on the same computer on which you have your electronic mailbox, either in the folder for old mail described above or in another place.

This probably is not the best idea, however, because you probably will not be doing very much with the computer except using it for e-mail. Few non-computer science or engineering students have much to do with Unix or VMS.

A second possibility is to download the file to the personal computer you are using to log onto the central computer where your electronic mailbox is located. This also may not be a good idea if you are using a computer in a public access computer lab unless you are careful to transfer the information to a floppy disk that you can take with you. On the other hand, if you are using your own personal computer, transferring information you wish to save from the central computer to your personal computer is appropriate.

There are several different ways to transfer information from a central computer to a personal computer. The first is to download the entire file as a unit. If you are working in VMS Mail, you must first copy the e-mail message to a separate file by typing "extract" after you have read the message. You then download the file to your computer. The exact procedure for this varies according to the communications software you use. In Unix and some VMS systems, you can download files by entering "sz" and the exact file name at the system prompt. This tells the host computer to send a file using Zmodem communications protocol. It is important that your communications software supports Zmodem. If you have received some lengthy messages, dozens of pages long, transferring messages in this fashion may be the best route to go, even if it is a little complicated. To learn the exact sequence of steps for your specific situation, you will have to work with your local computer support personnel.

There is another more straightforward method for transferring a message from your electronic mailbox to the personal computer on which you are working. You can use the *log* or *capture* feature of your telecommunications program. The log feature allows you to capture an electronic record of everything that appears on your screen directly to a file on your personal computer.

Consequently, as you read a message, you can save it directly on your personal computer, bypassing the potentially complicated procedures of transferring files from a central computer to your personal computer.

Using the log feature has its disadvantages, however. First, to capture a file, you must scroll through it entirely. If the message is long or you are under pressure, that could be too time consuming. Moreover, the file may be littered with extraneous information. Generally, as you read your mail, for example, a message at the bottom of the screen will tell you to hit the Return key for more information. That message may be included with every screen, full of information captured by using the "log" feature.

Nonetheless, the log feature is very simple to use. In the telecommunications program ProComm Plus, for example, you hit Alt-F1 to open a log file. In MacKermit for the Macintosh, Log On is under the File commands. In *NCSA-BYU Telnet* for the Mac, the Capture Session to File command is under the Session commands. In the Clarkson University NCSA TCP package (CUTCP) for DOS, the capture session command is Alt-C. In most cases, you can turn the log feature on and off and you can effectively *pause* the log feature, allowing you to pick and choose the information you wish to save. Once you have successfully transferred the information you want from your mailbox to the personal computer you are using, you can easily call it up in a word processor and read it or print it out.

Hard copy may be better

For shorter messages, you may simply wish to immediately print messages you want to save, rather that storing them electronically. You can do that in several ways. First, often the communications software on the personal computer you are using will have a print screen command that automatically prints the text on your screen. Let's say your professor has sent an assignment to you via e-mail that is only two paragraphs long. You read the assignment and want to save a copy on paper. You can simply choose the print screen command and the text will be printed on the printer that serves that personal computer.

Another alternative is to automatically print everything that appears on the screen. Many communications software programs have a feature that turns on a local printer. In ProComm Plus, for example, the command is Alt-L.

A third possibility, which is particularly easy if you are using a Macintosh OS or Windows-based personal computer, is to open your word processor, copy the information you want to save from the mail program, and paste it into a word-processing document.

Finally, you can also print messages directly from VMS Mail or Unix. In VMS, you use the "print filename queuename" command. The queuename is the location of the printer on the network you wish to use. Remember, if you are logged onto a central computer, the printer automatically associated with that computer probably will not be the printer closest to the personal computer you are using. Consequently, unless you understand how to use the queue command and know how to direct the central computer to use a printer close to you, this method for printing will be very inconvenient.

Discussion lists and listservs

In addition to person-to-person e-mail—e-mail that is sent to the e-mail address of one individual from the e-mail address of another individual—the Internet has tools that allow e-mail from individuals to be read by many people. Different forms of one-to-many communications will be discussed in more depth in Chapters 7 and 8. However, discussion groups and mailing lists have emerged as interesting forums for students and faculty from different universities to interact.

Discussion groups and mailing lists use e-mail to generate one-to-many communications. If you have e-mail access to the Internet, you can participate in these groups.

Electronic discussion groups have emerged for virtually all academic subjects as well as many other topics of interest for students and professors. Lists for specific disciplines will be described in Chapters 11 through 13. Discussion lists that may be of general interest to students range from the College Activism Information list to the Advanced Dungeons and Dragons list, and from the Coalition of Lesbian and Gay Student Groups list to the Conservative Christian Discussion list.

There are two parts to discussion groups. The first is the list service software, which is a specialized mailing program to manage these kinds of lists administratively. The second is the discussion list itself.

The most important primary functions of the list service software are to allow a person to subscribe to or terminate a subscription to a particular list. To subscribe, you would send a message to listserv@*the location of the list*. In the body of the message, you would enter subscribe *list name your name*. To terminate a subscription, you would send a message to listserv@*location of the list* and in the body of the message type unsubscribe *name of the list*. Instead of the unsubscribe command you can also use the signoff command.

For example, if your name were Jane Doe and you wanted to subscribe to a list called WISA, which stands for Women in Student Affairs, your mail dialog would look like this:

```
To: listserv@ulkyvm.louisville.edu
Subject:
subscribe WISA Jane Doe
```

And if you were John Doe and you wanted to subscribe to the Student Employment list, called STUDEMP your message to send dialog would look like this:

```
To: listserv@listserv.arizona.edu
Subject:
subscribe STUDEMP John Doe
```

Although the list service software is very popular, some mailing lists are managed by software that uses variations on this theme. Instead of sending the subscribe message to listserv@*location* you send it to *name of list*-request@*location*. There also is a growing number of sites where you address your correspondence to majordomo@*location* or to listproc@*location* rather than listserv.

Once you have subscribed to a listserv or similar discussion list, you will begin to receive the e-mail messages that are being sent to the list. With some active lists, you may receive 10 to 50 messages a day. Consequently, you should check your mailbox regularly. If you subscribe to four or five lists, you could receive more than 100 e-mail messages a day.

To post a message to a discussion group, you send e-mail to *name of the list@location of the list* and then follow the normal procedures for sending e-mail. To respond to a posted message, with most lists you can simply use the reply function of your mail program while you are reading the message. But be aware, when you reply to a message from a discussion list, your reply is mailed out to everyone on the list, not just to the person who sent the message to which you are responding.

In addition to sending and receiving mail, there are many other functions you can do with list service software. Many discussion lists save their messages in archives, and you can retrieve messages on subjects that are of interest to you. For instructions about how to access advanced commands, send the message "info refcard" to listserv@*location*.

Reading and participating in discussion lists can be a lot of fun and potentially useful as well. It puts you in contact with a lot of people who are interested in the same subjects you are.

Managing discussion list(s)

The challenge is to find a discussion list of interest to you or appropriate to supplement a class you may be taking. Currently, there are more than 4,000 active electronic discussion lists. Although you could retrieve a list of almost all the active lists by sending e-mail to listserv@listserv.net with the message "list global," that would return a file that holds more than 500K of information. Not only is that very unwieldy to search, it is too big to fit into many electronic mailboxes.

A better idea is to send a request list with a certain keyword. For example, suppose you were interested in chemistry. Send e-mail to listserv@listserv.net with the message "list global/chemistry." The word chemistry is the keyword. The response will contain only lists with the word chemistry in them.

In addition to discussion lists that people from across the country join, many campuses are establishing internal discussion lists to talk about campus issues. And some enterprising professors are setting up specialized electronic discussion lists for their students. For example, a discussion list was established for business students at Baldwin Wallace College, the University of Wisconsin at Milwaukee, McGill University and two other business schools to discuss international business problems. Along the same lines, students in the First Year Seminars at the College of Wooster were able to carry on in-class discussions and debates through an online environment. A list has also been launched for people involved in service learning at several campuses.

Many people face a dilemma after they have subscribed to a couple of lists. On the one hand, they are interested in the messages. On the other hand, they feel that a dozen or more messages a day creates a lot of clutter in their mailboxes. Listserv and Listproc software allow you to issue Set commands that help you to control the way you get your messages. Two such Set commands of particular interest here are *digest* and *index*.

Under digest, the listserv saves all the messages for the day and sends them to you in one bundle. Instead of twenty separate messages, you get one message from the listserv each day. At the top of that message will be a table of contents that summarizes the messages for the day. Then each of the messages follows in order. Set to index, the listserv still sends you only one message per day. But what it sends you is a two-line listing of each of the articles, the sender, the subject, and the article's number. If you want to read an article, you send a message to the listserv telling it to print that article for you.

If you want to stop your mail while you are on vacation, you could send the command "set *list name* no mail." When you return, you would send the same message without the word "no." Digest, index, mail, no mail, and other listserv commands are described in the listserv command reference card. The document you receive when you send the message "info" to listserv tells how to get the command reference card and other listserv information.

When you are going away for a period of time such as a semester break or summer vacation, either unsubscribe to the discussion lists or set your subscription to "no mail." When you subscribe to a discussion list, you should save the confirmation message you will receive for future reference. It provides the basic commands you need to manage the list.

The rules of behavior

In the winter of 1995, Jake Baker, a student at the University of Michigan posted a story to a computer bulletin board detailing what he later described as a fantasy about raping and killing a classmate. He also sent e-mail to another man about the fantasy. Shortly thereafter, Baker was arrested and charged with threatening the student who was the subject of the fantasy. Prosecutors argued that the writing of the e-mail message proved that Baker's musings had evolved from fantasy to a firm plan of action.

Although the charges against Baker were later dismissed (he did drop out of school), the episode raises several significant points about e-mail. First, although e-mail has the illusion of being private, it isn't. It has been well established that the enterprise that owns the computers on which an electronic mail account is lodged, can, under the right circumstances, read the messages in the mailbox. For example, companies can read the e-mail of their employees, and presumably universities can read the e-mail of their faculties and students.

Secondly, the same rules of speech that govern regular communication also apply to electronic communication. You can libel somebody online by spreading false information that will damage his or her reputation. You cannot threaten anyone. You cannot send or store illegal obscene material.

If you act in a way that violates the law, you can be prosecuted. Indeed, the way you behave online can put your university at risk as well. For example, in 1995 Prodigy, which is a commercial information service, was the subject of a lawsuit because of information one of its subscribers had distributed electronically. In another case, a person was arrested for having illegal telephone credit card numbers stored on his computer. He said that he had received the numbers via e-mail and didn't even know they were there. Nevertheless, he was prosecuted.

Being polite is important

In addition to the legal constraints concerning online communication, a code of etiquette, called *netiquette,* has evolved as well. You can be polite online, or you can be rude. As in life in general, most people prefer polite to rude.

There are several aspects of being polite online. First, check your e-mail regularly. Once you start communicating with people, they will want to communicate with you. Furthermore, if you use a central computer, you will want to delete old messages and download messages you wish to save to your personal computer in a timely fashion so that you do not exceed your disk quota.

Never assume that e-mail is private. Messages you send may be forwarded to others, and security in some systems is not what it should be. Consequently, you would not want to say anything via e-mail that you would not say face to face or that would make you feel uncomfortable if others heard it secondhand. Moreover, because your files are accessible to somebody who has system privileges, you will not want to store private information.

You want to make your e-mail messages as easy as possible for others to read and for them to respond to. Consequently, try to keep e-mail relatively short and to the point. Not only is it difficult to read long messages, the people to whom you send e-mail may not always be experts in operating their own mail utility programs. They may have problems negotiating back and forth through a long message.

The objective of e-mail is to communicate. So, when appropriate, don't forget to include your name, affiliation, e-mail address, and other ways to get in touch with you at the bottom of the message. Also, forwarding a private message to a discussion group without that person's permission is considered very rude.

Discussion groups have rules; lurk before you leap

In addition to those general rules, discussion groups generally have their own sets of rules. First, you should read the mail you receive from a discussion group for several days before you jump into a conversation.

Be sure that you understand the tenor of the conversation. If you participate in an ongoing discussion, try to keep your responses to the point and relevant. Also, discussion lists are not election campaigns. You don't have to chime in that you support a particular position unless you wish to add an additional perspective or new information.

Try to be constructive. Too often, discussion groups seem to bring out the Mr. Hyde in many people's personalities. Being online is no excuse for being rude or crude or launching personal attacks on other participants. Personal attacks in the online world are known as *flaming*. Because you don't know with whom you are communicating, you should refrain from flaming and also not respond if somebody flames you.

If you request information from persons in a discussion group, have them send their answers to your e-mail address rather than to the list itself.

If somebody else asks a question or requests information, answer or respond only if you are relatively sure you are correct. You do not help anybody when you share incorrect information.

Do not expect people on a discussion list to do your work for you. People deeply resent a student who announces he or she has a paper due in a couple of days and then asks the members of the list for input and direction. Do your own research. Tap the resources of the discussion for specialized or difficult questions.

In general, use common sense. Although you can mask yourself behind a cloak of anonymity, you should act as though you are face to face with others.

You can still have fun

Even with all the rules, e-mail and discussion lists are a lot of fun. For example, in addition to words, a whole vocabulary of little graphics has emerged to indicate the emotion behind certain messages. These symbols are called *emoticons*. So while it may seem strange for college students or faculty members to include little smiley faces in their regular correspondence, they are fair game in e-mail.

Veteran e-mail users also have developed a complete set of abbreviations for phrases that are used repeatedly. For example, IMHO means "in my humble opinion," and BTW means "by the way."

Using e-mail

For students and faculty, e-mail and discussion lists are quietly emerging as extremely useful channels of communication. The first, best application for e-mail is for individual teacher-student communication and consultation. Once a student and a professor can both use e-mail, they can be in much closer touch with each other. Students can conveniently send professors questions and professors can easily reply.

Some professors have their students turn in their homework via e-mail. Having homework in an electronic format often makes it easy for the professor to comment. It also makes it easier for students to make corrections and revisions once the homework has been returned.

E-mail also opens the world up to faculty members and students. Faculty members can easily communicate with their colleagues around the world. Students can correspond with their friends at other universities or studying abroad, their parents, and their classmates on campus. It can help students when they are working on group projects or when they wish to share information.

Though historically more used for recreation, discussion lists also can be extremely useful. For the first time students can participate as equals in discussions being conducted online by experts in areas in which the students wish to learn. And as faculty members learn to set up local discussion lists, a whole new dimension to the classroom experience could be created. In the long run discussion lists could be an integral part to the development of distance learning—allowing students across the country to participate in a single learning experience.

Finally, as more and more businesses use e-mail, it will be an important skill for students to master. By the time they graduate, it is very likely that many will be able to send their résumés to prospective employers electronically and otherwise use this dynamic new channel of interpersonal and group communication.

Chapter 4

Surfing the World Wide Web

When Katie Devine first received her assignment in an introductory communications class, she was thoroughly dismayed. She was to write a report on new developments for libraries. She worried that the topic would be as dry as the dust on a book not checked out in a dozen years.

But talking to a professor, she learned that the National Science Foundation had launched a multimillion-dollar initiative called the Digital Library. The idea is to convert books and other information into a format that can be accessed electronically by computers on the Internet.

With that tip, she sat down at a machine in her department's computer lab, which had access to the World Wide Web (WWW, or the Web). She entered the WWW location of the National Science Foundation and then searched a database of NSF grants. She read the abstract of the Digital Library grant proposal and learned that researchers at the University of Michigan were deeply involved. She then jumped to the University of Michigan WWW site where she found more information about the project, including the names and areas of expertise of several researchers working on the grant at Stanford University.

Katie was specifically interested in one part of the project. She clicked the computer mouse on the name of the scientist at Stanford involved in that task. She was automatically taken to his spot on the Web. There she viewed a picture of him, read his curriculum vita and list of publications, and found a short statement describing his work. She also got his e-mail address and telephone and fax numbers to contact him.

Now Katie, who went to school on the East Coast, had a friend who went to Stanford. So after she downloaded the information about the Stanford researcher, she went to the main Stanford Web page—also called the default page, and sometimes, incorrectly, the home page. From there she took an online tour of the Stanford campus to learn about the school and its offerings.

She also noticed a Web link to the Australian National Library, so she decided to follow it. As it turns out, the Australian National Library is connected to the Australian National Portrait Gallery. So Katie, who is interested in art history, made a quick stop, viewing several of the portraits on display as well as reading detailed explanations of the work.

Looking back, Katie realized that within an hour she had viewed, downloaded and printed information from the National Science Foundation in Washington, D.C.; the University of Michigan in Ann Arbor; Stanford University in Palo Alto, California; and then two sites in Australia. Yet she never left her seat in the computer lab. In a few hours, she had more than enough information for her report about the state of the art in library technology. By the time she was finished, she probably knew as much as many librarians about the future of libraries.

Katie Devine had been surfing the Web.

In this chapter you will

- Learn about the history and development of the World Wide Web.
- Understand the basic structure of the Web.
- Be introduced to the software you need to use the Web.
- Develop search strategies to effectively apply the Web to your work.
- Be instructed in the basics of building sites on the Web.
- Receive tips about how to avoid common pitfalls and resolve basic problems that occur when people use the Web.

The history and development of the Web

The World Wide Web began when Tim Berners-Lee, then a researcher with CERN, the European Particle Physics Laboratory in Geneva, developed what he called a hypermedia initiative for global information sharing. Since the mid-1970s, CERN had been a leader in developing and using computer networks. In 1988, CERN researchers had collaborated with scientists from the Amsterdam Mathematics Center to establish the European Internet, a network of European computer networks all running the TCP/IP protocol described in Chapter 2.

CERN quickly became the largest Internet site in Europe. Moreover, as a result of its activity in developing networks during the course of nearly 20 years, a culture based on distributed computing had developed among researchers at the laboratory. In a distributed computing environment, tasks are divided among many computers and researchers who then swap and share needed information.

There were many problems inherent in a distributed computing environment. Because different computers and software tools were not compatible with each other, it was difficult, time consuming and frustrating to share information among scientists. Moreover, it was virtually impossible to easily move through related information stored on different types of computers. For example, as Berners-Lee wrote in the original proposal for the World

Fig. 4-1: Home page for Mosaic provides links to many network resources.

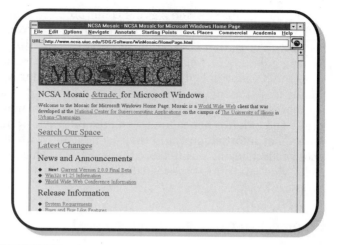

Wide Web, if a researcher found an incomplete piece of software online with the name of Joe Bloggs on it, it would be difficult to find Bloggs' e-mail address. "Usually," he wrote, "you will have to use a different look-up method on a different computer with a different user interface."

The World Wide Web was Berners-Lee's solution to that problem. The objective was to provide a single-user interface to access widely varied classes of information stored on different computers on the Internet. To achieve that objective, several elements had to be developed, including a simple protocol for requesting information stored on different computers that could be read by people (as opposed to information that can be read only by computers); a protocol so the information could be converted into a format that both the sending computer and the receiving computer understood; and a method for reading the information on screen.

To achieve those goals, Berners-Lee proposed a system based on the concept of hypertext. With hypertext, information can be organized and accessed in a nonlinear fashion. In other words, you can easily skip around to different sections of a document. For example, imagine you have a book and there is a footnote labeled number 3 on page 5. With hypertext you can move from the footnote number on the page to the footnote itself with the click of a mouse.

In Berners-Lee's vision, page 5 could be stored on one computer and the footnote on another. The development of hypertext links connecting text, sound, graphics and video information located on different computers became known as hypermedia.

Finally, the Web, Berners-Lee suggested, would use client-server architecture. As you know from previous chapters, within a client-server set-up, client software running on one computer sends a request to another computer running server software. The server then fulfills the request. Because in most cases, any computer on a network can serve as both a client and a server, the number of Web servers could proliferate dramatically. Linking different kinds of information stored on all kinds of computers scattered in disparate places, Berners-Lee suggested, would create a web of information. No single document would have links to all other related documents, but users could follow linked documents to find related information, ultimately linking up to the information they want.

Moreover, users could assemble their own collections of information stored locally and link to other computers on the Internet running Web server software. That information could then be accessed with Web client software. Those collections of locally stored information, which can be text, images, audio, video and other types of data, have come to be called *home pages, Web pages* or *Web sites*.

Graphical software gave Web a boost

Although Berners-Lee clearly laid out the structure of the Web and the strategy, the development that turned it into a widespread, global phenomenon was the creation of Web browsing software with a graphical interface. The browser is the client software used to navigate the Web and to display information.

While he was still an undergraduate at the University of Illinois–Urbana Champaign, Marc Andreesen led the project team that developed a browser called Mosaic. Mosaic allowed users to navigate through the Web simply by clicking a mouse pointer on icons, text and buttons. Mosaic was developed under the auspices of the National Center for Supercomputing Applications (NCSA) at the University of Illinois and was initially distributed free by FTP, a network protocol described in Chapter 6.

Andreesen left Illinois, and with Jim Clark founded Netscape Communications Corporation, which publishes the popular Web browser Netscape Navigator. Several companies also publish commercial versions of Mosaic. But reflecting their roots in academe, Netscape and Mosaic remain free for use in academic settings. Available by FTP from the TradeWave Galaxy site are graphical Web browsers WinWeb (Windows) and MacWeb (Macintosh). Cello is a graphical browser for Windows available by FTP at Cornell University Law School. Consequently, Web browsers should be available on many of the public computers in computer labs across campus. If not, talk to your computer support office to get Web browsers installed.

The popularity of the Web

After the emergence of Mosaic, the Web as a network resource literally exploded. In the summer of 1993, there were approximately 100 home pages on the Web. Now there are more than 4 million home pages. In May 1994 alone the equivalent of 2,300 *Encyclopedia Britannicas* of information traveled through the Web, and since then the quantity of Web traffic (measured in bytes) has been doubling every two to three months.

Fig. 4-2: Traditional magazines such as *Time* and *People* are available in graphical format on the World Wide Web.

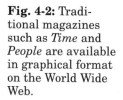

The popularity of the Web and its browsers can be attributed to two factors. First, they provide a seamless interface to the entire Internet. In many ways, Web browsers are like Swiss Army knives. In addition to the knife—or the Web protocols themselves—browsers provide an umbrella for most other Internet tools including Telnet, Gopher, Usenet, and other Internet applications you will learn about in subsequent chapters. These tools generally do not have graphical user interfaces. Consequently, they appear less friendly to use. You have to remember commands, and there are other inconveniences and difficulties. On the other hand, graphical browsers like Netscape and Mosaic operate like the Windows and Macintosh operating systems, so you can quickly master their primary commands.

The second reason the Web has become so popular is the variety of information available. Not only are colleges and universities making information available via the Web, all sorts of companies, from local Pizza Hut stores to Time Warner, the publishers of *Time* and *Entertainment Weekly* magazines, are scrambling to create a presence on the Web. As a result the Web is a lot of fun to use. You can find all sorts of interesting information, from academic research to city guides to directories and descriptions of microbreweries. Not only do many major libraries have a presence on the Web, so do most of the major movie studios. You can find advanced scientific studies, law journals, state-of-the-art literary criticism and reams of census data. You can buy CDs, order books, play advanced computer games, "tour" foreign countries, and download public domain software through the Web. For many people, the Web is useful both at work and at play.

For example, Stefani Manowski was assigned to write a report about the civil war in Bosnia. She normally would have done the research by reading newspaper articles, but using the Web, she was able to download a daily English language news service from Croatia, one of the front-line states in the conflict. Later, she was able to track the activities of some of her favorite music bands, also using the Web.

The structure of the Web

The Web is built on a three-part foundation: a scheme to identify and locate documents, protocols for retrieving documents, and a method for supporting hypermedia links to information stored in different files on different computers. The scheme for identifying and locating documents on the Web is called the Uniform Resource Locator (URL). The primary Web protocol is called the HyperText Transfer Protocol (http). The method for supporting hypermedia links is known as the HyperText Markup Language (HTML). For moving among home pages on the Web, understanding the URL is critical. For preparing information for distribution through the Web, knowing the basics of HTML is key. But to understand the reach of the Web, having a grasp of the notion of transport protocols is essential.

Web transport protocols

The main distinction between the Web and other ways to move information around the Internet such as Gopher, which you will learn about in Chapter 5, and WAIS, which you will learn about in Chapter 9, is the model of data they use. For example, for Gopher, data is either a menu, a document, an index or a Telnet connection (Chapter 6). With WAIS, everything is an index, linked to a document. In the Web, all data is treated as potentially part of a larger hypermedia document linked to other parts of the document residing on other computers. Consequently, in the Web, all data is potentially searchable.

Because of the model of data it uses, the Web is able to provide access to servers with information intended to be used with other transport protocols such as Telnet, Gopher, WAIS and Usenet. Nevertheless, a specific transport protocol—http—has been developed for the Web itself as well.

The http protocol underpins the entire World Wide Web. It has several significant attributes. First, it is what is called stateless and generic—that means it can communicate with different computers running different operating systems. Second, it is object oriented. Object-oriented software is a method that allows complex information to be treated as a single object. Third, it can recognize and represent different types of data. That means the mechanisms to transport data can be built independent from the data itself. Finally, it communicates with other Internet protocols and gateways.

You can think of it this way: http treats all data as if they were containers in shipping. A container can be transported on a ship, truck, train or airplane. It doesn't matter what is inside the container; that will be revealed when the container is opened at its final destination. In addition to sending the containers, http also handles all the paperwork needed to travel from port to port.

You really don't have to understand the mechanics of http. But you must keep in mind that http is designed to move data such as text, graphics, audio and video around the Web. Other tools are needed to actually see or hear the information when it arrives at its destination. Those tools will be fully explained on the section about browsers later in this chapter.

Finally, although http was developed for the Web, it also can communicate with other transport protocols. Unlike other Internet protocols, which can only work with the cyberspace equals of, let's say, ocean freight, http, can manage all the Internet methods of transportation. In many ways, the Web is the umbrella environment for the entire Internet.

The anatomy of an URL

To move information to and from a location, you must know that location's address. A Uniform or Universal Resource Locator (the names are currently interchangeable) is a method for locating resources on the Web. In its most basic formulation, an URL has two parts: the scheme or protocol used to access the information and an identifier of the information. The specific format of the way the information is identified depends on the protocol used to access the information. In general terms, an URL is presented this way:

<protocol>:<information-identifier>

Because most of the information you will access via the Web uses http as its protocol or method of access, most of the URLs you will see will be for http. The general format for an URL for http is

http://host computer(:port number)/file path/

The host computer is the server from which your browser is requesting information. (The port number is the communications port the computer is using and is generally included only if the computer is using a nonstandard port.) As you recall, every computer on the Internet has a unique identification or IP number. Those IP numbers are long strings of numbers and are very difficult to remember. Fortunately, there is a way to assign a name—called an alias—for those numbers. So instead of remembering the numbers for a computer, you can remember a name. For example, *Scientific Computing & Automation* magazine has an experimental home page running on a computer at the Center for the Advanced Study of Online Communication at Loyola College. The computer's IP number is 144.126.5.84. That computer has been assigned the name (or alias) of gordonpub.loyola.edu. The URL for *Scientific Computing & Automation* is http://gordonpub.loyola.edu. The computer running the home page of the television network CBS has been assigned the name www.cbs.com. The URL for CBS is http://www.cbs.com.

Once you get to the computer on which the information you want is stored, you then have to access the specific information in which you are interested. Information is stored on Web servers in the standard path/file format described in Chapter 1. The different directories, subdirectories and file names are separated in the URL by the / mark.

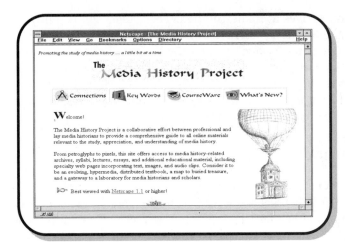

Fig. 4-3: The "History of Communication Media Technology" page is the production of Kristina Ross, assistant professor at the University of Texas–El Paso.

To fully understand the anatomy of an URL, consider this example. Kristina Ross at the University of Colorado has set up a Web site about the history of communication. The URL for the site is http://spot.colorado.edu/~rossk/history/histhome.html. That means the information uses the http protocol and is on a computer called spot.colorado.edu under the directory ~rossk and the subdirectory history. The file that will be accessed is called histhome.html. Undoubtedly that file will contain information, perhaps text and graphics, plus links to files of information stored on computers elsewhere on the Internet.

As noted earlier, in addition to http, the Web supports access to a wide range of Internet protocols including FTP, Gopher, Telnet, news and nntp (which are Usenet news groups protocols), mailto (electronic mail addressing), and other less-used protocols. Consequently, when you see an URL that begins ftp://, you know that you will be accessing information from an FTP server.

In most cases, however, while you are using the Web you will be using the http protocol. You will move from link to link in hypermedia documents, in the process jumping to new URLs. It is the hyperlinks that make the Web such a dynamic service.

Your browser—graphical or text

Understanding the basic elements of the Web will help you maximize your benefits. But to use the Web, all you need is a Web browser, which is the term used for the client software for the Web. Unlike e-mail, in which you need your own mailbox, with the Web you can basically use any computer running Web client software. The browser is the software that makes the requests to Web servers for information and then displays the information that is returned on your computer.

At most colleges you will find Web browsers on many of the public-access computers linked to networks connected to the Internet. Due to

Fig. 4-4: The Lynx browser is text-based. Words that are linked to other networked documents appear highlighted on the screen.

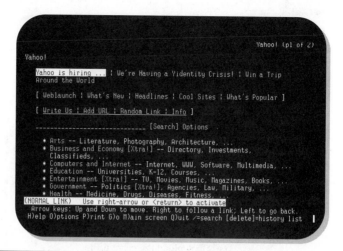

the Web's roots in academe, many browsers, including versions of both Netscape and Mosaic; are free for academic users. That is why virtually any school with Internet access should have Web browsers loaded on many publicly accessible computers. It may not always be the latest or best version of the browser, but most are sufficient to let you get a taste of the Web.

Some schools may not have graphical Web browsers. There is a text-based Web browser called Lynx, which you may find running on a central computer or in your campus labs. Using keyboard commands in Lynx may not be as easy as using a point-and-click graphic interface, but it works. Although it won't display graphics, Lynx will allow you to retrieve and display text files. And because it is text-based, it can be used by people who dial into a central computer and it can be accessed through Telnet connections (Chapter 6). You move around in Lynx by using the cursor arrow keys. For example, the Up arrow and Down arrow keys move your cursor selector up and down through document links. Pressing the Right arrow key selects a link and takes you to the document indicated. Pressing the Left arrow key takes you back to the previous document. You launch the dialog for opening a new site by typing a "g" (for Goto). A summary of Lynx keyboard commands is given in Figure 4-5.

Like other applications software, browsers allow you to perform many tasks. The most important, of course, is that the browser allows you to request information from Web servers and then displays the information. You may have the option to save the information to a file or download it to your computer. In addition, many browsers allow you to copy, cut and paste information from the screen into word-processing documents. There are also tools for setting and keeping bookmarks on the URLs of sites that you visit often and the sites you pass through. Some browsers allow you to send e-mail directly from them without exiting to an e-mail program.

Keyboard Commands for Lynx

Movement:

Down arrow .... Highlight next topic
Up arrow .... Highlight previous topic
Right arrow, ... Jump to highlighted topic
Return, Enter
Left arrow .... Return to previous topic

Scrolling:

+ (or space) .... Scroll down to next page
– (or b) .... Scroll up to previous page

Other:

? (or h) .... Help screens
a .... Add current link to your bookmarks
c .... Send a comment to document owner
d .... Download the current link
e .... Edit the current file
g .... Goto a user-specified URL or file
i .... Show an index of documents
j .... Execute a jump operation
k .... Show a list of key mappings
m .... Return to main screen
o .... Set your options
p .... Print to a file, mail, printers, or other
q .... Quit (Capital Q for quick quit)
/ .... Find string within current document
s .... Find string in an external document
n .... Go to the next search string
v .... View your bookmark file
= .... Show file and link info
\ .... Toggle doc. source/rendered view
! .... Spawn your default shell
Ctrl-R   Reload current file & refresh the screen
Ctrl-W .... Refresh the screen
Ctrl-U .... Erase input line
Ctrl-G .... Cancel input or transfer

Fig. 4-5: Common keyboard commands for Lynx, a text-based World Wide Web browser, follow many of the same conventions as Gopher, an earlier Internet browser described in Chapter 5.

Not all browsers are created equal

Although many browsers are available free on the Internet, not all can display all the information available on the Web. All can display text, but some browsers have difficulty displaying some images. Not all can play back audio and many cannot play back full-motion video. For example, many schools are running Mosaic 1.03, which does not automatically play back audio, video or some graphics formats.

The inability to load all data types is not just a function of how old the software is. It is a result of the Web being made up of many different types of computers. For example, many browsers running under the Unix operating system cannot play back Quicktime files, which are full-motion video files in a Macintosh format.

If the browser you use does not display all the different data types available, you should consult with academic computing support staff to load the necessary additional viewers. The viewers are available free via FTP, which you will learn about in Chapter 6. If you are setting up a browser to run on your own machine, it is fairly easy to locate GIF, JPEG, and MPEG viewers and audio-playback software. The names of some JPEG and GIF graphics viewers are Lview (Windows) and Jpeg View (Mac). Wham and Wplayany are sound players for Windows; Sound Machine is for the Mac. MPEG Player 3.2 is a full-motion video viewer for Windows; Sparkle is for the Mac.

A second factor to keep in mind if you are configuring a browser on your own computer is that the computer must be running TCP/IP. All Macintoshes with System 7.5 and above already have TCP/IP, as does Windows 95. With earlier versions of Windows or Mac systems prior to 7.5, however, you will have to install TCP/IP yourself. For the Macintosh you have to have MacTCP loaded at startup. For Windows 3.1, you can download the Microsoft TCP/IP stack from ftp.microsoft.com, or you can get a shareware program called Trumpet Winsock.

Finally, there is one drawback about graphical Web browsers that has limited their availability in many places: hardware requirements. Graphical Web browsers require not only the right network connection (direct connection or modem via SLIP or PPP), but they require fast machines with lots of memory. Mosaic, for example, requires 8MB of random access memory (RAM) whether it is on the Mac or a Windows machine. On the Mac, Mosaic requires System 7. On Windows, Mosaic 2 requires either Windows 95, or you must upgrade Windows 3.1 with 32-bit extensions. WinWeb, MacWeb, and Netscape are almost as demanding. Cello1.0 (a Windows only program), on the other hand, has been reported to run on 386sx machines with only 2MB of RAM. These hardware limitations—the need to have fast network connections and high-end computers—are largely limited to graphical browsers and in no way represent requirements for all network access.

Surfing the Web

When you start a Web browser, the first thing that happens is that it loads a home page. By default, the freeware versions of Mosaic generally call out to the home page (that is, information on the Web server) of the NCSA. Netscape calls out to the home page of Netscape Communications, its publisher. MacWeb and WinWeb are preconfigured to open the TradeWave Galaxy page.

Because these tend to be busy home pages, many people change the initial home pages—also called *default home pages*. In some browsers, the

Fig. 4-6: Activities in graphical Web browsers, such as "opening a location" using an URL or choosing software preferences, are done through drop/pull down menus.

default home page can be changed by pulling down on the Options menu across the top of the browser and choosing Preferences or Configure. Many schools use their own home page as the default. Others use the home pages of specific academic departments.

Once the browser is operating, you can then jump to virtually any location on the Web. If you know the URL of the information (or location) you want, you can pull down the File menu and choose Open Location (Netscape), Navigate (MacWeb or WinWeb), Jump (Cello), or something similar. You then enter the URL or the location from which you are requesting information.

When your browser requests information from a Web server, a three-part process occurs. First, if the Web server has an alias, the request is sent to what is called a Domain Name Server (DNS) to determine the IP number for the computer. Once the IP number has been determined, the appropriate server is contacted and the information is requested. Finally, the data is transmitted to the browser on your computer for viewing.

For example, let's say you are an environmental science student and you want to access information from the Earth and Environmental Science Center at the Pacific Northwest Laboratory. You heard the Web site there has descriptions of the research being conducted as well as a listing of hydrology resources accessible through the Internet. Under the File menu you would pull down to Open Location and then enter the URL, which in this case is http://terrassa.pnl.gov:2080.

The request from your browser is sent to the DNS to look up the IP number of the computer called terrassa.pnl.gov. The request is then sent to that computer and the information—in this case the Web site's opening page—will be transported to your browser for display. But let's say you are not interested in the research being conducted at the lab. All you want is the hydrology resource list. Then you can enter the URL http://terrassa.pnl.gov:2080/resourcelist/hydrology.html. In reply, you will receive the file that contains the list itself, which probably provides links to information found elsewhere on the Internet.

There are two important lessons to be learned from this example. First, every file available via the Web has its own, unique URL. You do not have to first call up the page that the people who have created the Web site present as their first file and then travel down layers to find what you want. Virtually every file of information on the Web is accessible from every other place on the Internet. Second, you don't actually log onto the remote computer. You simply make a request for information, which is then sent back to your computer for display.

Opening a specific URL is only one way to travel through the Web. The real power comes through when you automatically jump, or surf, from place to place using links the creators of the site have established. For example, let's say you are planning to go to graduate school and you want to find information about universities across the United States. You can open the URL http://wwwhost.cc.utexas.edu/world/univ/alpha, which is a file on the Web server of the University of Texas. You will receive a listing of 560 university Web sites. If you click your mouse on the name of one, you have requested information from that site be sent to your browser for, well, browsing. Depending on the links at that site, you can continue moving through the Web. It is this ability to follow links on the Web that gives users the sensation of surfing on a sea of information.

Where are you and how do you get back?

As you move from site to site on the Web by clicking on linked information, it is useful to know the URL of the Web servers you access. If you find useful information, you may want to return to the same site later.

The first step to staying oriented is knowing where you are. Under the Options menu on the tool bar in Netscape and Mosaic, you can click on Show Location. Then, as you move from Web site to Web site, the exact URL for each file you access will be displayed.

As you move through the Web, you may find that you want to move back and forth among several pages. For example, after you accessed the list of colleges and universities at the University of Texas Web site, let's say you then jumped to the home page of American University in Washington, D.C., at http://www.amu.edu/. There, you followed a link to its Department of Health Fitness and then another to the National Center for Health Fitness, which is located there.

From there, if you just want to return to the information about the Department of Health Fitness, you can click on the Back button (in Lynx you would use the left arrow). But if you want to return to the master list of universities at the University of Texas, the most efficient way is to pull down on the Go command on the menu bar of the browser. You will see a history of the sites you have visited during that session. Highlight the site to which you want to return, and you automatically jump back to there. Keep in mind, though, that if you visit a lot of sites during a single session, the history list may be truncated at some point.

If in the course of surfing the Web you find sites that you are sure you will want to return to regularly, you can bookmark these sites. When you are at the page of information to which you wish to return—perhaps the opening page of the site of a favorite magazine—you pull down on the Bookmark command on the menu bar and click on Add. The URL will automatically be added to a list of URLs saved earlier. To access an URL on the list, simply double click on it and off you go.

Remember, however, that if you are working at a computer to which other users have access, such as a computer in a computer lab, the other users could delete your bookmarks. To be safe, you may wish to compile a list of the URLs of your favorite sites on paper or on a floppy disk. If your list is on a disk, you can copy and place the URLs into the Open Location line when you wish to revisit sites.

Finding information on the Web

In the spring of 1995 there were more than 4 million Web sites on the World Wide Web. By August there were more than 6 million. And while it is a lot of fun to surf from site to site, happily discovering interesting information, the Web also is a dynamic source to find information that you need for a report or project or to simply give you a better insight into the subjects in which you are interested.

There are many different ways to locate information on the Web—some systematic and some based on understanding the way the Web works. For example, Tanya Zicko was assigned to write a report about budget cuts in public broadcasting. She went to the library, but all the books about public broadcasting were at least five years old and not much help.

But Tanya knew that many companies and organizations use a standard format for their URLs. The URL is www.company name or initials.domain. As you learned in Chapter 3, the domain indicates the kind of organization operating the computer network on the Internet. There are six top-level network domains in the United States.

So Tanya sat down with her Web browser and entered "http://www.pbs.org" at the Open Location line. She reasoned that the Public Broadcasting System would go by the initials PBS, and because it is a nonprofit organization, it would be in the .org domain. She was right. She accessed the opening page of the Public Broadcasting System's Web server. There she found many press releases and transcripts of congressional testimony relating to her topic. She also visited www.cpb.org, the home page of the Corporation for Public Broadcasting, PBS' parent organization, where she found additional information. Instead of being based on five-year-old information, Tanya's report was filled with the most timely facts, figures and perspectives.

Fig. 4-7: Several sites on the World Wide Web, such as Yahoo, shown here, provide keyword search engines for finding documents specific to your interest.

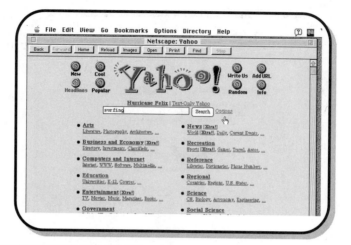

While many Web URLs follow the general format www.company or organization name.domain, many do not. Moreover, many times you will not know where the information in which you are interested is located. In those cases, there are two primary vehicles for finding information about the topics you want on the Web: Web search engines and Web subject listings.

As the Web began to grow in popularity, several teams of researchers began to explore ways to automatically index all the information available online. These researchers created software *robots* that travel through the Web to identify new Web pages. They then index the pages according to keywords and other mechanisms. The researchers then created methods to access the index according to keywords. Taken together, the indexing and accessing of Web information serves as what is called a search engine.

Keyword searches

Currently, there are several active search engines available to users of the Web. Among the more popular are
- Infoseek (http://www.infoseek.com).
- Lycos (http://lycos.cs.cmu.edu).
- Webcrawler (http://webcrawler.com.html).
- World Wide Web Worm (http://www.cs.colorado.edu/home/ mcbryan.wwww.html).
- OpenText (http://opentext.uunet.ca:8080/omw.html/).
- TradeWave Galaxy (http://galaxy.einet.net) .
- Jump Station (http://js.stir.ac.uk./jsbin/js).

The University of Geneva, Switzerland, publishes what it calls W3 Search Engines (http://cuiwww.uniqe.ch/meta-index.html), which provides access to 19 different search engines including some for other Internet protocols like Gopher and WAIS.

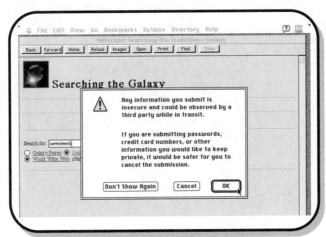

Fig. 4-8: Security warnings occur frequently in Netscape when you submit information in a form—even in a routine search. These warnings are gentle reminders that it is easy to intercept credit card information unless it is encrypted.

In general, the search engines work like this: Once you access the search engine, you enter keywords describing the information you want (Figure 4-7). For example, let's say you want information about molecular modeling in chemistry. The results may be a list of sites from the Web, Gopher, news groups, and others in which the title of the site or some of the key information matches the keywords you have entered. Every entry on the list is linked to the site, so you can then jump from site to site, looking for the precise information you want.

As you could tell from the URLs, some of the search engines are being operated by commercial companies, while others are offered by academic institutions. As a result, each search engine has somewhat different parameters. For example, Infoseek runs a public access service and a commercial service. The public access service, which is free, will return up to 10 appropriately linked URLs. The commercial service, which charges 10 cents per query, will return up to 200 matches. Carnegie Mellon University's Lycos allows you to search two different databases—one larger than the other. You receive results from the smaller database faster.

While search engines are very powerful tools, they have notable limitations. First, a search engine often will only return a small percentage of the Internet sites that actually match your search. For example, Webcrawler found 476 Web sites with the keywords "molecular modeling" and returned a list of 25.

Second, because searches are driven by keywords, the results may not always match your intentions. For example, let's say you want to learn the proper form for citing information found on the Internet. You enter the words "citation form." The resulting list of Web sites will include everything from the Mouse Genome Database to the Chiropractic

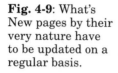

Fig. 4-9: What's New pages by their very nature have to be updated on a regular basis.

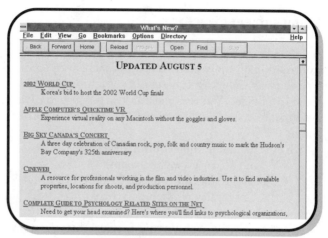

Page. Although each page has both keywords, "citation" and "form," neither has the information you seek.

Moreover, once you have run a query in a particular location, it will always return the same subset of sites. In other words, if there are 100 Web pages that match your keywords but the search engine will list only 10, you will get the same 10, no matter how many times you re-enter the keywords. Some of the Web search engines allow you to expand or to narrow your results list. But it will still be a tedious task to survey several hundred potential sites for information.

Consequently, to conduct a thorough search you will want to run several searches, varying your keywords from search to search. Furthermore, you will want to use several different search engines when you are actively seeking information.

Initially searching for information via search engines is a lot like searching for needles in hay stacks. You may find yourself looking at many irrelevant pages before you find something appropriate. Once you find a good source, you will probably want to follow links on that page to other appropriate pages. To return to the results of your search, you can use your browser's history list described earlier.

As might be expected, the major search engines are extremely busy. In one week at the end of June, 1995, when most colleges were already on vacation, more than 1.6 million Web pages were viewed from searches conducted with Lycos. With that kind of traffic, you must be sure to tailor efficient searches based on keywords that have a high possibility of identifying the information you want without having to churn through a lot of inappropriate URLs. Moreover, major search engines sometimes are too busy to respond to your requests. You may have to try several times before you can successfully complete a search.

Using subject directories

Subject directories represent an alternative to search engines for finding information on the Web. In this approach, once again, the Web is monitored by a software robot. But instead of searching the index, the pages are categorized by subject. You can click on the subject Art History, for example, and get links to 40 or 50 sites on the Web with information about Art History on them.

Six of the major subject directories are
- Yahoo (http://www.yahoo.com).
- Clearinghouse for Subject-Oriented Internet Resource Guides at the University of Michigan (http://http2.sils.umich.edu/~lou/chhome.html).
- World Wide Web Virtual Library (http://www.w3.org/hypertext/dataSources/bySubject/overview.html).
- Yanoff List (http://www.uwm.edu/mirror/inet/services.html).
- TradeWave Galaxy (http://galaxy.einet.net/).
- Whole Internet Catalog (http://gnn.digital.com/gnn/wic/newrescat.toc.html).

Another growing subject guide is being developed by City University London (http://web.city.ac.uk/citylive/pages.html), and still others pop up frequently. A directory of Web servers by location is maintained at http://wing.buffalo.edu/world. Users can click on a world map to find Web servers literally around the globe.

If you know exactly the kind of information you want, subject guides are often a productive way to start a search on the Web. Using subject guides is comparable to using the subject guides in libraries. You can easily scroll through many listings looking for the most promising material.

On the other hand, search engines often turn up resources you would never find via subject guides. For example, many college students and professors are creating their own home pages with links to a lot of interesting other Web sites. Search engines treat the home pages of college students the same as all other home pages and often will link you to an obscure but useful page of information you would not have otherwise found.

As you search for information, keep in mind that new Web servers with information are coming online every day. One place to track new pages is through What's New With NCSA Mosaic at http://www.ncsa.uiuc.edu/SDG/Software/Mosaic/Docs/whats-new.html. In addition to carrying announcements about new Web pages, it has information about new Web-related software. Netscape has What's New (http://home.mcom.com/escapes/whats_new.html/) (Figure 4-9) and What's Cool (http://home.mcom.com/escapes/whats_cool.html/) buttons on its menu bar.

If you are using Netscape, or some versions of Mosaic, using search engines and subject directories is extremely easy. Simply click on the appropriate button on the menu bar and you are automatically connected to the right page to begin the search. Otherwise, you may enter the URL for the engine or directory you wish to use with the Open Location command.

Searching the Web for information can be time consuming. Consequently, if you know that you are going to be working on a project over a period of time, it is worthwhile to subscribe to one of the appropriate online discussion groups described in Chapter 3. Web sites of interest are usually posted in discussion groups. Moreover, after you are familiar with the flow of information among group members, you can post a message asking for good sites with information about your project.

When you find what you want: printing and saving

Usually, the primary purpose of surfing the Web is to locate information you can use for class projects and assignments. In most cases, that means you will want to save the information you find.

One approach is to print the information you wish to save for future use. Most browsers allow you several options to save and print information. In fact, most have a Print command under the File button on the menu (Lynx, the text-based browser, also has a print command.) When you hit the Print command, the file at which you are looking is printed at the printer associated with the computer you are using. Remember, that printer may not be the one closest to you. So, if you are going to simply print the file directly from the browser, be sure to know where that file will be printed.

Printing from the browser has some drawbacks. The file at which you are looking may be quite long. Don't be fooled because a file is presented in fairly small chunks and there are hyperlinks from section to section in the text. For example, it is easy to find A Beginner's Guide to HTML online. The first screen you see is a table of contents. Click on any entry and you move to that section of the document. But the whole guide is only one file, 14 pages long. If you simply press the Print command, the whole file will be printed, even if you only wanted to save one page on troubleshooting.

If you do want to save a long file, you may want to store it electronically on your personal computer. You can do this using the Save As command under the File menu on the browser. Alternatively, you can mail the file to your e-mail address. To use the e-mail feature or the Netscape browser, however, you must know how to configure the mailer. You will need to know the IP number or alias of your mail server and other information. Moreover, if you are using a public access computer, anybody can change the configuration.

Most often, you will be interested only in a small part of the information you view. For example, you may not need the graphics on the page. If you only want to save parts of a document, you should open your word processor and copy part of the Web file to your computer's clipboard. Then you can paste it into a document on your word processor. The Copy and Paste commands are on the Edit menus in your browser and your word processor. After you have copied and pasted all the information you need, you can treat the file as a regular word-processing document.

The copy-and-paste approach is very effective if you wish to save bits of information from different pages. It is also a good approach if you wish to use the information on a personal computer off the network. If you use the copy-and-paste approach, be sure to carefully document where you found the information. The easiest way to accurately document the site from which you accessed information is to copy and paste the URL from the Show Location line.

Citations in cyberspace

To effectively use material you find on the Web and elsewhere on the Internet in an academic setting, you are going to have to document your work. In other words, in your footnotes, you will have to indicate where you found the information you are using.

There are two problems with footnoting information you have found in cyberspace. First, there is no universally accepted standard format for citing sources on the Internet. Second, the Internet is always changing. There is no assurance that the information will still be at the same location, should somebody want to check the sources sometime later. In fact, most of the basic background information about the Web itself has been transferred from the server at CERN in Switzerland called info.cern.ch to one at MIT called www.w3.org. While in this case users are forwarded to the new location, that will not always be the case.

The most widely used manual for citation forms is *Electronic Style: A Guide to Citing Electronic Information* by Xia Li and Nancy B. Crane (Westport, CT: Meckler, 1995). The citation format they have selected is based on the *Publication Manual of the American Psychological Association*, which is commonly used in the sciences and social sciences. A wider listing of citations for Internet protocols will be discussed in Chapter 9. For the Web, a basic acceptable form is "Author, Title, (Online), (Date, Date Retrieved), Available: protocol://host(port)/directory/subdirectory/file.name."

Although it has not been universally accepted, this citation form does address both problems of Internet citations. First, it provides a basic form. Second, it lets readers know when the information was at the given location even if it is no longer there.

Creating your own Web page

One of the reasons so many Web pages have been created is that simple Web pages are very easy to create. Indeed, many college students have created their own pages. Some professors currently require their students to build pages.

Fig. 4-10: HTML script for the Web page shown in Fig. 4-11 has more tags than it has text. The tags, enclosed in angle brackets <>, tell Web servers and clients where to get linked files and how to display text. The script shown here includes all the straight text displayed in Fig. 4-11.

```
<html><title>Welcome to SportsWorld</title>
<body bgcolor=ffffff>
<img align=left src="gif/bar.gif">
<center>
<img src="gif/sportsw&.gif">
<p>
<b><i><font size=5>W</font></b></i>elcome to
Sportsworld.line.com<br>
The REAL TIME Total Sports Web Service.
<p>
<h2>Our sponsors</h2><p>
<b><i><font size=5>P</font></b></i>lease take the
time to click into our sponsors' cool sites.<p>
<a href="/captain_morgan"><img border=0
 src="gif/clippers_sm.gif"></a><p>
<a href="/proform"><img border=0 src="/proform/gif/
prozissis.gif"></a>
<a href="/abflex"><img border=0
src="abflex/gif/abbut.gif"></a>
<a href="rogaine/rogaine.html"><img
```

The only requirement for creating a Web page is for students to be able to post HTML documents on a Web server. They can then write HTML documents with links to other appropriate files on the server, and they are online.

HTML is a plain ASCII text script language. Scripts can be created using any word processor or text editor. Documents are named with the .html file extension (or .htm if you are working in the DOS/Windows environment). HTML allows you to format a document and link sections and documents by embedding tags within text. Together, the tags and text are called the source code. See Figure 4-10 for the source code of Figure 4-11.

Tags are embedded using angle brackets < >. Some common tags are <title> for the title of the document, <h1>, for a header and <p> to separate paragraphs. A title is generally displayed separately from the text and is used to identify the contents. There are six levels of headers (h1 to h6), with h1 being the most prominent. Unlike word processors, HTML text needs the <p> to separate paragraphs. Browsers ignore indentations and blank lines in the source code. See Figure 4-10 for an example.

The main feature of HTML is linking documents and sections of documents—either text or images. Browsers highlight hypermedia links so that users know to click on them to be connected to another file. All links use the anchor tag <a>. The link includes the name of the document to which the link connects plus the text or image that is to be highlighted. The name of the document begins with the letters HREF and is enclosed by quotation marks. The full form for an anchor tag is <a href=*name of document*>*highlighted text*</a>. This form can be used to link documents running locally on the Web server and documents that are running on different servers.

Fig. 4-11: The Sports World Web site has a simplified text content augmented by many graphics. The HTML script for this page is given in Fig. 4-10.

Most Web browsers can also display what are called in-line images; that is, images next to text. In most cases, the images should be in a GIF or JPEG format. To include an in-line image on your Web page, you use the tag <img src=image_*url*>. The URL is the file name of the image and must end in either .gif for GIF files or .jpeg or .jpg for JPEG files. By default, the bottom of the image is aligned with the text.

The tags outlined above are enough to create very simple Web pages. More sophisticated pages use short computer routines called CGIs to enable database searching, creating links to parts of images and other advanced features. Moreover, HTML is still being developed, and there are many other tags that can be embedded. Several HTML text editors have been released and are available via the Internet. Moreover, several leading text processors such as Microsoft Word and Novell Word Perfect now allow for automatic conversion into the HTML format.

A good way to learn HTML programming is to study other pages on the Web. To see the source code for pages you are viewing, simply click on Source under the View button on your Web browser.

Error messages (when the Web goes wrong)

Many people believe that the Web is the prototype for the Information Superhighway. And it may well be. But nonetheless, even in that scenario, it is still just a prototype and does not work flawlessly.

Perhaps the main problem with the Web is that few people realized how popular it would become in such a short period of time. So, much like the streets in a rapidly developing city, there is a lot of traffic and an occasional traffic jam.

For a user, a traffic jam makes itself felt in several ways. First, if you are requesting large amounts of information, it may take a long time for the information to arrive and be viewed by your browser. In general, text is the fastest to load. Images represent a lot more data than simple text and take a longer time to be displayed. Audio and video are data intensive. Depending on the exact link to the Internet, it may take several minutes to retrieve 20 seconds worth of audio.

The speed at which information is transferred and viewed depends on the traffic on the Internet itself, the speed at which information is transferred from the Internet to the network on which the computer you are using is located—the computer that manages the transfer is called your gateway computer—and the traffic on your local network. The busier the Web and your local network, the slower the information will be transferred.

Sometimes the traffic jam is not on the Web, or your gateway or local network, but at the server from which you request information. Servers can only manage requests for information from a set number of browsers at any one time. If that limit has been exceeded, you may receive a message indicating that your connection has been refused and you should try again some other time. This is a fairly common occurrence with very busy Web sites. A less friendly "Connection refused by host" often means the same thing.

Another common problem is that the connection between your browser and the network will be unexpectedly cut off. You may not realize that you are offline for some time, particularly if you are mainly looking at pages that have been cached onto the hard drive of your computer. If you have lost your connection, you may receive a message saying that the Domain Name Server cannot find the computer even when you request information from an URL you know is good. Or, the browser may just say "host not found." If you receive that message consistently as you try different servers, you can be almost certain your connection has gone down and you should restart your browser.

As you know, URLs are generally made up of long strings of characters. It is very easy to make mistakes when you enter an URL into the Open Location line. If you have incorrectly entered the name of the Web server on which the information you want resides, you will receive the message "host not found." When that happens, you should check the first part of the URL.

If you incorrectly entered the directory path and file name for the information you want, you will probably receive a message which says "404 File Not Found." That means you have sent your request to a legitimate Web server but the specific file you asked for could not be located.

Finally, as you surf the Web, from time to time you will come to sites that will ask you to register. Some will allow you to buy things online. While it is up to you to decide if you wish to register at a site, for the most part, transactions on the Internet are not yet secure. That means people can intercept and monitor information as it travels through the networks. Until further notice, you should never send any credit card information or other confidential data to sites on the Web. It is much safer to handle those kinds of transactions offline. You should consider the Web a public place and act accordingly.

Alternative access

To fully enjoy and exploit the Web, you want to have a browser running a graphical user interface on a personal computer. If for some reason your school does not provide graphical browsers but does have Internet access, you can experience the Web by telnetting to either the University of Kansas (ukanaix.cc.ukans.edu), where you log in as www and can run Lynx, or to the New Jersey Institute of Technology (www.njit.edu), which also offers public access to a full-screen Web browser. There are also public-access browsers located in other parts of the world including Israel (vms.huji.ac.il, login: www), Hungary (fsev.kfki.hu, login: www) and Finland (info.funet.fi, login: www). Many Gopher sites also provide access to Lynx clients.

Conclusion

With the World Wide Web, the whole world is your library. Literally millions of people are making information available on Web servers to be accessed by people with Web browsers. Browsers with graphical user interfaces like Mosaic and Netscape are easy to use and if your school has not yet loaded them on accessible computers, you should request that they do.

On the other hand, with the World Wide Web, it is as if the Library of Congress just opened but nobody has ever seen a book before. It is thrilling to be able to access all sorts of information. But inevitably, at some point you will want to locate information for specific purposes.

Finding specific, high-quality information is still a challenge. To integrate the Web into your work, you will have to invest time to gain experience. You will want to develop your own hot list and bookmarks. You should leave enough time in each project to follow links to see where they lead. You should explore.

As you get access to more information, you will face new demands. For example, in an ethics course, Kara Kiefer decided to write about assisted euthanasia. In the middle of the semester, she read an article in the *New York Times* which referred to a New York State Legislative Report on law and dying.

In the past, citing the article in the *Times* would have been sufficient. But Kara wasn't satisfied. She went up on the Web and, working through subject directories, found a copy of the original report on the Web site of the Indiana University Law School.

Kara's success meant that she then had to read a long, complicated report. Finding the report on the Web meant she had to do more work. But her finished product was also much better. More importantly, she had learned more and had more fun doing it.

Chapter 5

Gopher tunnels through Net

The assignment was typical for an advanced sociology class. Each student was supposed to do research on a major social problem, gathering as much hard data as possible. Students were even encouraged to locate databases on which they could perform their own statistical analysis.

But if the assignment was routine, the approach some students took was not. Instead of just traipsing to the library to look at the usual sources, two turned to the Veronica search engine for Gopher servers around the world. One student looking at teenage pregnancy found that by some accountings the rate of teenage pregnancies was actually declining. A second student, who had selected child abuse, was connected to the National Data Archive on Child Abuse and Neglect, which offered a rich archive of data sets for analysis.

How did they know to turn to Gopher? A friend of theirs in a religion class had been assigned to do a report on a religious group she knew little about. A native of New York, she had read about the Chabad-Lubavitch community of Jews whose headquarters was in Crown Heights, Brooklyn. She discovered that Chabad ran its own Gopher server. Indeed, it served as the main source of information for her project.

The student in the religion class had also discovered Gopher by word of mouth. She had attended a session on substance abuse at her campus and the presenter had mentioned that there was information posted on the Campus Wide Information System. She had a friend who she thought had a substance abuse problem and she wanted to know how to access the information. Gopher was the way.

In this chapter, you will learn how to
- Use Gopher to quickly navigate among network sites worldwide and to bring information quickly into the student's personal computer.

- Use Veronica and Jughead programs to locate information stored on Gopher servers.
- Use Gopher servers as a gateway to access FTP, Hytelnet, Usenet and other network resources.
- Gain access to Gopher clients if one is not freely available on your host.
- Become acquainted with a few Gopher clients that run on personal workstations.

This chapter assumes that you are already comfortable with using your campus computer account and that you know how to log into that account. Although generally we discuss several Internet finding tools separately, the tools are in many ways interconnected. Both Gopher and World Wide Web browsing clients provide gateways to nearly all the other Internet tools. Most of the examples described throughout this chapter refer to text-based Gopher clients of the type available on campus central host computers operating under VMS or Unix system software. The section labeled "Some other Gopher clients" near the end of the chapter discusses the kind of clients available for personal workstations. Regardless of the client you are working with, you will be able to perform the same actions, subject to the restraints mentioned in the text.

A short history of Gopher

As recently as 1991, the only way to pull information from the Internet was unfriendly and often complex. That was before Gopher. Before Gopher, people who used the Internet with any frequency might keep notebooks full of network addresses near their computers. Almost any network move required you to type out long addresses and sometimes complicated commands. No two places on the Net had exactly the same appearance and command structure; therefore, you might keep small notebooks telling you how to get around at each of your favorite network sites. Furthermore, it was difficult to do anything on the Net unless you knew the Unix computer operating system. Network navigation could be most intimidating.

Then late in 1991 some folks at the University of Minnesota, where the school mascot is the Golden Gopher, released a piece of software known as Gopher. It put a uniform face on the Internet so that one site looked the same as the next and responded to the same commands in the same way. By mid-1992, the Net was buzzing with Gopher fans. All you had to do was to point a cursor at an item of interest (or type in its menu number) and hit the Enter key. Gopher then went out, tunneled through the Internet, and brought back to your computer the thing you asked for.

Gopher can find and retrieve anything from weather reports in Pittsburgh to movie listings in Paris. Gopher can bring back to you reports on earthquakes and other disasters from around the world; student newspapers across the United States; full, searchable text of great literary works; or the *CIA Factbook* reports on nations around the world. Newer Gopher software can also fetch and display photographs and artwork as well as digital audio recordings of music, debates and other sounds.

In short, Gopher can be a powerful ally in your quest for mastery over the Internet. Like Mosaic, Netscape and Cello, Gopher is browsing software. But while the World Wide Web organizes network files into a web of hypermedia links, Gopher arranges network server information into hierarchical menus generally ordered around topic areas.

Campus Wide Information Systems

In 1991, folks at the University of Minnesota Computer Center needed a more efficient way of passing along instructions for using computers on the campus. At the same time, another group on campus was looking for a computer-based document delivery system. The Computer Center people wanted a simple, easy-to-use and easy-to-support program that supported browsing of documents (scrolling through documents backward and forward to support online reading). Through the summer and the fall, a Minnesota programming team led by Mark McCahill developed Gopher software that would run on Macintoshes, PCs, Unix machines, and NeXT workstations.

Minnesota's release late in 1991 of this new Internet navigating program drew interest from other universities. Cornell University had been looking for a way to place campus information services into a network environment that would make it available at workstations throughout the campus. Instead of designing their own program, they adopted Gopher. Others followed suit. In the months that followed, campuses throughout the United States adopted Gopher to serve as a friendly face for online campus information. Students, staff and faculty now had an easy-to-use system that gave them calendars of campus events, access to college catalogs, directories for the campus community, access to the library and more. Gopher didn't care whether you used phone lines to dial into the campus computer system from some other place or you sat at a machine on campus. The menus were the same, and Gopher always responded to the same commands. Gopher appeared to be an elegant solution to the need many schools had for a Campus Wide Information System—CWIS for short.

But Gopher provides access to more than just the campus. As easily as it opened and displayed a University of Minnesota campus calendar or class schedule, it could reach across the network and display the same from Rice University in Houston, the University of California at Los Angeles, or the University of Alabama in Tuscaloosa. All the Gopher user has to do to access campus documents is to point at a menu item describing the document in question and then hit the Return key to retrieve the document, whether it is a menu or a text file.

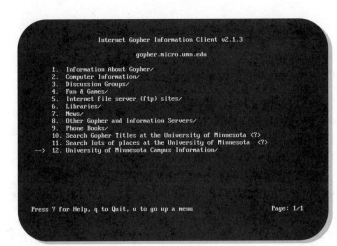

Fig. 5-1: Gopher organizes Internet information into menus. Cursor keys move a selector arrow (here on choice 12) up and down. Hitting the Enter key or Right arrow key selects the item on which the pointer rests.

The ability to reach with the same ease across campus, across the state, the nation, or the globe brought with it some challenging side effects. To tame the flood of information made available by Gopher, the information needed to be organized in some logical manner, and there needed to be some convenient way to search across the network for widely scattered documents relating to the same topic. Veronica and Jughead (discussed later) provided the searching mechanisms, and Gopher's built-in menuing structure suggested grouping pointers to documents on related topics under the same menu or group of menus.

Menu hierarchies

If your campus host computer has a gopher client, you connect to the University of Minnesota main Gopher server by typing

gopher gopher.micro.umd.edu <CR>

or by telling your Gopher client to "open the location" gopher.micro.umd.edu. In either case, you are greeted by a simple menu offering you twelve choices, the last of which promises information about the University of Minnesota campus (Figure 5-1).

To select the campus information you would do one of three things. First, you might type the number of the entry you want to select (12). Second, after using your Down arrow to point at menu choice 12, you might either hit the Enter key on your keyboard, or third, you might hit the Right arrow key. Gopher brings a new menu to your screen that displays 18 choices and tells you that you are looking at the first of two screens. (The lower right-hand corner of the screen in Fig. 5-2 says says "Page: 1/2.") You selected one menu choice that took you to another menu rather than to a text file (or graphic or sound file). In turn, the new menu might take you to yet another menu.

Fig. 5-2: Having selected "University of Minnesota Campus Information" from Minnesota's top Gopher menu, you are greeted with a new menu that is two screens full. The lower right-hand part of the screen tells you that you are on page (screen) 1 of 2.

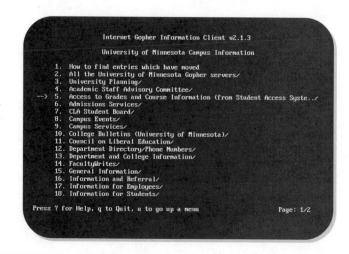

```
              Internet Gopher Information Client v2.1.3

                University of Minnesota Campus Information

        1.  How to find entries which have moved
        2.  All the University of Minnesota Gopher servers/
        3.  University Planning/
        4.  Academic Staff Advisory Committee/
    --> 5.  Access to Grades and Course Information (from Student Access Syste../
        6.  Admissions Services/
        7.  CLA Student Board/
        8.  Campus Events/
        9.  Campus Services/
       10.  College Bulletins (University of Minnesota)/
       11.  Council on Liberal Education/
       12.  Department Directory/Phone Numbers/
       13.  Department and College Information/
       14.  FacultyWrites/
       15.  General Information/
       16.  Information and Referral/
       17.  Information for Employees/
       18.  Information for Students/

    Press ? for Help, q to Quit, u to go up a menu            Page: 1/2
```

This structure of layering or nesting menus one beneath another is known as a hierarchical menuing system. It is characteristic of Gopher and used at many Telnet sites (Chapter 6). Under such a system, you select one menu choice after another, burrowing deeper into the information system, until you open a terminal document, usually text. It could be a graphic or other file, or you might wind up selecting a menu choice that tells Gopher to hand you off to a Telnet session or to some other network client (such as a Lynx World Wide Web browser).

Navigating GopherSpace

GopherSpace—as that part of the Internet accessed by Gopher clients is called —is by nature organized into menus, which in turn are organized in hierarchical fashion, generally with menu items on related topics. You call up (bring to your screen) Gopher documents by moving a cursor device to the item of interest and select it by hitting the Enter key, or the Right arrow key, by typing the number of the menu item, or, in some graphical clients, by double clicking your mouse pointer on the item.

Once you have selected a document and brought it to your screen, you may have options to print the document, e-mail it to yourself, save it to disk, or close it. Gopher allows the option of doing many other things as well. From within Gopher you may visit other sites by *pointing* your Gopher at them. You may set, retrieve, edit, and view bookmarks. You may launch sessions with other Internet tools such as WAIS, Hytelnet, Telnet and FTP. You may call up searching mechanisms such as Archie, Veronica, and Jughead. You may scroll backward and forward through documents and move up and down the menu hierarchy. You may call up information about a document without actually retrieving the item in question. All of these actions are available through a small set of keyboard commands. Graphical Gopher browsers

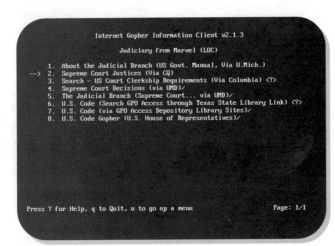

Fig. 5-3: This Gopher menu lists three different kinds of choices indicated by the character at the end of each line. A slash mark (/) denotes another menu; a bracketed question mark (<?>) suggests a search dialog; and no mark or a period marks a text document.

permit you to do these things through the use of drop-down or pull-down menus activated by a mouse.

Some Gopher commands and conventions

The way Gopher lists menu items gives the user information about the menu listing. In Figure 5-3, menu lines 4, 5, 7 and 8 end with a slash mark (/), indicating that each line marks a directory that will have further choices if it is selected. The selector arrow in Figure 5-3 points to menu choice 2, which has no punctuation at the end of the line. Lines with no punctuation or with periods at the end indicate text files. If you select one of them, the text displays on your screen.

The bracketed question marks (<?>) at the end of choices 3 and 6 denote menu choices for which the user will be asked to provide search terms. You could search for U.S. Court clerkship requirements (item 3) or for matters covered by U.S. codes of law (item 6). Sometimes one finds a Gopher menu item labeled Under construction, which means that choice may not be fully functional. In Gopher, as with other network programs and utilities, patience is indicated. It is not unusual to find Gopher menu choices for which no information is available. When such an item is selected, Gopher returns a message telling you that nothing is available. You might want to try that choice again at a later date. There are other kinds of temporary frustrations encountered on the network.

When you hit your Return key (Enter key) or Right arrow key, Gopher goes to work retrieving the item in question. If it is a directory (items 4, 5, 7 and 8 in Figure 5-3), that directory will appear on the screen when it has been retrieved from its point of origin. The menu item in question may be on the currently logged computer or on another computer halfway around the world. While Gopher is working, a message in the lower right-hand corner of the computer screen reports "Retrieving xxxxxxxx /." The xxxxxxxx may be a file or a directory, and the slash mark spins to show work in progress. When Gopher has retrieved the item in question, messages across the bottom of the screen report status and user options. Across the bottom of the Gopher menu screen runs a list of three basic commands:

- Entering "?" for help produces a list of Gopher commands and their results (see Figure 5-4).
- Typing "u" moves the user up one level on the Gopher menu hierarchy.
- A "q" starts a dialog asking whether you really want to quit Gopher. (A "Q" quits without question.)

If you select a file from the menu, that file displays on your terminal one screen at a time. Across the top of the screen (bottom on some clients), a message reports what percentage of the file has been viewed. After you have viewed the entire file, some clients provide a screen prompt indicating that you can download the file to your personal computer by entering "D." On some clients the message does not appear, but the command is still available, as are commands to save the file or to have it mailed to you.

A list of common Gopher commands is given in Figure 5-4. Gopher is case sensitive. If you are looking at a menu comprised of your bookmarks and you want to download a file you are pointing at, you would enter "D." However, if you want to delete a bookmark you are pointing at, you would enter "d." Also worth noting about Gopher is that commands for moving around often have synonyms. To move down a screen, you could hit the Pg Dn key. However, if you are logged into a host system using a communications program that is command compatible with ProComm, Pg Dn starts the download process, so you would want to use the spacebar or the + key to move down a screen.

"u" for up or "b" for back?

Two actions that at first seem identical are not. These are typing "u" and "b." Figure 5-2 shows the first page of a Gopher menu that is two pages long. Some Gopher menus (All the Gophers in the World, for example) may be more than 100 pages. The bottom right-hand corner of a Gopher menu screen tells you where you are in the current menu. You could get to the second page (or subsequent pages) by pressing your Down arrow key repeatedly. When the arrow moves below the last item on the current page, the next screen displays. A quicker way, however, is to use the spacebar, which will take you to the next page. So will the + key, the > key, or the Pg Dn key (if you have that key, and it is not intercepted by your communications program). This is where entering "b" becomes handy. If you are several pages into a Gopher menu, entering "b" moves you back one page of the menu. Entering "u," however, takes you entirely out of your current menu and moves you up one level in the menu hierarchy.

Pressing the = key in Gopher brings to the screen a report that tells the networker where (what machine, in which directory) the selected item is physically located (Figure 5-5). Here is another distinction between Gopher and Telnet. When you use the Telnet protocol to access a distant computer,

Gopher Keyboard Commands

To move around

    Use the arrow keys or vi/emacs equivalent

Right, Return .... "Enter"/Display current item.

Left, u .... "Exit" current item/Go up a
                              level.

Down .... Move to next line.

Up .... Move to previous line.

>, +, Pgdwn, Space . View next page.

<, -, Pgup, b .... View previous page.

0-9 .... Go to a specific line.

m............................. Go back to the main menu.

Bookmarks

a .... Add current item to the bookmark list.

A .... Add current directory to bookmark list.

v .... View bookmark list.

d .... Delete a bookmark/directory entry.

Other commands

q .... Quit with prompt.

Q .... Quit unconditionally.

s .... Save current item to a file.

S........... Save current menu listing to a file.

D .... Download a file.

r .... goto root menu of current item.

R .... goto root menu of current menu.

= .... Display information on current item.

^   .... Display information on current directory.

o .... Open a new gopher server.

O .... Change options.

f .... Connect to anonymous FTP server.

w .... Connect to http, gopher, FTP, or telnet URL

/ .... Search for an item in the menu.

n........... Find next search item.

g .... "Gripe" via e-mail to administrator of item.

L .... Change language of messages (VMS).

!, $ .... Shell Escape (Unix) or Spawn subprocess
             (VMS).

Ctrl-L, Ctrl-R, Ctrl-W   Redraw (Wipe) the screen.

Ctrl-T .. Show host's local date and time.

Fig. 5-4: Common keyboard commands for Gopher are summarized in a chart like this when you ask Gopher for help.

Fig. 5-5: The Gopher link information screen tells you about the menu item to which your cursor is pointing. Invoked by typing the = key, it tells you the host computer, the type of document, path to the document, and the URL.

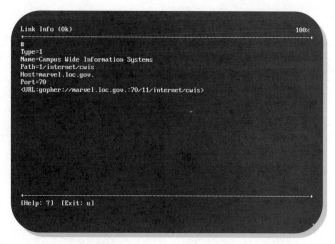

```
Link Info (0k)                                                        100%
+------------------------------------------------------------------------+
#
Type=1
Name=Campus Wide Information Systems
Path=1/internet/cwis
Host=marvel.loc.gov.
Port=70
<URL:gopher://marvel.loc.gov.:70/11/internet/cwis>




+------------------------------------------------------------------------+
[Help: ?]  [Exit: u]
```

you are a captive of that site. With few exceptions (some large government sites especially offer gateways to other government sites), your menu choices do not connect you to computer networks other than the one you first connected to.

In Gopher, however, you might start with a root menu that resides on a machine in your home town. You pick a menu choice that calls up a new menu/directory. That menu, and any number of items on it, may actually be called up from a machine in another state or even another country. It is possible that the 10 to 15 menu items on a typical Gopher directory could be located in 10 to 15 different places. Point the selector arrow at the piece you desire. Gopher knows where the requested file or directory resides and goes out and fetches it for display on your screen. Whether the requested file or directory comes from France or rests on a machine next door, you see the same dialog, the same kinds of displays. Again, pressing the = key will give you a report of where your menu choice really resides.

Using Gopher bookmarks

Because Gopher facilitates movement so easily from one menu to another and another and another and so on, it is very easy to lose track of where you are. Two Gopher features help keep track of where you are. The = key already mentioned is available to anyone, even with only Telnet connections to Gopher.

Assume for a minute that you connected to Gopher by Telnet to consultant.micro.umn.edu or some other Telnet host. Browsing, you moved down through a series of menus until you happened onto a menu full of the very crime statistics you need. You suspect from signatures on some of the files that they are updated regularly, and you would like to return to this menu later, but you have not kept thorough notes. You could point at a file or

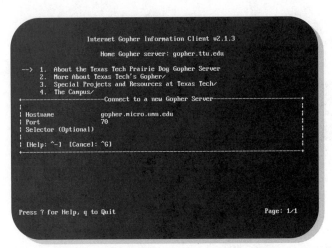

Fig. 5-6: The "Other Gopher" dialog is launched by typing "o" at any Gopher menu. You then type in the host address, and if necessary, the port number.

a menu, press the = key, and write down the host address and the path information provided. (See Chapter 6 for path shorthand.) The next time you want to get to your precious crime statistics you start by connecting to your usual Gopher. Once connected, you type "o" and the host address you recorded from the earlier dialog. That at least will get you to the right host, and with luck (or good path notes) you will again find the files you seek.

There is a more graceful way of keeping track of where you are in GopherSpace. If the machine you use as your connection to the Internet houses a Gopher client, you may employ Gopher bookmarks. Placing bookmarks in GopherSpace is very easy. If you want to mark an item on a Gopher menu, just move the selector arrow to the item and type "a." A dialog box pops onto your screen highlighting a suggested name for the bookmark. This is the name that will appear on your bookmark menu when you recall your bookmarks. If you want to return later to the menu now on your screen, type "A" and you will get the same kind of dialog box. If you accept the suggested name, just hit the Enter key and the bookmark is recorded. Otherwise, you may type in a name to suit your taste. The display given when you press the = key (Figure 5-5) is actually the information stored in your bookmark.

To recall your bookmarks, you type "v" (for view). Gopher displays your list of bookmarks in menu format, replacing whatever menu was on the screen with your bookmark list. Again, just point your selector at the menu item (or type in its number), and hit the Enter key (or Right arrow key) to call the item to your screen.

Searching with Veronica and Jughead

Many Gopher sites offer as a menu choice something like "Search GopherSpace using Veronica." The menu listing may be followed by a <?> because the user must provide search parameters. Such a choice is offered on the Library of

Fig. 5-7: Veronica searches accept Boolean logic. In this search we are asking for a list of Gopher items that have both words, "campus" and "crime" in them.

```
              Internet Gopher Information Client v2.1.3

                 Search Gopherspace using Veronica
                             o

     3.  Find GOPHER DIRECTORIES by Title word(s) (via NYSERNet   ) <?>
     4.  Find GOPHER DIRECTORIES by Title word(s) (via PSINet) <?>
     -----------Search GopherSpace by Title word(s) (via PSINet)-----------
    :                                                                      :
    : Words to search for                                                  :
    :                                                                      :
    : campus AND crime                                                     :
    :                                                                      :
    : [Help: ^-]  [Cancel: ^G]                                             :
    +----------------------------------------------------------------------+
    -->  13.  Search GopherSpace by Title word(s) (via PSINet) <?>
         14.  Search GopherSpace by Title word(s) (via SUNET) <?>
         15.  Search GopherSpace by Title word(s) (via U. Nac. Autonoma de MX.. <?>
         16.  Search GopherSpace by Title word(s) (via UNINETT/U. of Bergen) <?>
         17.  Search GopherSpace by Title word(s) (via University of Koeln) <?>
              Simplified veronica chooses server - pick a search type:

    Press ? for Help, q to Quit, u to go up a menu                Page: 1/2
```

Congress Gopher, marvel.loc.gov. From the root menu choose Internet Resources (choice 11 at this writing) and then choose Veronica and Jughead (choice 13 at this writing). You then will be asked to input the term(s) you want to search for. One of the strengths of Veronica is that it allows you to narrow your search using Boolean (AND, OR, NOT) logic.

Figure 5-7 displays a typical search dialog in which we have asked Veronica to find all the Gopher files and directories (wherever in the world they might be) that use both "campus" (the search is not case sensitive) AND "crime" in their names. When Veronica is done searching, it reports the results of the search in Gopher menu format. That is, you are given a customized Gopher menu that looks like any other Gopher menu. It also works like any other Gopher menu. You select an item in any of the normal ways, and Gopher goes out and connects you to that site.

Sometimes Veronica search results report what seems to be multiple occurrences of the same item. They could, however, represent Gopher directory choices with the same names but in different locations. To tell the difference, you have only to point at each item and press the = key to get Gopher's report on the item location. You sometimes get duplicate listings because Gopher administrators (the people who set up the server offerings) in different locations may elect to establish menu choices leading to the same document. Because the same menu item occurs in multiple locations, Veronica reports once for each occurrence.

Jughead operates much the same way as Veronica. In fact, you could conduct precisely the same search with Jughead that we made in Veronica and get similar results. There are, however, some subtle differences in search capabilities. At each Jughead and each Veronica site there are files describing search parameters of the respective programs. If you wish to become a Gopher guru, you will want to study each document. Most sites have short documents explaining how to do searches. Veronica has been out a little longer than Jughead and is more widely distributed.

Some great Gophers

Your own campus information is probably not the only network resource you will find listed on your campus Gopher server if your campus has one. Many colleges and universities have special areas in which they excel. The Massachusetts Institute of Technology and Cal Tech in Pasadena, California, are noted for outstanding science programs. Harvard is known for its business school. Schools have done much the same thing on the Internet. Cornell and Washburn Universities have developed outstanding online resources in the field of law. Sam Houston State University has an especially rich collection of pointers to economics resources online.

Several schools have set up Gopher servers that are distinguished in some way or another as gateways to a wide variety of resources. A few outstanding Gophers include

- University of Minnesota, where Gopher was created.
- University of Michigan Library.
- Live Gopher Jewels site at the University of Southern California.
- Rice University's Riceinfo Gopher.
- University of California Irvine's PEG.
- University of California Santa Cruz's InfoSlug.
- Library of Congress.

University of Minnesota

Minnesota's Gopher may be reached at gopher.micro.umd.edu. As the mother of all Gophers, the Minnesota Gopher provides access to a lot of other Gopher servers. In fact, one of the menu choices at the Minnesota Gopher promises All the Gophers in the World. If you select this choice, you will be asked to select a continent or subcontinent first, and then you choose from a menu of nations. Within nations you might be asked to select regions or states, and gradually you are taken to a list of local Gopher sites.

This process may be useful to you if you know (or suspect) ahead of time that the information you desire is located at a certain site. Because many Gopher sites provide phone books or directories, this resource can be very useful. If you know someone is affiliated with Washington and Lee University, for example, you could start at the Minnesota Gopher, select All the Gophers in the World, North America, then United States, Virginia, and so forth until you get to Washington and Lee. Choose the phone book entry if it's available, and search for the person you need.

This ability to reach All the Gophers in the World is useful to enough people that many Gopher sites offer it as a choice. In some of those cases, that menu choice actually points at the menu choice of that name at the University of Minnesota. Thus, even though you started at your own home

Gopher, when you make this choice you actually are connecting to the Minnesota server.

University of Michigan subject-oriented guides

Instead of organizing information geographically, sometimes it is more useful to group documents according to subject or topic. Libraries assign catalog numbers to books based upon subject area classifications. Hence, different textbooks for introductory biology will be placed on the shelves in the same area in the library. They all will be grouped together. Similarly, many Gopher servers follow subject-area organization.

Just as the Minnesota Gopher points to Gophers worldwide listed by geography, a Gopher server at the University of Michigan Library points to Gophers worldwide organized by subject areas. The Clearinghouse of Subject-Oriented Internet Resource Guides at the University of Michigan may be accessed at una.hh.lib.umich.edu by selecting choice 11, Inetdirs.

Live Gopher Jewels at Southern California

Rich Wiggins is a Gopher scholar who has maintained a list of outstanding Gopher sites. To qualify for inclusion in the Gopher Jewels list, a site must exhibit a truly outstanding collection of information resources on one topic. Wiggins has also maintained a discussion list inhabited by others who are interested in outstanding collections of information made available by Gopher servers. Contributors to the list often suggest or discuss inclusion of Gopher sites on the list. The subject-oriented list is available from many sites. But at the University of Southern California, the list is live, meaning you can actually call up a site by selecting it from the list.

The live Gopher jewels may be reached at cwis.usc.edu choosing first Other Gophers and then Gopher Jewels. While the USC Gopher is home to the Live Gopher Jewels, other sites have pointers to USC, and still others around the world *mirror* (provide a working copy of the resource) the site at Southern Cal. What distinguishes the Gopher Jewels site from other subject-oriented sites is that all sites included on the list have been examined and certified as excellent resources.

Rice University's Riceinfo Gopher

A number of universities have set up Gopher servers with the stated purpose of providing excellent general information resources. Rice University is one such site. The Riceinfo Gopher is basically the campus-wide information server. But two of its main menu items provide pointers or links to a wealth of other resources. One menu choice is Information by Subject Area. This choice gives links to the University of Michigan Clearinghouse of Subject-Oriented Internet Resource Guides (mentioned earlier in this section), to Jughead and Veronica searching programs, and to a menu of subject-oriented directories. Another choice from the root menu at Riceinfo promises Other Gopher and Information Servers. This last choice in turn contains links to two different All the Gophers in the World lists. You access the Riceinfo Gopher at riceinfo.rice.edu.

UC Santa Cruz's InfoSlug

Another Gopher site billed as a superior all-around resource is located at the University of California at Santa Cruz. The InfoSlug gets its name from the university mascot—the large, bright yellow banana slug that inhabits redwood forests in California coastal areas. InfoSlug provides pointers to many outstanding Gopher resources. If you select The Government from InfoSlug's root menu, you will have access to an outstanding list of California state and United States federal government information sources.

If you select The Community, you are presented with a long list of Santa Cruz area resources of particular interest to students. Similarly, selection of The World from the root menu calls up a directory containing a handful of menu choices that lead to other worldwide network resources. InfoSlug may be accessed by pointing your Gopher at gopher.ucsc.edu.

UC Irvine's PEG

If you ask Gopher to open cwis.uci.edu, you open the Campus Wide Information Service for the University of California at Irvine. One of its menu choices is Accessing the Internet. On the menu retrieved by selecting Accessing the Internet, one menu choice is PEG. PEG is an acronym for Peripatetic Eclectic Gopher. As the name implies, PEG has wide-ranging (eclectic) interests providing links to an expansive range of topic material.

PEG's directory links to mathematics, medicine, politics and government, physics, and women's resources are especially rich. And PEG's Virtual Reference Desk provides access to scores of reference documents and to other Gopher sites offering reference materials on a wide range of subjects.

Library of Congress

For many reasons, it is understandable that if the United States Library of Congress wanted to provide information by Gopher, it would have a far-reaching Gopher server. That in fact is the case. Accessed at marvel.loc.gov, the Library of Congress Gopher provides pointers to the same kinds of worldwide resources mentioned for other Gophers as well as pointers to United

States government information servers and to the extensive holdings of the Library of Congress itself.

Some other interesting Gophers

By following links on any of the Gophers just described, you could ultimately find your way, as one frequent menu choice suggests, to All the Gophers in the World. Or following subject leads on the Gophers just described, you could find information on just about any topic you might find of interest. A few other Gophers you might find of interest are

- Texas A&M Gopher, gopher.tamu.edu, a good general, all-around Gopher.
- University of Melbourne (Australia) gopher.austin.unimelb.edu.au that has among other things great sources on medicine and health, as well as telephone and e-mail directories from throughout the world.
- Environmental Protection Agency gopher, gopher.epa.gov.
- United States Department of Education, gopher.ed.gov.
- United Sates Congress at gopher.senate.gov and gopher.house.gov.
- United Nations at nywork1.undp.org.
- Cornell University Law school at fatty.law.cornell.edu provides access to a wealth of legal material including searchable indices of United States Supreme Court decisions.

File-capturing options

One of the more common reasons for finding files in GopherSpace is to retrieve documents needed as source material for research papers. When you find a document of use to you in GopherSpace, you may wish to print it out or to save it to a file on your computer. Gopher permits these and other options. To do any of these things, you need to be aware of two things: where the Gopher client software you are using is located and how that software is configured with regard to printing.

If you have gained access to Gopher through a Telnet link (described later in this chapter), you will not be able to print files directly because the Gopher client in question sits on a computer somewhere far away from you. If you gain access to Gopher through a central host on your campus, then you need to find out from your computing services people where files are printed.

On some campuses where you access Gopher on a central host, your files will not print on paper at all. Instead, if you tell Gopher to print a document, that document is *printed* to a computer file in your disk space on the host computer. It might be given a name such as

"Gopherprint$123456." Whatever name it is given, you now have the job of printing out the file. That may be as simple as issuing a command such as print queue Gopherprint$123456 <CR>. Instead, you may have to download the file to your personal computer or workstation and then print from there. You need to ask your instructor and/or your campus computer systems people the proper course to take.

If, on the other hand, your Gopher client software resides on your personal computer or workstation, your document may well print out on whatever printer is connected to your computer or its network. Ask the person in charge of the lab you are using.

Even if you gain access to Gopher by way of a Telnet connection (see section on Alternative Access), you can e-mail the document to your mailbox. When you are viewing a Gopher text document, typing the letter "m" will initiate the mail option dialog. This option is also open to you if you access Gopher through a local client or a central host client on campus; you just would use a different command sequence.

The third option for capturing documents in Gopher is through the save command. Again, when you scroll through a Gopher text document, you have the option of typing "s" to save the document. If you choose this option, the document will be saved on your disk space if you are using a client on a central host on campus. You then have to download the file to your computer or print from the central host. If your Gopher client is on the computer you are using, then you may save to the computer's hard disk or to a floppy one. Having done that, you now have the option of importing the file (or portions of it) into your word processor and doing with it anything you normally do with a word processor document.

Finally, there is the download option for those who access Gopher through telephone lines. When you are viewing a Gopher document, all you need to do is to type "d" to initiate the download dialog. You will be asked what communications protocol (such as Xmodem, Zmodem, Kermit) to use for the file transfer. And you may be asked to give a name for the file.

Dealing with network gridlock

Because the volume of Internet traffic has exploded since 1992, more popular network sites may be more in demand than the existing network structure can manage. If you try to connect to a site where there is already too much traffic, you are likely to get one of three kinds of messages. The friendlier, more enlightening messages (less common) tell you something like "there are already too many people connected to 123.456.78." The second kind of message simply says something like "unable to connect to 123.456.78." Another common occurrence is that your computer screen just sits for several minutes with a message like "trying to connect" or "retrieving directory" and finally comes back with a message about being unable to connect because the connection process "timed out."

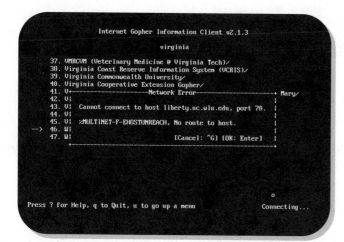

Internet Gopher Information Client v2.1.3

virginia

37. VMRCVM (Veterinary Medicine @ Virginia Tech)/
38. Virginia Coast Reserve Information System (VCRIS)/
39. Virginia Commonwealth University/
40. Virginia Cooperative Extension Gopher/
41. V+-----------------------Network Error-----------------------+ Mary/
42. V| |
43. V| Cannot connect to host liberty.uc.wlu.edu, port 70. |
44. V| |
45. V| %MULTINET-F-EHOSTUNREACH, No route to host. |
46. W| |
47. W| [Cancel: ^G] [OK: Enter] |
    +---+

                                                          o
Press ? for Help, q to Quit, u to go up a menu   Connecting...

Fig. 5-8: A "Network Error" message typical of gridlock. The Gopher at Washington and Lee University is popular, so it sometimes has more requests for connections than it can handle, as this message suggests.

A student confronted with any of these situations might adopt the following strategy:

1. Try going to an alternative site for the same information. If you can choose an alternative from the same menu, do so. If you have to go to another Gopher or perhaps a Telnet site, do so.
2. If you got the message when you selected a menu item from Gopher, you might try asking Gopher for the address of the site (pressing the = key) and then connecting there directly from your system prompt if possible.
3. If the site is accessible by another method (Telnet, http), try that method.
4. Just try again in a few minutes.

When Gopher hands you off to another client

Gopher is easy to use and can put you in touch with a lot of information. The Gopher menu and command structure are uniform worldwide. Whole libraries of information are made easily available. Gopher administrators have grouped gateways to like information together in many instances, making it easier to find what you are looking for. Veronica and Jughead searching tools expand the finding capabilities for a student on the prowl for some particular kind of data.

One of the limitations to Gopher, however, is that there is a lot of information that is available on the network but may not be indexed to Gopher searching devices. There is even more information that is not stored at Gopher sites or under the Gopher umbrella. You might find pointers to some of that information if a Gopher menu happens to point to a Telnet or http site. But to get to the Telnet site, you must leave Gopher. And Veronica and Jughead won't tell you what is at the Telnet site other than what is on the Gopher menu pointing to that site.

However, many Gopher servers offer a menu choice something like Internet Resources or Other Internet Resources. The Library of Congress Gopher server (marvel.loc.gov) has such a choice on its root menu. Typically, selecting this menu choice brings up a new menu populated with several selections offering use of network tools that reach beyond the limits of Gopher. The Internet Resources menu from the Library of Congress Gopher offers access to Archie and FTP (Chapter 6), university Campus Wide Information Systems, Free-Net systems, Hytelnet (Chapter 6), WAIS servers (Chapter 9), and to Veronica and Jughead servers. One can also find guides to mail lists (Chapter 3), Usenet Newsgroups (Chapter 7), and to World Wide Web.

Alternative Gopher access

For the user, a Gopher session at first glance looks and behaves very much like a Telnet session (see Chapter 6). Once connected, the network user faces a menu of less than 20 choices. Figure 5-3 shows the Judiciary menu from the Library of Congress Gopher. If the local host has a Gopher client (each student will have to ask the network access provider), one has considerably more freedom in moving around GopherSpace. Usually all that is necessary to start a Gopher session (if your host has a Gopher client) is to type the word "gopher" at the system prompt and then hit Enter. Typing the word "gopher" followed by a Gopher server's address takes the student to the Gopher site she chooses. For example, one might access the Library of Congress Gopher by typing

gopher marvel.loc.gov <CR>

Another way to get to the Library of Congress Gopher from a local Gopher site would be first to launch the local Gopher, then to "point" the Gopher at a chosen destination site. Typing "o" brings up a window (Figure 5-6) in which you are asked to enter the address of the destination Gopher (the one you want to connect to). In this case, you would type simply

marvel.loc.gov <CR>

Finally, one may access some public Gopher clients by using the Internet Telnet program (Chapter 6). Thus, typing the command

telnet consultant.micro.umn.edu <CR>

launches a remote log-in to the Great Mother Gopher at the University of Minnesota. Some other public Telnet addresses that allow access to Gopher clients include

• gopher.who.ch, log in as "gopher."

- gopher.uiuc.edu, log in as "gopher."
- info.anu.edu.au, log in as "info" (Australia).
- gopher.chalmers.se, log in as "gopher" (Sweden).
- ecnet.ec, log in as "gopher" (Ecuador).
- gan.ncc.go.jp, log in as "gopher" (Japan).
- panda.uiowa.edu, log in as "panda."
- gopher.ora.com, a commercial site, log in as "gopher," specify VT100 terminal.

Not all Gopher servers may be accessed via Telnet. Some may be reached only through another Gopher client or other network front end. If you have to telnet to access Gopher, you will not be able to take advantage of Gopher's bookmarks feature nor the save (file) feature. But one great feature about Gopher that sets it apart from Telnet is that Gopher presents the same *face* and responds to the same commands wherever the Gopher server is. With Telnet, on the other hand, each site has its own face and responds to its own commands.

Some other Gopher clients

The discussion in this chapter so far has described Gopher as it is seen and used from a local or remote host computer. If you have direct network access from your workstation, then you may be able to use one of the other Gopher clients such as:

- TurboGopher for Macintosh.
- PC Gopher for DOS.
- WS Gopher or BC Gopher for Windows.

Each of these clients is mouse sensitive, permitting you to make Gopher menu selections by pointing and double clicking. In each case, these clients strip away the Gopher menu item numbers, so you lose the option of making Gopher choices by entering menu item numbers. What you see instead are bracketed letters (PC Gopher) or graphics denoting whether an item is a folder (directory), a file, a search, or a handoff to another client (Telnet or Lynx). And in each case, bookmark information is stored on the local computer.

This last characteristic, storing bookmarks on your personal workstation, means that if you are using a machine that other students use, your bookmarks are liable to get mixed up with other people's bookmarks. There are ways to deal with this. Under Configuration, PC Gopher allows you to specify the location of your bookmark file. You could specify a floppy disk (which will mean slow access) or some private directory on your machine's hard drive. With the other clients, there are solutions commonly referred to as *workarounds*.

What is involved here is that you identify the file in which the bookmark information is stored. To begin your workaround, you make a copy of this file

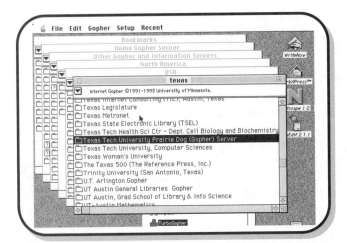

Fig. 5-9: Graphical interface Gophers such as TurboGopher, shown here, may open several windows at once, giving you a stairstep track of the menu choices you have made.

(called a duplicate on the Mac) and give it some other name, like "bookmark.bak." During your Gopher sessions, you store all your bookmarks as you wish. At the end of your Gopher session, you rename your bookmark file to something like "mybkmark.lst" and save it to your floppy disk for safekeeping. Before you end your session, you must remember to rename the bookmark.bak file to its original name so that people using the computer after you will have bookmarks. In BC Gopher, bookmarks are stored in a file called bcgbkmrk.ini stored in the \windows directory. For WS Gopher, the bookmarks are stored in the wsgopher.ini file in the directory where WS Gopher program files reside. You must be especially careful with your handling of this file, because it governs a lot more than just bookmarks for WS Gopher. For TurboGopher, you have the option under the File menu to save a bookmark file wherever you choose. Then under the Gopher menu you may import a bookmark file.

Each of these clients opens a new window on your screen when you select a Gopher menu item. It is common to have several windows cascading across your screen as you choose one item after another. Beware, however, that you can tax your system resources with too many windows. Each window you have open requires a piece of memory. At some point—maybe five windows, maybe a dozen—you will find that the client does not want to open any more windows.

Conclusion

Regardless of the client you use, Gopher software organizes network information into hierarchical menus. Browsing software allows you to read documents on screen, moving forward and backward through the document and through Gopher menus. When you find a document of special use to you, your client may permit you to print the document, save it on disk, or send it to yourself as e-mail.

Each client allows you to get information (location, name and type of document) about documents toward which your software is pointing. Each client allows you to store this information in bookmarks so that you can easily retrieve the document again. Some Gopher clients will retrieve and display (or play) graphics and sound files, but generally Gopher caters best to text files.

Veronica and Jughead programs allow you to search GopherSpace for keywords. Several Gopher sites offer subject-oriented menu trees to a vast expanse of information stored worldwide. Whichever Gopher client you use, the client software puts the same face on Gopher sites wherever they are. In the final analysis, Gopher is a powerful, rich, and useful tool for navigating the Internet.

Chapter 6

Foundation tools: Telnet & FTP

Jeff McCormick, a senior, faced a tough, semester-long assignment. His task was to become an expert on a specific industry, such as autos or entertainment, and write a report outlining the key issues and leaders in the industry and defining the jargon associated with the sector. But as a journalism major, Jeff had little formal training in business and economics.

As he approached the problem of educating himself about this complicated area, he learned that the business school on his campus had a subscription to Dow Jones News Retrieval, a commercial online service operated by the same company that publishes *The Wall Street Journal*. DJNR is an excellent source of daily and historical business information. So Jeff sat down in front of a computer in a public-access laboratory at his school and used the Telnet program to connect to the DJNR computer.

When Dow Jones News Retrieval appeared on screen, Jeff had to complete a log-in routine, providing the account name and password reserved for use by the students at his school. Once logged in, he had to learn the commands used specifically by DJNR to navigate through the database. The computer at which he was sitting could still perform basic Macintosh commands such as copying material and pasting it to another file. But for accessing information, it served basically as a dumb terminal.

Telnet, the program Jeff used to access DJNR, allows computers on the Internet to connect to each other. Once the connection is made, however, the user must know the log-in procedures and the necessary commands to move among the files and directories on what has become the host computer.

During her senior year, Elaine Lazarte was a student programmer at the University of California at Davis. In some of her classes, she was required to write computer programs involving networking. To facilitate the process, the students were allowed to use software libraries, collections of standard computer subroutines.

A computer subroutine is a program that does one task in a larger computer program. For example, spell checking can be considered a subroutine in a large word-processing program.

When one of her professors identified the location of an appropriate library of subroutines, Elaine wanted to download the routines to use in the programs she was writing. Sometimes she used her World Wide Web browser to retrieve files. But frequently she had to use the Internet's file transfer protocol, or FTP. FTP is a way to move files among different computers on the Internet.

World Wide Web browsers, like Swiss Army knives, have lots of tools on them and, in a pinch, will do lots of things. But you wouldn't want to use a Swiss Army knife to build a cabinet. To take full advantage of the Internet, you need to know about all the tools available. Telnet and FTP are basic, or core, Internet applications. They were the first tools available to facilitate the swapping of files and information back and forth among computers, the primary function of the Internet. Consequently, as you search through the Net with your Web browser, you will be pointed to Telnet or FTP sites. To use the information, you will have to know how Telnet and FTP work.

At the end of this chapter, the reader should be able to

- Log into remote computer systems.
- Navigate menus during a Telnet session.
- Capture remote text files on your personal computer.
- Move comfortably through FTP server directories.
- Fetch ASCII and binary files using FTP.

Telnet lets you *drive* distant computers

The basic function of Telnet is to allow you to log into another computer on the Internet and view the information and use software available there. The

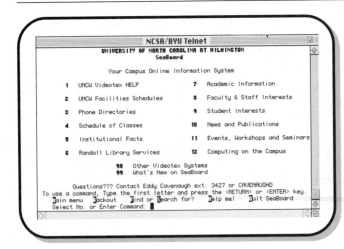

Fig. 6-1: Main menu of the SeaBoard system at the University of North Carolina at Wilmington presents a typical Telnet BBS series of choices.

computer may be far from your campus or in the lab next door. For example, some schools do not support several of the more fun Internet applications such as Internet Relay Chat (IRC), which is like talking via computers and will be described in Chapter 8. Through Telnet, you can log onto a computer that does support IRC and join the fun. To play with IRC in the past, some students using Telnet have logged onto computers as far away as Taiwan.

On a more academic level, Telnet allows you to search the library holdings at colleges throughout the world. The CARL public-access library system described in Chapter 2 is based on the Telnet protocol. Furthermore, many Campus Wide Information Systems (CWISes) are accessible via Telnet. Let's say you are going to visit a friend at the University of Pennsylvania but you need information about the campus. You can Telnet from your campus to the PennInfo CWIS system. For scientists, Telnet allows researchers in one location to use sophisticated software stored on computers elsewhere.

Accessing distant computers is an exciting feature of Telnet. But Telnet is also becoming a common method for connecting to computers on different parts of campus. For example, let's say your e-mail account resides on a central VAX computer and you are working at a public-access lab. You can use Telnet to connect to the VAX to check your e-mail.

Using Telnet clients

On one level, Telnet is the easiest Internet tool to use. On another level, it is difficult. Indeed, Telnet does only one thing—it establishes a connection from one computer to another. In essence it is a way for your computer to *call* another computer and open a line through which you can communicate.

In many implementations, Telnet is not a point-and-click operation in which you use your mouse. Instead, you type out a command telling your computer you wish to call another computer. You use this command-line entry to launch the Telnet program and to enter the Internet Protocol (IP) number of the computer with which you wish to establish communications. (IP numbers were explained in Chapter 2.) On many computers, to launch the Telnet client, you type the word "telnet" followed by the appropriate IP number (or character address).

On clients running through graphical operating systems, the Telnet client works much like other software designed for the specific environment. For example, on NCSA-BYU Telnet (Figure 6-5), a popular Telnet client running on Macintosh computers on campus, you click on the Program icon to launch the Telnet client. Then, under the File command on the button bar, click on Open Connection. At that point you enter the IP number in the appropriate box. A similar process occurs in Windows Telnet clients.

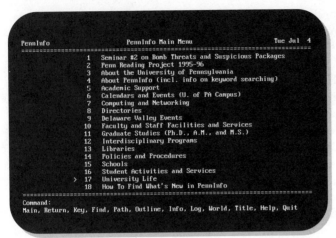

```
PennInfo                      PennInfo Main Menu                    Tue Jul  4
=============================================================================
             1   Seminar #2 on Bomb Threats and Suspicious Packages
             2   Penn Reading Project 1995-96
             3   About the University of Pennsylvania
             4   About PennInfo (incl. info on keyword searching)
             5   Academic Support
             6   Calendars and Events (U. of PA Campus)
             7   Computing and Networking
             8   Directories
             9   Delaware Valley Events
            10   Faculty and Staff Facilities and Services
            11   Graduate Studies (Ph.D., A.M., and M.S.)
            12   Interdisciplinary Programs
            13   Libraries
            14   Policies and Procedures
            15   Schools
            16   Student Activities and Services
         >  17   University Life
            18   How To Find What's New in PennInfo
=============================================================================
Command:
Main, Return, Key, Find, Path, Outline, Info, Log, World, Title, Help, Quit
```

Fig. 6-2:
PennInfo's CWIS employs a selector arrow to make menu selections. Here, the selector arrow has selected choice 17, University Life.

In addition to NCSA-BYU Telnet, there are several other Telnet clients that can run on personal computers. For the DOS platform, many universities make available a package from Clarkson University called Clarkson University TCP, or CUTCP for short. Like NCSA-BYU Telnet, CUTCP contains both Telnet and FTP clients. If you use CUTCP, what you will see on the screen is very much like Figures 6-2 through 6-4 except that the bottom line of your screen carries certain messages. Typically the left part of that line would have the first part of the address of any machine to which you are connected.

QVT Net is a multiclient package for the Windows environment that is popular on many campuses. It does Telnet, FTP, e-mail, and serves as a Usenet News reader. When it is launched in Windows, the program places a small button bar on the screen (Figure 6-6). A single click launches a terminal (Telnet), FTP, or Usenet News reading session.

Regardless of the client you use, once you have launched the Telnet application, you will have to enter the computer to which you want to connect. Remember, as with the World Wide Web, the people responsible for computers on the Internet can associate a name with the IP number. (The naming scheme was described in Chapters 2 and 4.) In those cases, instead of entering the IP number itself, you can just use the name of the computer. For example, let's say you want to telnet to the library catalog at the University of California. You don't need to know the IP number of the computer on which the catalog resides. If you know the computer is named melvyl.berkeley.edu, all you need to do is type in "telnet melvyl.berkeley.edu." Or if you are using a graphical Telnet client, type "melvyl.berkeley.edu" in the Open Connection box.

Opening a connection via Telnet is easy; closing a connection can be a little more challenging. Using NCSA-BYU Telnet, you click on Close Connection under the File button on the button bar. If you are not using

Fig. 6-3: Having selected University Life from the main menu at PennInfo, the system user receives a second menu from which to choose.

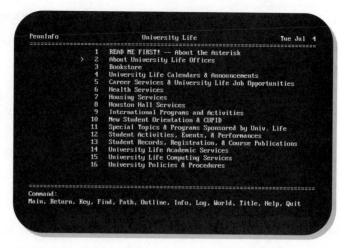

```
PennInfo                    University Life                    Tue Jul  4
=========================================================================
           1   READ ME FIRST! -- About the Asterisk
       >   2   About University Life Offices
           3   Bookstore
           4   University Life Calendars & Announcements
           5   Career Services & University Life Job Opportunities
           6   Health Services
           7   Housing Services
           8   Houston Hall Services
           9   International Programs and Activities
          10   New Student Orientation & CUPID
          11   Special Topics & Programs Sponsored by Univ. Life
          12   Student Activities, Events, & Performances
          13   Student Records, Registration, & Course Publications
          14   University Life Academic Services
          15   University Life Computing Services
          16   University Policies & Procedures


=========================================================================
Command:
Main, Return, Key, Find, Path, Outline, Info, Log, World, Title, Help, Quit
```

NCSA-BYU Telnet or another client with a graphical interface, the process can get a little tricky. When you first connect to a site, you don't know what kind of computer is at the other end or what kind of software it is running, so you cannot be sure exactly what command will close the connection. After you have opened a connection, for the most part, you have to use the commands of the computer you called.

Sometimes information detailing how to disconnect is provided to you when you first connect. A site might tell you, for example, "Escape character is '^]'." What that means is that by typing Ctrl-], you can escape the program and disconnect.

The combination (Ctrl-]) is common on the Internet. Other common ways of leaving programs include
- Typing "Q" or "QUIT."
- Typing "E," "X," "EXIT," or "Ctrl-X."
- Typing "Ctrl-Z."
- Typing "Bye," "Goodbye," or "G."

Logging in—on and off campus

Opening and closing connections mark the beginning and end of a Telnet session. It is what happens in between that counts. Accessing information stored on the computer you called is the hard part. First, while thousands of computers are accessible via Telnet, many are not open to the public. You have to know specific log-in procedures. If you are logging onto a computer on your own campus, presumably you know the log-in procedures. Except for libraries, most Telnet sites require that you have a username and a password (i.e., an account on that machine or knowledge of a public-access account). For example, if you telnet to Arizona State University by typing the command

telnet asu.edu <CR>

Fig. 6-4: Three menu levels into the PennInfo system, we still have choices that will lead to yet other menus before we get to documents answering our questions.

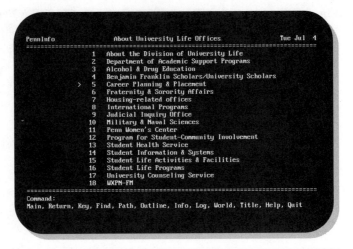

```
PennInfo              About University Life Offices              Tue Jul  4
==============================================================================
                 1   About the Division of University Life
                 2   Department of Academic Support Programs
                 3   Alcohol & Drug Education
                 4   Benjamin Franklin Scholars/University Scholars
              >  5   Career Planning & Placement
                 6   Fraternity & Sorority Affairs
                 7   Housing-related offices
                 8   International Programs
                 9   Judicial Inquiry Office
                10   Military & Naval Sciences
                11   Penn Women's Center
                12   Program for Student-Community Involvement
                13   Student Health Service
                14   Student Information & Systems
                15   Student Life Activities & Facilities
                16   Student Life Programs
                17   University Counseling Service
                18   WXPN-FM
==============================================================================
Command:
Main, Return, Key, Find, Path, Outline, Info, Log, World, Title, Help, Quit
```

you will be informed that the system is for authorized use only. If you do not have an appropriate username and password, you will not be able to log on.

Fortunately, publicly available Telnet resources frequently give out some kind of public password allowing limited access to the system. If you issue the command

telnet vxc.uncwil.edu <CR>

for example, once you are connected you are greeted by a screen message that announces the "system is for the use of individuals authorized by the University of North Carolina at Wilmington's Office of Computing and Information Systems only," and you are asked for "USERNAME." However, if for the username you type "info," you gain immediate access to the UNCW campus-wide information service, called SeaBoard, and you are taken to the system's main menu (Figure 6-1).

Before you connected to UNCW you may have observed a screen message that said, "Trying ... 128.109.221.1." The number sequence is the IP number truly recognized by machines connected to the network. Had you typed

telnet 128.109.221.1 <CR>

you would have achieved the same result as you did by "vxc.uncwil.edu."

Other public Telnet sites may provide you with connect screens that offer advice for logging in to access special services. If you telnet to archie.sura.net, for example, a screen message tells you on connection that if you type "qarchie" at the log-in prompt you will have access to the Archie client, which will be described later in this chapter. FedWorld is a BBS-type system available through Telnet. To get to FedWorld by Telnet, type

telnet fedworld.gov <CR>

and when you connect you are prompted for your name. The first time you log in you enter "new," and FedWorld asks you to fill out a form giving your organizational affiliation (your school), phone number, and address. You then choose a password, and you are encouraged to write it down so that future log-ins will proceed more quickly. FedWorld offerings include gateways to more than 120 BBS systems run by various federal government agencies.

Usernames and password procedures are sometimes just the first steps in the log-in process. Some Telnet sites require you to specify a terminal type during the log-in process. This is done so that the host computer, that is, the computer to which you have connected, knows how to read your keyboard and in turn how to speak back to your computer. Most communications software and Telnet client programs allow your computer to *emulate* one of several different dumb terminals often connected to larger computers.

Probably the most commonly accepted terminal on the Internet is the DEC VT100. If the site you are connecting to asks for VT100 or some other emulation, be sure you configure your software to that specification. A few sites require an IBM 3270 terminal emulation. If you do not know what is required or accepted, try VT100 or TTY first.

Because most Telnet sites require you to log in by giving a username and password, you might want to practice telnetting to the following sites:

Address	Log-in procedure	Resource
vienna.hh.lib.umich.edu	mlink	Mich. libraries
cap.gwu.edu	login guest, pwd visitor	Washington, D.C., info
neis.cr.usgs.gov	username: QED	USGS earthquake info
fdabbs.fda.gov	login bbs, pwd bbs	FDA info
info.umd.edu	none	University of Maryland
debra.dgbt.doc.ca 3000	none	AIDS, epilepsy

Note that the last entry in the list above concludes with a space and a number after the computer's name. The number designates the port or place on the computer that manages Telnet connections. It is known as the port number. If a standard port is used, the port number is omitted. If a port number is included in the address, it is important that you include it when you try to telnet to that computer. Some Telnet clients have other means for entering port numbers into the addressing scheme; you need to know the requirements of your Telnet client. In all instances you will want to be alert to uppercase and lowercase designations—sometimes the case makes a difference.

Menu hierarchies and other logic

Once you have successfully logged onto a computer via Telnet, you can begin to explore the material available. In most cases you will find only files of text material organized according to directories and subdirectories. Let's say you want to explore the Campus Wide Information Service at the University of Pennsylvania called PennInfo. You launch Telnet by typing

telnet penninfo.upenn.edu <CR>

At this site you don't need a username or password. Once connected, you are given a menu of 17 numbered items from which to choose (Figure 6-2). Those items include access to the university libraries, campus calendars, faculty and staff services, student activities and services, and other choices. You type the number of your choice and hit the Return (Enter) key on your keyboard.

The first screen you see is generally called the main, or top, menu. In this case, it also includes a list of commands for maneuvering through the directories.

Selecting items from the top menu takes you to lower-level menus. The menu structure is generally organized by topic. Choices on secondary menus may in turn lead to new menus and so on until you locate a text document containing the information you sought in the first place. This hierarchical menu structure, found frequently at Telnet sites, is the same type of arrangement found at Gopher servers (Chapter 5).

In the case of the PennInfo site, delving three menu levels deep (Figures 6-2 through 6-4) still did not produce any files with the information we wanted in them. Moreover, if you study the choices given in the lowest level (Figure 6-4) of the PennInfo system, you find menu items not intuitively associated with the menu choices above. This is common in Telnet and other hierarchically organized menu systems. The nature of building menu systems is such that only so many choices can be offered at each level, and clear, logical pathways to useful material do not always suggest themselves. Frequently you must explore to locate the most worthwhile information when using most menu-based information systems.

Don't get lost

Telnet clients do not have handy bookmark utilities, as World Wide Web and Gopher clients do, that allow you to mark a site that has information that you may want to use again and then automatically return to that place. You have to keep track of how you got to the information you wanted.

Working through Telnet sites is an adventure somewhat like the one described in the Greek myth of Theseus and the Minotaur. In that tale, the hero Theseus was able to slay the monstrous Minotaur and escape a maze by marking his movements with a ball of string. Entering a Telnet session is much like entering a maze in search of the monster called information. It is easy to move randomly about the computer site's menus, browsing among information that is neither useful for any school assignment nor particularly interesting.

However, when you do find something that you expect may be useful now or in the future, you will want to be able to get back to that information.

If you want to get back, unravel a ball of twine along the way. You do this with notes. Record the Telnet address. Then as you move down through menus, keep notes of which choices you selected.

For example, let's say you are concerned about job opportunities after you graduate. Browsing through PennInfo, you happen onto the menu shown in Figure 6-4. Your eye catches menu item 5, Career Planning and Placement. Graduation is still some time off for you, but you want to keep current on your opportunities. You think you might want to periodically check information offered under PennInfo. If you were casually browsing — without unraveling your ball of string — you might have a hard time finding that resource again.

Here's how to get there:

1. Connect to PennInfo through Telnet by typing "penninfo.upenn.edu."

2. At the PennInfo main menu (Figure 6-2) select item 17, University Life.

3. From the University Life menu (Figure 6-3) choose item 2, About University Life Offices.

4. At the About University Life Offices menu (Figure 6-4) item 5 opens up the Career Planning and Placement menu, which leads to desired files.

A relatively standard shorthand for tracking network navigation would summarize the actions this way:

Path = 1/17 University Life/ 2 About Un. L. Offices / 5 Career Plan

The shorthand means start at the top menu (1) and choose item 17, then item 2, and then item 5. The first word or two of each menu choice is kept with that choice's number as a security check. The path shorthand would be attached to the site address (penninfo.upenn.edu) in order to provide a full record of where you had been.

Capturing a Telnet session with log utilities

When you bring files to your computer screen during a Telnet session, you are doing just so much reading unless you take advantage of a utility built into nearly every communications program on the market—session logging. Session logging is like computerized photocopying. It copies all the text that passes your screen and writes it to a disk file that you name. You then have the full text on your computer so that you use it without having to re-enter it.

If you are using a PC with ProComm communications software, you start a log file by typing Alt-F1. If you are networked using DEC Pathworks, the command is Ctrl-F1. In either case, you are prompted to name the file you wish the session log to be stored in. If you are using Clarkson University's Telnet package (CUTCP described earlier), you launch what the software calls a capture session by typing Alt-C. The resulting log file is saved under

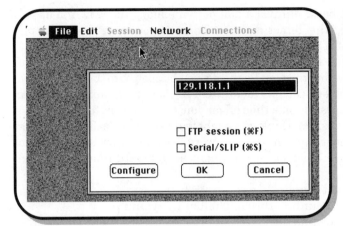

Fig. 6-5: The NCSA/BYU Telnet program for the Macintosh also has FTP capabilities.

the name of Capfile. In the NCSA-BYU Telnet package the Session Capture option is under the Session menu. Whatever your software, consult your manual (or your instructor) for the procedure to start a log file or to log a session.

Most programs also allow you to suspend the log temporarily during a session. In ProComm, once a log file is started, it may be toggled on and off with the command Alt-F2. In Pathworks, the Ctrl-F1 combination is a toggle. In the Clarkson University package, Alt-C acts as a toggle to turn the capture procedure on and off.

In Macintosh or Windows-based computers, you have a second option for saving information you find in a Telnet session. You can highlight text and copy it to the clipboard. You can then paste the text to a document in your word processor. In Windows or in Macintosh System 7 (or later) you can actually have the word processor running in the background and switch between the word processor and your Telnet client.

Getting help

As you explore your possibilities with Telnet, at times you may get confused about what to do. You can generally get online help in one of three ways:

- Type "?"
- Type "H" or "HELP."
- Enter the number, letter or name of a menu choice.

Fig. 6-6: QVT Net software for Windows offers Telnet (terminal) and other Internet clients.

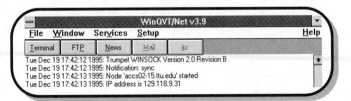

For example, in the top menu of SeaBoard (Figure 6-1) the help function is accessed by typing "1." At PennInfo (Figure 6-2) help is accessed by typing "H."

Help screens generally summarize available commands. If you are accessing the network by telephone, be alert to the commands of your software program. For example, Ctrl-] is a common Telnet escape command we have noted. However, if you are using ProComm communications software, that key combination merely toggles on and off a status bar across the bottom of the screen. The command is not passed on to the Telnet host.

Finding directions with Hytelnet

While FTP, Gopher and the World Wide Web have extensive search tools to help you locate information you may want, the tools for Telnet are less developed. From time to time a World Wide Web search will lead to a Telnet server. Sometimes you will read about a good Telnet site. The tool developed (by Peter Scott at the University of Saskatchewan) for helping you use Telnet to find information is called Hytelnet.

Hytelnet is a client program that puts a menu interface on publicly accessible Telnet sites and gives you online help logging onto remote sites. Library systems, CWISes, and community Free-Nets (public Internet systems maintained in a specific location) are among the more interesting sites indexed by Hytelnet.

On the Hytelnet menu, menus and submenus are organized by subject. Terms in brackets (< >) are selector items, and the cursor highlights them one at a time. When you choose a highlighted item by pressing the Enter key, you either get a new menu, a text document, or a Telnet connect dialog box telling you about the site you have chosen. The dialog box usually provides the Telnet address, log-in instructions, and a brief description of what you will find at the remote computer.

The simple command structure for Hytelnet can be confusing at first. It can take a little time to get used to the difference between using the Left arrow which takes you to the previous document, and typing "b" or "-," either of which takes you back one screen in the same document. To quit Hytelnet, type "q."

While Hytelnet facilitates the use of Telnet sites, it does not have keyword searching capability. You cannot enter a keyword and locate Telnet sites that have that information. Moreover, Hytelnet is not widely distributed. If your school does not have a Hytelnet client, you can access by telnetting to

- hytelnet.cwis.uci.edu (login: "hytelnet").
- pubinfopath.ucsd.edu (login: infopath, use selection 9).
- laguna.epcc.edu (username: library).

Additionally, some Gopher sites provide links to public Hytelnet clients.

```
Password:
<                      Welcome to
<                 THE OAK SOFTWARE REPOSITORY
<          A service of Oakland University, Rochester Michigan
<
< If you have trouble using OAK with your ftp client, please try using
< a dash (-) as the first character of your password -- this will turn
< off the continuation messages that may be confusing your ftp client.
< OAK is a Unix machine, and filenames are case sensitive.
<
< Access is allowed at any time.  If you have any unusual problems,
< please report them via electronic mail to archives@Oakland.Edu
<
< You are user #229 out of 400 maximum users on Thu Jul 13 08:53:22 1995.
<
< Oak is also on the World Wide Web, URL: http://www.acs.oakland.edu/oak.html
<
< File searching is now available!  Example command:  site exec index 4dos
<
<Please read the file README
<   it was last modified on Fri Mar 24 18:59:19 1995 - 111 days ago
<Guest login ok, access restrictions apply.
OAK.OAKLAND.EDU>
```

Fig. 6-7:
Oakland
University's Oak
Software
Repository's
FTP greeting
message lets you
know of a
shorter log-in
process peculiar
to the Oak site.

Why use Telnet

Although Telnet has been surpassed by more advanced Internet tools, it would be worthwhile to gain experience using it. First, there is still a lot of good information available via Telnet servers. As mentioned earlier, often World Wide Web and Gopher searches will lead you to Telnet sites.

Second, Telnet is a good confidence builder. As you learn to move through Telnet sites, you will also gain the skills needed to make more sophisticated use of the Internet tools at your disposal.

Moving files with FTP (file transfer protocol)

Although reading and logging information found via Telnet serves many purposes, often you will find information on the Internet that you will want to grab and transfer to your own computer. It may be a large file located somewhere else or it may be a great piece of software available on the Net. Telnet, or other Internet applications, generally would not have helped Elaine Lazarte, who wanted to integrate computer subroutines stored elsewhere on the Internet into her computer programs.

Instead, once she located the subroutines she wanted, she could transfer them to her computer using FTP, or file transfer protocol. FTP is also an excellent method for getting Frequently Asked Question (FAQ) files about Usenet Newsgroups, which will be discussed in Chapter 7.

Like Telnet, FTP is one of the basic Internet applications. It is the method used to transfer files among computers on the Internet. File transfer protocol is a name given by computer programmers to a series of conventions that enables one kind of computer operating under its own set of rules to send/receive files to/from another kind of computer operating under another set of rules. Thus a UNIX machine connected over a network passing through a

Fig. 6-8: The FTP dir command produces a detailed directory. At the far left of each line is a listing of descriptors that tell you whether the object is a file or a directory. At the far right of each line is the object's name.

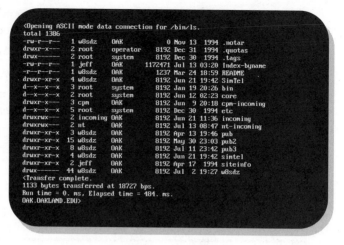

```
<Opening ASCII mode data connection for /bin/ls.
total 1386
-rw-r--r--    1 w8sdz     OAK           0 Nov 13  1994 .notar
drwxr-x---    2 root      operator   8192 Dec 31  1994 .quotas
drux-------   2 root      system     8192 Dec 30  1994 .tags
-rw-r--r--    1 jeff      OAK     1172471 Jul 13 03:20 Index-byname
-r--r--r--    1 w8sdz     OAK        1237 Mar 24 18:59 README
drwxr-xr-x    4 w8sdz     OAK        8192 Jun 21 19:42 SimTel
d--x--x--x    3 root      system     8192 Jan 19 20:26 bin
d--x--x--x    2 root      system     8192 Jun 12 02:23 core
drwxr-x---    3 cpm       OAK        8192 Jun  9 20:18 cpm-incoming
d--x--x--x    5 root      system     8192 Dec 30  1994 etc
drwxrwx---    2 incoming  OAK        8192 Jun 21 11:36 incoming
drwxrwx---    2 nt        OAK        8192 Jul 13 08:47 nt-incoming
drwxr-xr-x    3 w8sdz     OAK        8192 Apr 13 19:46 pub
drwxr-xr-x   15 w8sdz     OAK        8192 May 30 23:03 pub2
drwxr-xr-x    8 w8sdz     OAK        8192 Jul 11 23:42 pub3
drwxr-xr-x    4 w8sdz     OAK        8192 Jun 21 19:42 sintel
drwxr-xr-x    2 jeff      OAK        8192 Apr 17  1994 siteinfo
drux-------  44 w8sdz     OAK        8192 Jul  2 19:27 w8sdz
<Transfer complete.
1133 bytes transferred at 18727 bps.
Run time = 0. ms, Elapsed time = 484. ms.
OAK.OAKLAND.EDU>
```

machine running VMS can exchange files with an IBM mainframe operating under still another set of rules and then pass the file on to your Macintosh or PC.

From the user point of view, there are some similarities between Telnet and FTP. Both are found on any computer connected to the Internet running TCP/IP. In their basic format, both are command-line driven. In both cases you connect by naming the protocol (FTP or Telnet) and then adding the Internet address of the host or server to which you wish to connect. In both cases, you frequently go through a log-in procedure once you are connected.

FTP is perhaps the least friendly of all the Internet protocols. It is "strictly business" and assumes you know the rules. Fortunately, there are only a few simple rules to learn. Those rules govern 1) connecting to and disconnecting from FTP sites, 2) getting and reading directories, 3) moving between directories, and 4) retrieving files with the proper protocol.

Making the FTP connection

FTP connections are made exactly the same way Telnet connections are. Using an FTP client, you make your FTP connection by typing "ftp" and the name or IP number of the computer with which you want to connect.

For example, there is a large repository of software available at Oakland University in Rochester, Mich. To begin the process of transferring files from there to your computer you would type

ftp oak.oakland.edu <CR>.

As an alternative, you can launch the FTP client first and then from its prompt (typically "ftp>"), type

open oak.oakland.edu <CR>

and get the same results.

In either case you are greeted by the dialog shown in Figure 6-7. At the log-in prompt type "anonymous," and when you are asked for the password enter your complete e-mail address. This process of logging in with the username "anonymous" and your e-mail address as your password is known as Anonymous FTP.

In addition to being the prime method for serving up software on the Internet, Anonymous FTP is the way to get many text files. For example, one

---

Fig. 6-9: The more commonly used FTP commands help you move through the remote server directory structure, get directory reports and retrieve files. Commands that turn features on, such as hash, bell, and interactive, can be turned off by issuing the same command with "no" added to the front of the word. For example, "nobell" turns off the bell that sounds at completion of file transfer.

Basic FTP Commands

Command	Description
abort	Terminate current operation
ascii	Set file transfer mode to ascii
bget	Retrieve a file in binary mode
bput	Send a file in binary mode
bell	Ring bell when file transfer completes
binary	Set file transfer mode to binary
bye	Close the connection and exit
case	Toggle mapping of local filenames to lowercase
cd	Change current working directory on remote host
cdup	Change working directory on remote host to parent directory; synonym = cd ..
dir	Display contents of a directory in long form
dis	Close the connection
get	Retrieve a file from remote host
hash	Print # for each packet sent or received
help	Display help messages for all FTP commands
interactive	Prompt with each filename for mget, mput and mdelete commands
ls	Display contents of a directory in short form
mget	Retrieve a group of files from the remote host
open	Open a connection to a remote host
put	Transfer a file from client machine to remote host
pwd	Print remote host's current working directory
quiet	Do not display transfer statistics
remotehelp	Display list of FTP commands implemented by the server
stat	Display contents of a directory in short form
show	Show current status
verbose	Display server replies and transfer stats

can get the text of Federal Communications Commission rules and proposed rules, the text of Supreme Court decisions, National Institutes of Health data files, Securities and Exchange Commission filings, and Commerce Department data. Also available by Anonymous FTP are U.S. Navy policy and strategy documents, immigration information, NASA documents on and graphic images from space missions, and gigabytes of software for all kinds of different computers.

Because anybody can log in using Anonymous FTP, host sites grant limited, or *restricted* access to people doing so. The FTP greeting screen at Oakland University, Software Repository (Figure 6-7) concludes with the line "Guest login ok, access restrictions apply." If you have an account with the host site, you would give your assigned username and chosen password. You then presumably would have more liberal access than people logging in anonymously. In either case, each site is limited in the number of persons who can log in at one time. The Oakland University site greeting screen says that its limit is 400 users. Other sites may handle fewer.

Navigating FTP server directories

One reason that using FTP is complicated is that once you have connected to the host computer, you will be using UNIX-like commands. The commands and results will look very cryptic to people accustomed to Macintosh and Windows interfaces.

For example, after you have logged onto the FTP server at Oakland University, you will be staring at a command-line prompt with no menu. If you type "dir" you will see a detailed directory. Figure 6-8 shows the results of asking for a directory immediately after logging into the Oakland University FTP site anonymously. FTP reports back that the "PORT" command was successful, that an ASCII (text) file is being opened (the file is actually the directory), and that the transfer of information from the distant server to your local client is complete. Before displaying the list of files and directories, FTP reported that there were 10 files and directories.

The fifth item listed in Figure 6-8 is a README file that you are encouraged to read. (To read the README file, you will have to get it using the procedure outlined below and then open it using a word processor.) Most of the remaining objects listed are directories. You know this because the first character in the 10-character string at the left of the lines describing those items is a "d" followed by an "r." The left-most characters on the line describing the README file are "-r."

Near the end of the list in Figure 6-8 are three directories labeled "pub," "pub2," and "pub3." These are standard designations for publicly accessible directories. You change to the pub directory by using the cd (for change directory) command:

cd pub <CR>

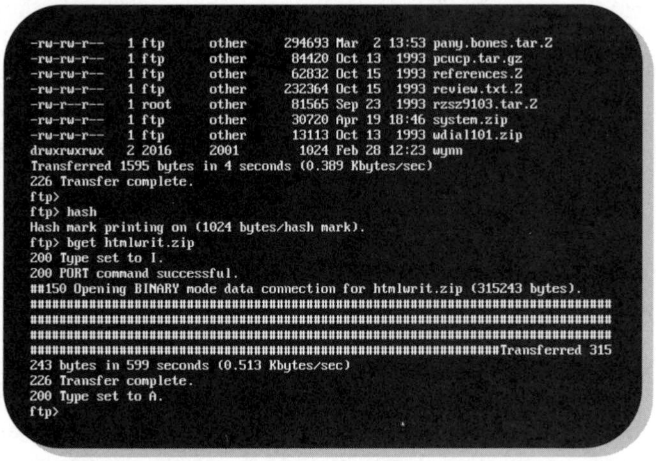

Fig. 6-10: The entire process of downloading a binary file using FTP marked by hash marks (#) is shown.

```
-rw-rw-r--    1 ftp      other       294693 Mar  2 13:53 pany.bones.tar.Z
-rw-rw-r--    1 ftp      other        84420 Oct 13  1993 pcucp.tar.gz
-rw-rw-r--    1 ftp      other        62832 Oct 15  1993 references.Z
-rw-rw-r--    1 ftp      other       232364 Oct 15  1993 review.txt.Z
-rw-rw-r--    1 root     other        81565 Sep 23  1993 rzsz9103.tar.Z
-rw-rw-r--    1 ftp      other        30720 Apr 19 18:46 system.zip
-rw-rw-r--    1 ftp      other        13113 Oct 13  1993 wdial101.zip
druxruxrux    2 2016     2001          1024 Feb 28 12:23 wymn
Transferred 1595 bytes in 4 seconds (0.389 Kbytes/sec)
226 Transfer complete.
ftp>
ftp> hash
Hash mark printing on (1024 bytes/hash mark).
ftp> bget htmlwrit.zip
200 Type set to I.
200 PORT command successful.
##150 Opening BINARY mode data connection for htmlwrit.zip (315243 bytes).
###############################################################################
###############################################################################
###############################################################################
#########################################################################Transferred 315
243 bytes in 599 seconds (0.513 Kbytes/sec)
226 Transfer complete.
200 Type set to A.
ftp>
```

Be very careful to observe differences in uppercase and lowercase letters because many FTP sites are case sensitive. FTP will report back to you that the PORT command was successful if you typed it properly.

Below the "pub" directory are several other directories occupied by still other directories in a hierarchical fashion. A close relative of the dir command is ls for list. The ls command gives you a short directory, listing only the names of files and no other information about them. The ls command tends to give you results more quickly than the dir command, but you have less information reported. Consequently you don't know if an item in the list is a directory leading to files or if it is a file. Still, if all you need to know is the exact name of a file so that you can get or bget it, then ls does the trick.

Getting or bgetting a file

Usually the reason for using FTP is to retrieve a file you already know something about. FTP is not an especially friendly or efficient browsing tool. You may know, for example, that the most recent set of Supreme Court rulings are at ftp.cwru.edu or that data from the National Archives are at nih.gov. If you've done an Archie search, which will be discussed later in this chapter, you have full path information. In other words, you will know which directories you have to move through to arrive at the directory in which the file you want is located. In most cases, using FTP, you know where you are going and what you want to do ahead of time.

Let's say you are in a class in which the professor has you post information to a server and you want a piece of software that will give text posted electronically the look and feel of paper-produced magazines. By monitoring a mailing list, you learn that the Html Write program will meet your needs and has had been placed on an FTP server at Brigham Young University. It has the file name htmlwrit.zip and is located in the /tmp directory. Figure 6-10 shows the dialog with the FTP server that occurs during the process of retrieving the file.

You connect to the BYU server by typing

FTP ftp.byu.edu <CR>

and then type "cd" (change directory command) to move to the "/tmp" directory. From there, the "dir" directory command to

- Confirm that the file was where it had been reported.
- Get the exact name of the file, noting case of letters.
- Ascertain the approximate size of the file.

The ls command would have given you the first pieces of information but would have provided no insight into the file size. Because the file is more than just a few bytes, it is prudent to enter the FTP hash command, which tells the FTP server to report the progress of the file transfer. It does so by sending hash marks (#) to the screen for each *packet* of file data it sends out. After entering the hash command, the actual transfer can begin.

Html Write is a binary file to be read by a computer and not a text file (for reading by human beings). There are two common command sequences for retrieving binary files. Typing the command "bget" followed by the file name (in this case, htmlwrit.zip) tells the server to get a file in binary mode with the specific file name. In a two-step process you could enter the commands

binary <CR>

get htmlwrit.zip <CR>

If the file you want is a text-only (ASCII) file with no special formatting commands or any other programming code, you can use FTP in the ASCII mode, which is its default generally. In that case, you can use the get command, rather than bget. Sometimes several files are stored together. To transfer them as a group, you can use the mget command.

Most types of files require binary transfer. You can usually determine the type of file it is by its file extension, the part of the file name that follows the period. Some common file extensions requiring binary are .sea (Macintosh self-extracting archive), .ps (PostScript), .exe (an IBM executable file), as well as graphics files with extensions such as .tif, .pnt, .pcx, .gif, .cgm, and .mac. The most common file name extension for ASCII (text) files is .txt.

Interestingly, you may successfully transfer text files in binary mode, but you may not move binary files in ASCII mode. Users of popular Macintosh client programs such as NCSA-BYU Telnet must first turn on MacBinary (under the File menu) to transfer some files successfully. It is generally advisable to enable MacBinary at each FTP session.

When the server is done moving the file, it reports the time required (599 seconds in the example) and the rate of transfer.

Handling and using files

Once you have mastered the steps in grabbing a file and transferring it to your computer, there are several other factors to consider. First, if you are transferring the file to your account on a central computer, you have to be sure that you have enough disk space to receive the file. If you don't, the transfer will be automatically terminated.

Second, if you transfer the file to a central computer, you will probably want to download it to a personal computer so that you can open it and read it using a word processor (if it is an ASCII file) or use it (if it is a piece of software). Many files that are transferred using FTP are compressed. Not only do compressed files take up less storage space on a hard drive, they are more quickly transferred across the Internet. However, once you receive a compressed file, you must first decompress it before you can use it.

By convention, the file extension—the part of the file name after the period—indicates if a file has been compressed and, if it has, by what compression method. The name of the file used in the example was htmlwrit.zip. The extension .zip indicated that the file had been compressed and archived using a program such as PKzip. In order to use the Html Write program, it

---

Table 6-1: File extensions provide clues to the nature of a file's contents and storage format. This table summarizes some of the more common file extensions encountered on the Internet.

File Ext.	Archive?	PC?	Mac?	Extraction program to use
ARC	yes	x		PKUNPAK, ARCE
ARJ	yes	x		ARJ
COM	maybe	x		If archived, is self-extracting
CPT	yes		x	Compactor
DOC	no	x	x	Usually text-only file; may be MS Word (PC) file
EXE	maybe	x		If archived, is self-extracting
HQX	yes		x	BinHex
LZH	yes	x		LHARC
MAC	no		x	Is a runnable application
PIT	yes		x	PackIt
PS	no	x	x	PostScript coded file; send directly to PS printer
SEA	yes		x	Self-extracting
SIT	yes		x	Stuff-It
TAR	yes			Should be decompressed on host/server
TXT	no	x	x	ASCII (text) file readable on any computer
WK*	no	x	x	Lotus 1-2-3 files usable by spreadsheet programs
WP	no	x		Word Perfect file
Z	yes			Should be decompressed on host/server
ZIP	yes	x		PKUNZIP, UNZIP

Fig. 6-11: FTP clients such as Fetch (here) and WS-FTP put a point-and-drag interface on the FTP process.

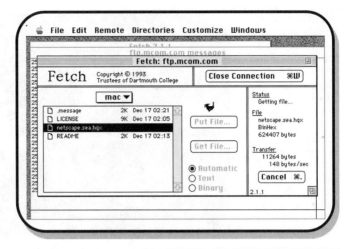

would have to be *unzipped* or decompressed. PKunzip and PKzip, IBM-compatible shareware programs widely available on college campuses, bulletin boards, and the Internet, are used to compress and decompress files.

Other common compression/decompression schemes are Stuffit/Unstuffit for the Macintosh (file extension: .sit) and Compress/Uncompress (file extension: .Z) and Pack/Unpack (file extension: .z) for Unix. Finally, many people use a program called Binhex to convert Macintosh files into a binary format. They have to be read and reconverted using Binhex as well. All compressed and Binhex files must be moved through the Internet in a binary format.

Fortunately, most compression software programs, as well as Binhex, are available via FTP. Some FTP sites will tell you in their welcoming screens about other compression schemes that the host site can uncompress "on the fly" if you follow instructions. See Table 6-1 for a list of common file compression/archive formats and the software needed to unpack the archive.

The final step

When you get a file with FTP, the file is moved from the remote server to the machine where the client software resides. If you are dialing in with a modem to access a host machine that has the FTP client you use, FTP brings the file to your disk space on the local host. You then will have to download the program to your computer using Kermit, Zmodem, or some other protocol your host recognizes. If, on the other hand, you are directly connected to the Internet with a network card and hard wire, or if your dial-in host provides SLIP access, then the file moves directly to your personal computer— if your FTP client software is on your computer.

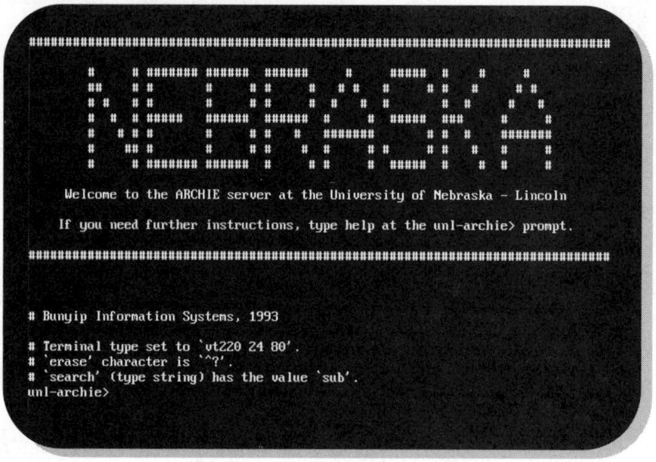

Fig. 6-12: The Archie startup dialog at many sites (here the University of Nebraska, Lincoln) reports default search settings. When you start your search, you are given a time estimate required for the search you have requested.

```
####################################################################

        #   # ####### ###### ######   #     ##### #   #   #
        ##  # # #     #   #  #    #   #     #   # #  #   # # #
        # # # # #     #   #  #    #   #     #   # # #     #   #
        # # # ##### ###### ######   #     ##### ###   #   #
        #  ## #     #    # #    #   #     #   # #  #   #######
        #   # ####### ###### #   #   #     ##### #   #   #   #

        Welcome to the ARCHIE server at the University of Nebraska - Lincoln

        If you need further instructions, type help at the unl-archie> prompt.

####################################################################

# Bunyip Information Systems, 1993

# Terminal type set to 'vt220 24 80'.
# 'erase' character is '^?'.
# 'search' (type string) has the value 'sub'.
unl-archie>
```

Making FTP easier

If FTP sounds complicated, it can be. But it is also one of the most efficient ways to transfer large files, software and data. FTP is also key to much of the collaborative work done by scientists on the Internet. For example, the Co-operative Human Linkage Center is a collaborative effort among research-ers to map the human genome. In it, experimental data collected at the Uni-versity of Iowa is automatically transferred via FTP for analysis at the Fox Chase Cancer Research Center in Philadelphia.

Fortunately, tools are developing to make FTP easier. Sometimes, if you are absolutely sure of the precise name and location on the network of a file stored on an FTP server, you can use your World Wide Web browser to re-trieve the file. Under the right circumstances your Web browser may even provide for you some directory listings and let you browse through those directories on a remote site. The standard format to access an FTP site with a World Wide Web browser is FTP://ftp.*computername.domain* / *filedirectory* / *filename*.

The Telnet clients for Macintosh, DOS and Windows described ear-lier in this chapter also permit you to do FTP. For Macintosh and for Windows machines there are also some very nice stand-alone clients that partially overcome the command line interface limitations of FTP. In the Macintosh program, Fetch, and in such Windows programs as WS-FTP, you get a point-and-drag type of interface. In either program you simply point your mouse at the file on the remote server and drag it to a folder (directory) on your machine (Figure 6-11). These programs also allow you to display on your screen text files (such as README files) that reside on the distant server.

Finding files using Archie

Archie and FTP go together. Like its comic book cousins Veronica and Jughead, which you learned about in Chapter 5, Archie is a network detective. Archie scours a constantly updated index of databases and archives for any hits on keywords you provide. What Archie comes back with is a list of directories and files whose names contain the word you have given.

The listing of those files and directories is organized by host site (Fig. 6-12). Below the name of each host site is a list of the directories and files whose names match your query. Archie tells you if the matching object is a file or a directory and then reports full path information for getting to the directory or retrieving the file by FTP.

Because it is used frequently by scientists and computer programmers to find software, Archie is often one of the first Internet clients system administrators put on a host. If your computer runs Archie (it will often be on the central computer on which you have your e-mail account), to launch an Archie search, you type the word "archie" followed by a keyword describing what you want to find.

If your host does not have an Archie client and you do not have one on your machine, you have two options for accessing a public Archie client. You could access Archie clients by using Hytelnet or Gopher (Chapter 5) clients. At a general Gopher site or Hytelnet site, Archie access is usually found under an Internet Resources menu. The advantage of using Gopher is that you may not have to start a separate FTP session to fetch a file if you find one you would like. Some World Wide Web clients also permit this.

You also could use Telnet to connect to an Archie client. Some publicly accessible sites include

- archie.ans.net (Advanced Network Services in Michigan).
- archie.unl.edu (University of Nebraska, Lincoln), log-in: archie (hit Return at password).
- archie.doc.ic.ac.uk (United Kingdom).
- archie.sura.net (a consortium of Southern universities).
- quiche.cs.mcgill.ca (McGill University in Montreal, the home of Archie).

In all cases, the log-in word is "archie." Table 6-2 lists addresses of Archie clients around the world. You should always use the client nearest you when possible.

When you launch Archie, either from your host computer or from a remote site, you are given a brief message that tells you the default settings for searches at the site to which you are connected. You must take note of these settings; they determine whether Archie's search is case sensitive and whether Archie looks for whole words or reports a match when your search string shows up anywhere. This setting will impact heavily on the results of your search. Figure 6-13 shows the possible settings for an Archie launch.

Fig. 6-13: When
Archie completes
your search, you
get a report with
files and directo-
ries grouped by
host site.

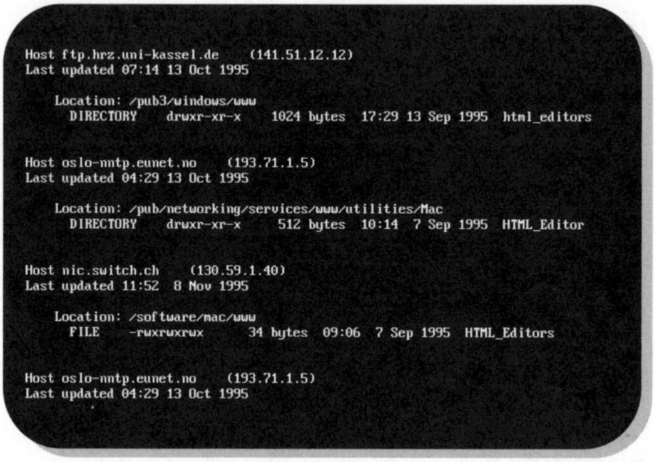

```
Host ftp.hrz.uni-kassel.de    (141.51.12.12)
Last updated 07:14 13 Oct 1995

    Location: /pub3/windows/www
       DIRECTORY    drwxr-xr-x    1024 bytes  17:29 13 Sep 1995  html_editors

Host oslo-nntp.eunet.no    (193.71.1.5)
Last updated 04:29 13 Oct 1995

    Location: /pub/networking/services/www/utilities/Mac
       DIRECTORY    drwxr-xr-x     512 bytes  10:14  7 Sep 1995  HTML_Editor

Host nic.switch.ch    (130.59.1.40)
Last updated 11:52  8 Nov 1995

    Location: /software/mac/www
       FILE       -rwxrwxrwx      34 bytes  09:06  7 Sep 1995  HTML_Editors

Host oslo-nntp.eunet.no    (193.71.1.5)
Last updated 04:29 13 Oct 1995
```

To use a specific setting, you append it to the end of the Archie command. For example, to launch a search that ignores the case of the letters you would type "archie-s." This generally is the best kind of search. When you ask Archie to report the names and locations of files and directories containing a specific string of characters, you don't know ahead of time whether the name of a file is uppercase or lowercase; nor do you care, so long as it has useful information in the file.

Public Archie Clients

archie.unl.edu	USA (Nebraska)
archie.internic.net	USA (New Jersey)
archie.rutgers.edu	USA (New Jersey)
archie.ans.net	USA (New York)
archie.sura.net	USA (Maryland)
archie.doc.ic.ac.uk	United Kingdom
archie.edvz.uni-linz.ac.at	Austria
archie.univie.ac.at	Austria
archie.funet.fi	Finland
archie.th-darmstadt.de	Germany
archie.rediris.es	Spain
archie.luth.se	Sweden
archie.switch.ch	Switzerland
archie.unipi.it	Italy
archie.au	Australia
archie.uqam.ca	Canada
archie.ac.il	Israel
archie.wide.ad.jp	Japan
archie.kr	Korea
archie.sogang.ac.kr	Korea

Table 6-2: Addresses of publicly accessible Archie clients. Using Telnet and logging in as "archie," anyone may have access to the Archie client software at these sites.

Figure 6-14 reports that default search parameters at a remote site are set at sub, which means that the search is case insensitive and that anywhere Archie finds a match—whole word or partial—a match will be reported. Other Archie search settings include exact, subcase and regex. Exact will report only exact matches (same case, whole word). Subcase looks for matches in terms of case, but does not require whole word matches. Regex sets the search to look for strings in Unix terms. If Archie tells you that the search type is anything but "sub" you may want to change the setting. You do that by typing the command

set search sub <CR>

Starting an Archie search

If you are at an Archie prompt (which is the case when you launch the program from a remote site), the way that you initiate an Archie search is by typing "prog" or "find" followed by a space and the string of characters you want to find. Hitting the Enter key starts the search. Otherwise, just enter the word "archie" and the search string.

Let's say you have an assignment to create a page for a World Wide Web site and you want to find an HTML editor to help you. So you conduct an Archie search using the keyword HTML_editor. The underline was included because keywords are often found in file names and file names cannot have blank spaces in them.

When Archie has completed the search, you get a list of files and directories matching your search terms. Figure 6-13 displays partial results of the search for the key word HTML_editor. A standard search did not return any results, but a case-insensitive search found several matches.

The report contains several tiers of information. The first tier (all the way to the left of the screen) reports the Anonymous FTP host site. The first two entries in Figure 6-13 are "extro.ucc.su.oz.au" and "ftp.cic.net." The second tier reports the "Location," which actually is the directory path leading to the object that registered the hit.

In Figure 6-13, the top hit is at "extro.ucc.su.oz.au." The location entry reads "Location: /pub/inet-apps/mac." What this means is that on the computer at extro.ucc.su.oz.au. there is, first of all, a directory called pub. This is standard designation for a directory accessible to the public. Within the pub directory is another directory devoted to the inet-apps, which are probably several software applications for the Internet. And finally, within that directory is another directory called mac, which is where the file in question resides. This directory path is very much like the hierarchical menu structure we have already seen in Gopher and at some Telnet sites.

The third and final tier describes the object itself. In the case of the extro site, only one object was found, a file called "HTML_Editor_1.0.sit.hqx." The name in this case tips you off that the file is a Binhex file compressed using

Stuffit because it ends in ".sit" and ".hqx," which are standard designations for such files. Archie reports the size of the file (554564 bytes), as well as the time (23:16 or 11:16 p.m.) and date (Mar 30, 1995) it was last revised. The time and date information can be of help if you are looking for information on a particular event or a specific version of a piece of software. The size information will give you a sense of whether you're looking at a novel-length document, a huge software program, or a one-page document.

As the Archie report results scroll past your screen, you can stop the scrolling by typing Ctrl-S. Once stopped, you start the scroll again with Ctrl-Q. If your communications program permits, you can of course create a log file and capture the Archie report as it passes. You also have the option of mailing the results to yourself. At the end of the search, you remain in the Archie program and have the option of issuing a number of commands. To mail the results of your search, you type

mail *username@host.domain* <CR>

where you would substitute your e-mail address for the string "username@host.domain."

When you are done with Archie, you type "q" for quit. Generally you will be released back to your host. The qarchie server at archie.sura.net (log-in: qarchie) accepts an abbreviated set of commands and does not drop you immediately back to your host. Help, in Archie, is accessed by typing "help" just as it is in many of the Internet programs. When you ask for help, you are given a set of help topics upon which you may get further information. If you want to see a full set of Archie commands and what they do, you give Archie the command

manpage <CR>

and you will see an Archie manual which is about 20 typewritten pages long.

While you can find text files on the Internet in this way, Archie and FTP are uniquely suited to finding and retrieving software archived at FTP sites around the world. But it is not always easy to tell whether a file is a text file or a binary (program) file. The naming conventions — discussed under FTP — provide clues. The Archie whatis command can also provide information about files. If you type

whatis baseball <CR>

for example, whatis searches the Archie Software Description Database for the string "baseball," ignoring case. In the database are names and short descriptions of many software packages, documents and data files on the Internet. When Archie finds a match, it will report proper file names and their descriptions. A prog or find search on the file names will then tell you where to get the files. That is a job for FTP.

Words of caution

Whatever way you bring text and software *down from the Net,* remember that much of it is copyrighted. With software, shareware programs put you on your honor to pay for them if you decide after a reasonable trial period that you like a program well enough to use it. Freeware is, as the name implies free, but is still copyrighted. Other programs are in the public domain, which means that nobody holds the copyright.

Still other programs available in Internet archives are software in some state of testing. During testing periods, users are encouraged to report software bugs to the authors in exchange for free use of the program.

Whatever the case, it's up to you legally and ethically to know the terms under which the software is distributed. Generally there is some kind of notice provided with each program, often in the README file or the opening screen.

Chapter 7

Sharing through Usenet

The 1995 vote of the regents of the University of California to terminate the system's affirmative action program sparked a storm of debate in forums around the country. From college campuses to Capitol Hill, people debated the merits of programs designed to increase the percentages of different population groups at universities, in industry, and elsewhere.

In one particularly spirited exchange, a student from Cornell University in Ithaca, New York, argued that the net effect of affirmative action was to allow unqualified people into better positions. That argument brought a heated response from an employee at Duke University in Raleigh, North Carolina. "Why is it always assumed that any black person who is not pushing a broom or a mop MUST be unqualified?" the employee at Duke wondered. A student at a third school observed that "blacks are blamed for everything," while a fourth participant in the debate countered that to point out specific instances of troubling behavior involving African Americans "does not constitute blacks being blamed for everything."

Participants in this particular debate didn't know each other. Nor is it likely that they will meet, or even see each other face to face. They had conducted their conversations over the soc.college Usenet Newsgroup. Affirmative action was not the only topic of discussion in that news group at that time. A graduate student at Ohio State University was circulating a manifesto predicting that the Internet would lead to a revolution in the way the philosophy and the humanities in general are taught. Yet other students on soc.college were musing about how to get the most out of college.

One student opined that "School is what you make of it." A colleague at Carnegie Mellon University disagreed. "Not entirely," she wrote. "The resources of a school, the quality and effort of the professor's research, and teaching greatly influences one's education."

The discussions on Usenet Newsgroups are not restricted to college issues. When Jerry Garcia, the leader of The Grateful Dead band died, thousands of people consoled themselves via Usenet Newsgroups. When the bombing of the federal building in Oklahoma City was linked to the activities of right-wing militia, the claims were hotly discussed in scores of Usenet Newsgroups. And when Senator James Exon of Nebraska introduced a bill to curb obscene material on the Internet, a portion of the information to which he objected could be found in Usenet Newsgroups.

In this chapter you will
- Learn what Usenet is and how news groups are organized .
- Understand how to navigate through Usenet menus.
- Be introduced to the basics of good Usenet behavior.
- Take a tour of one set of Usenet Newsgroups.

What Usenet is—and what it isn't

Usenet Newsgroups, which are sometimes referred to collectively as network news, make up a huge distributed conference system in which people with similar interests across the world can interact with each other. Perhaps the best way to imagine Usenet is as thousands of computer bulletin boards, each devoted to a different topic. People can come to a specific bulletin board, read the notices, and then post a reply if they are so moved. All the messages (sometimes called *articles*) on a particular bulletin board are distributed to interconnected computers via the Internet or other networks.

Global distribution through the Internet can be a powerful convenience for some students. Sandra Pulley began her college career at Baylor University in Texas. But she had graduated from high school in Wurzburg, Germany, where her father had been stationed with the U.S. Army. Thousands of miles from Wurzburg, Sandra gradually lost touch with her high school classmates. Then in her senior year Sandra learned to navigate the Internet in one of her classes.

On the Internet, Sandra discovered a news group called alt.culture.military-brats where she learned how to get in touch with her alumni association online. She found an organization called Military Brats of America that runs a bulletin board service (BBS) on America Online. Through these *virtual communities* she was able to re-establish contact with people who had been important to her during the three years she had spent in Wurzburg.

Usenet history

Usenet was born in 1979, when two graduate students at Duke University developed a system to exchange information among computers running the Unix operating system. The first two sites were at Duke and the University of North Carolina. In 1986, software using the Network News Transfer Protocol (NNTP) was released. This protocol allowed users to transfer news articles via TCP/IP, integrating Usenet into the Internet. From that point, as long as they were coded correctly, Usenet news articles could be accessible and stored on computers running different operating systems.

In many ways, Usenet Newsgroups resemble the discussion lists described in Chapter 3. But they are not the same. Discussion lists operate via e-mail, and once you subscribe to a list, you receive every message posted to the list as e-mail in your account.

Messages to Usenet Newsgroups are posted to servers that communicate with each other through agreements among system administrators. When one server receives news group postings from another, that is known as a news feed. When you read the messages posted to a news group, you are reading messages that are located on a server, not in your own account. In the same way, when you post a message, the message is posted to a server. It is not automatically distributed to thousands of people. Instead, the message is distributed to the servers that receive the news feed of that particular news group.

This arrangement has advantages and drawbacks. All you need to subscribe to and participate in a discussion list is e-mail. As messages come in, you can read them at your convenience, perhaps download them from a central account to your personal computer, and manage the mail in a way that is appropriate for your needs.

News servers are selective

With Usenet, you need to have a news reader and access to a news server. At most campuses, officials in the campus computing office will determine which news groups are received on the server on campus. Few carry all available news groups—by current count there are more than 10,000. Many campuses limit the range of news groups they carry either because they do not want to use the hard disk space needed to store a lot of messages—many megabytes of messages travel through Usenet every day—or because the administrator is uncomfortable with the topic of the discussion. The site administrator has control of the Usenet news feed to the site. Distinct from discussion groups, the user is not in control.

Moreover, with Usenet, because the system administrator decides how long to archive messages, you may miss interesting information if you do not check in regularly. With discussion lists, all the messages are saved in your mailbox. You determine when to discard them.

But the weaknesses of Usenet are also its strengths. If you leave campus or do not wish to participate in a news group for a period of time, you do not have to worry that your electronic mailbox will be stuffed to overflowing with unwanted messages. Moreover, the amount of information is enormous. By some estimates, more than 100,000 servers carry Usenet feeds and more than 370,000 articles, representing 20,000 pages of information, are transmitted daily. Most servers subscribe to at least 1,500 news groups; so if you are on a campus with a Usenet news feed you will have no shortage of choices.

As you explore Usenet, you should keep in mind that Usenet is not an organization, company or public utility. It is the network of servers that receive Usenet news feeds. You have no *right* to access Usenet; that is controlled by your system administrator. Moreover, Usenet is not centrally controlled or distributed. News moves from one machine to another at various rates of speed. The way news arrives at the server that you access and the order in which you see articles are controlled by your local system and the neighboring systems that feed the news.

Access to Usenet news

Like other Internet applications, Usenet news is a client/server application. The easiest and most efficient way to access Usenet Newsgroups is for the system administrator on your campus to arrange for a news feed to your local system and to mount news readers (client software) on different computers for you to use.

Most of the early news readers were written to run under Unix. Three of the most common news readers in the Unix environment are called nn, rn and tin. If you have an account on a Unix machine, to see if you already have access to network news enter "nn," "rn" or "trn" (an updated version of rn), or "tin" at your system prompt. If those don't work, you might also try "news" (which on some systems gives you news only for the system), "unews," "usenet," or "netnews." You can also consult your system administrator.

Written in 1984, rn uses a full-screen (as opposed to just a single command-line) interface. It includes many useful features, including the ability to read, discard and process articles in ways the user can decide. A superset of rn, trn groups articles according to their subject matter. Series of articles that are responses to a single subject are known as *threads*. Developed in 1989, nn, like e-mail, presents a directory of article subject lines and the senders' addresses, allowing you to preselect articles to read. Like trn, tin supports threads and the indexing of subject lines and sender names.

Some popular news readers for DEC computers running VMS include VMS/VNEWS and FNEWS (which also runs on Unix). For personal computers, Trumpet and WinVN are available for DOS/Windows computers and Nuntius, Hypernews and Newswatcher run on the Macintosh platform. Netscape supports a network news reader and QVT Net for Windows contains a news reader as one of its elements.

As you can see, there are several different places on campus in which you may find access to Usenet news readers and news groups. If you simply do not have access on your campus—some system administrators fear the large message volume will strain their systems—you may be able to configure a news reader to access a news feed from another campus.

Another alternative is to access Usenet through a Gopher site. For example, you can point your Gopher (see Chapter 5) to Michigan State University by typing "gopher gopher.msu.edu." If you select item 6, News and Weather, and then item 13 you can explore Usenet as well. If you gopher to Washington and Lee University (gopher gopher.wlu.edu), choose item 2, Netlinks, then item 11, Usenet Readers, you will receive a list of connections to all public-access Usenet news readers. Because everything changes on the Internet, by the time you try this some of the news readers on the list will no longer support public access.

There are several drawbacks to using a public-access news reader for Usenet. First, you cannot configure the system to show only the news groups in which you are interested. Consequently, it can take several minutes for the system to load the menu of available news groups. Secondly, the whole process is very slow. You need a lot of patience. So while you may want to experience network news via a public news reader, if you plan to get involved, you will want to lobby your campus to carry a feed and make news readers available locally.

Finally, many Web browsers, including Netscape, can now double as news readers. To use Netscape as a news reader, click on the news button. To configure it for a specific news server, pull down the preferences menu.

The news group hierarchy

Before learning how to participate in news groups, it is important to understand the overall structure of network news. Network news groups are organized according to hierarchies going from the general to the specific. The name of each news group is divided from its parent and various subgroupings by a period. For example, the news group sci.math.num-analysis was formed by people interested in discussing problems in numerical analysis. The originator of the discussion placed the group in the hierarchy of news groups reserved for discussion of science. All news groups in this hierarchy begin with sci.

The second element in the news group name math designates math designations. There are many other science-oriented news groups, including physics, biology, medicine, archeology, astronomy and more.

Traditionally Usenet Newsgroups have fallen into seven categories listed in Figure 7-1. Over the years, however, that number has expanded dramatically. There are now major designations for the humanities (humanities), users of VMS/VAX computers (vmsnet), high energy particle physics research (hepnet) and Russian language news groups (relcom).

News groups can also be created locally, designed just for discussion on a specific campus. So often you will find top-level designations by geographic designation (country, state and city) or organization. Often a college campus will have its own top-level Usenet designation. Because system administrators can arrange for news feeds for any group that is of interest, many locally created groups are widely and generally considered part of the Usenet Newsgroup family.

The most popular designation for the locally created news groups is the alt prefix, which stands for *alternative* news groups. Many of the wild and extreme discussions about curious topics take place in news groups with the alt designation. For example, fan clubs fall under the alt designation. Fan

Seven Major News Categories

comp . Computer science and related topics
news . Network news itself
rec ..... Hobbies, recreational activities
sci ..... Scientific research and applications
soc ..... Social issues, either political or simply social
talk ... Forum for debate on controversial subjects
misc .. Anything that doesn't fit into the categories
     above

Fig. 7-1: Traditional top-level domains for naming of news groups. Others include alt, biz, and bionet.

clubs have formed around public figures ranging from Newt Gingrich to O.J. Simpson. Some other common designations include bionet for topics of interest to biologists, biz for business-related subjects, and rec for recreational hobbies and leisure-time pursuits.

Although it seems as if much of the publicity given to Usenet Newsgroups in the media has focused on groups talking about topics like bestiality or bondage, the range of discussion on Usenet is extensive. A recent discussion in the sci.math.num-analysis news group looked for a solution to a problem involving the Fast Fourier Transform. The Macfarlane Burnet Center for Medical Research in Australia was recruiting researchers studying HIV infection. A woman posted a message to the misc.kids group wondering if she and her husband should have a baby. And in the rec.humor news group, somebody shared a bad joke with the punch line, "Rudolph the Red knows rain, dear."

There are news groups about major political events and leaders in both the alt and soc hierarchies. The soc.politics designation includes politically oriented news groups. Soc.rights.human is a news group that discusses human rights issues. Finally, most major professional sports teams as well as many entertainment activities and industries are the topics for news groups in both the alt and rec hierarchies. For example, in the rec hierarchy there is rec.sport.baseball, rec.music.bluenote for discussions about jazz and the blues, and rec.mag for discussion about magazines.

Navigating Usenet levels

When you read Usenet news, you enter a program that functions on three tiers: 1) a group-listing/directory level, 2) an article-listing/directory level, and 3) an article-reading level. Additionally, you may be in screen mode or command mode at either directory level, depending on the specific reader you are using.

Your first task when you access network news is to designate which news groups you want to follow. Local servers typically offer access to 1,500 to 5,000 news groups or more. In many cases, when you first begin to read network news, the system assumes that you may want to read all the news from all the news groups. It asks you, one group at a time, if you want to subscribe. Consequently, the process of eliminating news groups can be time consuming.

In newer news readers, the opposite occurs. If you have not yet designated which news groups you wish to access, you must load all of them. That may take a few minutes. Most news readers, both old and new, have features that allow you to select a subset of all available news groups to follow. In newer readers, such as the news reader available in Netscape, the process consists of *subscribing* to the news groups of your choice. In older readers, and particularly on most readers running on Unix and VMS-based machines, the process involves eliminating news groups in which you are not interested.

With that in mind, most news readers can eliminate news groups according to major designations and categories. For example, you may not be interested in anything that has to do with computer science, so often you can exclude all news groups that begin with the comp. prefix. If you have a local news feed and local reader software, the specific commands you need should be available in the help files.

Once you have gone through the process of selecting (or deselecting) news groups, most news readers keep a log of the news groups to which you subscribe and which articles within that group you have already read. That way, when you select that group again, you are brought directly to messages that have been posted since you last read the postings.

Fig. 7-2: Levels of Usenet news operations are graphically illustrated by these three windows from a Nuntius news-reading session. One selects a news group from a list (left window), then an article from a list within the group, and finally reads the article (foreground, right).

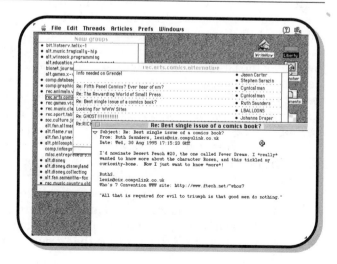

The NEWS.RC file tracks your reading

This information about which news groups you wish to follow is stored in a file frequently called NEWS.RC on the machine where the news-reading client resides. If the client is on your Internet host, it is stored in the space you are allocated on the host. If you have a client on your personal computer, the file (or its equivalent) will be stored there. If you are using public access to Usenet through a Telnet or Gopher connection, you do not have the benefit of the NEWS.RC file tracking.

A word of caution regarding the NEWS.RC file and the way you exit from your Usenet reader. Both quit and exit commands may take you out of the news reader. However, when you quit from some programs, the reader does not update your NEWS.RC file. When you exit, it does. Thus if you quit, the reader keeps no record of what you have read or your subscription list.

The group directory level

When you first launch the news-reading program, you enter at the group directory level. Figure 7-3 illustrates a directory of news groups. The message across the top of the screen indicates that this particular news server carries 2,818 news groups. The directory lists 20 groups to a screen. The top line also tells us the news-reading program we are using (VMS News) and the version (1.24). Beside the number of the news group is the news group's name. The top-domain categories for the groups shown here are info, a broad information category; junk, an active, nondescript category; k12, a grouping for teachers and students in elementary and secondary schools; la, a grouping for subjects about Los Angeles; and the ubiquitous misc. category. Only this last category is one of the seven traditional top domains of Usenet news.

In the news group directory, to the right of the news group's name is a number that corresponds to the number of the last article posted to the group. The group k12.chat.teacher has had 590 postings to it, and la.general has had 3,744. The first two groups in the misc. domain have the word Mod to the right of the posting number. This indicates that these groups are moderated. In such a group, a moderator screens all incoming messages before posting them for all readers to see. In unmoderated groups, people can post just about anything they please. The vast majority of Usenet Newsgroups are unmoderated.

Using your cursor arrow keys you can move the selector arrow through the list in order to choose the group you want. Or you can also enter a number and the news reader will take your selector arrow to that number. Because group numbers change, they are not reliable bookmarks for getting to the group you want. If you know the name of the group you want, you can enter the command "Group" followed by the group's name to send your selector arrow to that group. A shortcut for the "group" command in the VMS

Fig 7-3: The group directory level displays news group listings from a Usenet News server. To select a group, you point to it with the selector arrow (here on group 1992) and hit the Enter key.

```
UMS NEWS v1.24 --- Newsgroups [TOTAL] 2818 (Posting OK)
==> 1992  info.sun-nets                          -     2
    1993  info.sysadmin                          -     1
    1994  info.theorynt                          -   448
    1995  info.wisenet                           -  3071
    1996  junk                                   - 659693
    1997  k12.chat.teacher                       -   590
    1998  la.eats                                -  2181
    1999  la.general                             -  3744
    2000  la.news                                -   221
    2001  la.seminars                            -   247
    2002  la.slug                                -    44
    2003  la.test                                -    77
    2004  misc.activism.progressive              - 13780 Mod
    2005  misc.answers                           -   621 Mod
    2006  misc.auto                              -     8
    2007  misc.books.technical                   -  2703
    2008  misc.comp.forsale                      -    65
    2009  misc.computers.forsale                 -   232
    2010  misc.consumers                         - 32466
    2011  misc.consumers.house                   - 31720
NEWS:
%NEWS-I-GRPSEL, Newsgroup news.answers with 1319 articles selected
%CLI-W-IVVERB, unrecognized command verb - check validity and spelling
```

News reader is simply typing "g." Thus if we wanted to read messages in the group misc.consumers, we could enter the command

g misc.consumers <CR>

and our selector arrow would point to that group. Many of the news readers running on the Macintosh or under Windows use the familiar point-and-click method to move among news groups.

You can scroll through the list of news groups a screen at a time by entering the command "down" to go down 20 groups or "up" to go up 20 groups. If you aren't sure of the exact name of a group, you may search for matches using the asterisk wild card. Thus, if you want to find a group aimed at consumer interests you can enter the command

g *consumer* <CR>

and the news reader program will take your selector arrow to the next group that has "consumer" in its name. If what you get is not the group you wanted, you may repeat the command until you find the right group.

The article directory level

Once you have chosen an appropriate group, you get a listing of the articles available by hitting the Enter key while the selector arrow is pointing at the chosen group. While the examples here are taken from VMS News, other readers have similar—often identical—commands. In any case, you will understand how the news-reading and posting process works and what commands to look for when you issue the help command to your reader.

Figure 7-4 shows a listing at the article directory level of the group alt.california on the day an earthquake hit in Northridge, California. You

```
VMS NEWS v1.24 --- alt.california (#42) 4342 - 4383
==>  4361 Re: Quake Status.....??
     4362 Re: SO CAL EARTHQUAKES                                    1
     4363 Help passing 818 area-code messages?                      1
     4364 quake and Northridge                                      1
     4365 Re: SO CAL EARTHQUAKES                                    4
     4366 Re: Quake Status.....??
     4367 Quake Report 94 Jan 17                                    8
     4368 Re: SO CAL EARTHQUAKES                                    3
     4369 Re: quake and Northridge                                  3
     4370 Earthquake updates from Los Angelinos                     3
     4371 Re: Quake Status.....??
     4372 Re: Quake Status.....??                                   1
     4373 (213) 485-5191                                            1
     4374 Re: Quake Status.....??
     4375 Re: (oh s___!) Church and Child Molesters                 3
     4376 Re: Earthquake updates from Los Angelinos                 4
     4377 quake and Northridge                                      2
     4378 Re: Help passing 818 area-code messages?                  4
     4379 Re: Quake Status.....??
     4380 Re: Quake Status.....??
NEWS:
%NEWS-I-NOARTSRV, Newsgroup la.news contains no articles [SERVER ERROR]
%NEWS-I-GRPSEL, Newsgroup alt.california with 42 articles selected
                                               Receive: On
```

Fig 7-4: A directory of article postings to the news group alt.california on the day of the Jan. 17, 1994, earthquake in Northridge. News of the quake dominated the group as it did other groups affiliated with the Los Angeles area.

select articles in a fashion similar to the way you select news groups. You move the selector arrow to the article you want and hit the Enter key. As an alternative, you can type "go" followed by the number of the article to move your selector arrow to that article. When you are in the article directory, you must type the whole word; the "g" shortcut only works in groups.

Screen mode versus command mode

In both of the directory levels, you are automatically placed in *screen mode* until you type something other than a number, a Return key or a cursor arrow key. As soon as you type a letter (or hit the spacebar), you are taken into the *command mode*. In command mode, your Up and Down arrow keys do not move the cursor. Neither does the Return (Enter) key select anything; instead, a Return signals to the news reader completion of a command. Most of the time this screen mode vs. command mode is fairly intuitive, and it goes on unnoticed. But if you find peculiar things going on at one of the directory levels, you might wish to note whether you are in screen or command mode.

Once you select an article to read, you can scroll through the article one line at a time by using your down arrow, or you can scroll a screen at a time by typing the command "down." Typing the "dir" command or its shortcut "d" moves you up a level in Usenet News. If you are reading an article, typing the d command takes you out of reading the article into the article directory. If you are in the article directory when you type the "d" command, you are taken to the group directory.

When you select news group messages to read, what you see onscreen has all the appearance of an e-mail message or a message posting to a bulletin board. If you wish to respond, you have the option to write a *followup* message, which then will be displayed to the network. Or you can *reply,* which will send a mail message privately to the originator of the message. See Figure 7-5 for a summary of commonly used news reader commands.

If you choose the followup or the post command, you start a header dialog that has a few more options than a mail header. Figure 7-6 shows a

Fig. 7-5: Some of the more commonly used Usenet News commands appear here in their VMS News incarnation. Other news readers will have similar commands. It is wise to invoke "help" to get instructions specific to your program.

Basic Usenet News Commands

Bottom	Moves cursor to the bottom of the display. Goes to last entry in the group or article list.
Directory	Displays a directory of news groups or news items within a group. Moves up one level in tier structure. Synonyms = "dir" and "d."
Down	Moves down one screen. In directory level, moves cursor down 20 items. In article-reading level, scrolls to end of article or down one screen, whichever is first.
Exit	Leaves the news reader program, updating your NEWS.RC file.
Extract	Saves the current news article in an output file that you name on the same command as "extract." Thus "extract filename." Synonym = "Save."
Followup	Starts a dialog that posts to an entire news group your reply to news item.
Go	Selects (goes to) an article or news group specified by the number that follows the word "go."
Group	Selects (goes to) the news group named following the word "group." Accepts wild cards (*). Synonym = "g."
Help	Calls up the help facility, from which you may gain more detailed instructions.
Mail	Starts program to mail message to individual, not the group.
Mark	Marks specified articles as read/unread by user.
Next	Only in article-reading level, this command takes you to the next article in the group. Synonym = "n."
Post	Initiates process of posting an article to the news system.
Reply	Posts a mail message directly to the sender of a news item without putting the message out to the whole Net.
Scan	Command is followed by a pattern to search for. Works in article-reading level. Useful for finding a string in large articles. Example: Scan "*searchterm*" (quotes necessary).
Subscribe	Marks a group as one you want to monitor, so the news reader program keeps track of what you have read.
Top	Moves cursor to the top of the display.
Unsubscribe	Reverses "subscribe" command.
Up	Opposite of "down"; moves up one screen.

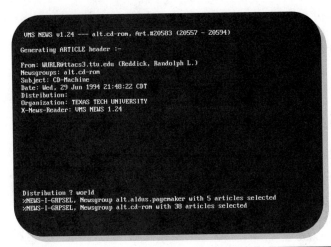

Fig. 7-6: The Article Header dialog in Usenet News. When you issue the post or the followup command, the news reader asks you for header information, suggesting default values for you. For some fields here you may have no options. Here we are defining the scope of distribution as worldwide.

posting header dialog. You should pay attention to the Distribution field. What you put in the Distribution field governs how far your message will be disbursed. If you select "world," your posting or followup will go out worldwide. If you select "local," it will generally stay at the site you post to. Other acceptable distribution categories are

- CA, OH, NY, TX, etc. = specified state.
- can = Canada only≥.
- eunet = European sites only.
- na = North American destinations.
- usa = United States-based servers.

An important restriction on distribution codes is that your site must be included within the zone you designate. If you post from Canada, you may not specify "eunet" distribution. If you post from Florida, you may not specify "PA," but you may specify "usa."

Most news readers track what you have read through a system of marking files. When you are in the article directory level, you are reading articles that are described by a one-line subject tag. You may know that you don't want to read certain articles. By typing the "mark" (or "skip" in some systems) command, you tell the news reader to treat the article as if it had been read.

Most simply, the mark (skip) command marks the article at which your cursor is pointing. You can also add qualifiers (or arguments) to the command. Thus "mark /all" will mark all of the current postings as if they have been read. More commonly you would give the command "mark num1-num2," where you would substitute the actual numbers of the articles you want to skip.

Proper Usenet behavior

After you have followed the discussions on a Usenet Newsgroup for some time, you will probably want to participate. When you want to post a followup remark, you should keep several factors in mind.

First, even though you don't know the other people posting messages and probably never will meet them face to face, in a news group, you are involved with a group of people—real people. Unfortunately, many people hide behind the anonymous nature of the Internet to act in ways they never would act in public. They express their opinions in intemperate terms or launch personal attacks against people with whom they disagree. These attacks are known as *flames* and they are simply not necessary. What you post to a news group will be read potentially by hundreds or even thousands of readers. You should conduct yourself accordingly.

In an effort to control the tenor of the conversation, some news groups are moderated. Messages must first be sent to and screened by a person who ensures that only appropriate messages are distributed. But even in unmoderated groups, you should work hard to moderate yourself.

Second, don't dominate the discussion. Even though you may have an opinion about every topic and every comment on every topic, you do not have to share every thought that passes through your mind. You may wish to conceive of a news group as a real conversation. Hearing the same person's opinion over and over again gets tedious. If you are too aggressive, people will start to skip reading your messages.

Third, try to be accurate. Many times, people use news groups to get advice or to have questions answered. If you don't know the answer to the question, don't answer.

Fourth, don't use the news group to send personal messages. If you find something in the discussion of private interest to you, correspond with the person via e-mail rather than via the news group.

Fifth, although it is easy to have your message seen by thousands of people by sending it to different news groups simultaneously, some people feel that violates the Usenet culture. As they see it, Usenet Newsgroups are mechanisms in which to interact and not a one-directional publishing medium. Usenet veterans in particular resent messages that are widely broadcast to a lot of different lists. Some people typically ignore messages sent to more than one list.

Also, you don't have to post information about major news events, such as the bombing of the federal building in Oklahoma City, to a Usenet Newsgroup. Conventional media are still more effective in circulating that kind of message. If you wish to discuss a breaking news event, however, you may wish to look at the misc.headlines news group.

Usenet writing style

The way you interact with other participants of a news group will have an impact on the value of the experience. The way you write news group posts is significant also. News groups are a new channel of communication. If you do think of a news group as an ongoing conversation, you should keep in mind that people are always entering and exiting. Moreover, participants don't have a lot of time, and the medium does not lend itself to long speeches. Moreover, the readers of your message not only do not know you very well, they have no clues other than the words and emoticons (graphics created using keyboard characters to express emotions) on their screen by which to understand what you are trying to say.

With this in mind, in most cases you should try to keep your messages short and to the point. Try to say what you want to say as quickly as possible and then stop. If your message extends for more than one computer screen, you may want to add subtitles between sections or visually break up the message into more easily digestible chunks.

For many reasons, subtlety and humor are often lost in cyberspace. People from all sorts of different backgrounds and cultures are interacting and if you are too cute, too subtle, or try to be too funny, many of your readers just won't get it. Sometimes, if you are trying to be clever, adding an emoticon such as a smile :-) or a wink ;-) or a frown :-(can alert a reader not to take your comments at face value.

Rules of Usenet Netiquette

Never forget that the person on the other side is human.
Don't blame system administrators for their users' behavior.
Never assume that a person is speaking for his or her organization.
Be careful what you say about others.
Be brief.
Your postings reflect upon you; be proud of them.
Use descriptive titles.
Think about your audience.
Be careful with humor and sarcasm.
Only post a message once.
Please rotate material with questionable content.
Summarize what you are following up.
Use mail, don't post a followup.
Read all followups and don't repeat what has already been said.
Double-check followup news groups and distributions.
Be careful about copyrights and licenses.
Cite appropriate references.
When summarizing, summarize.
Mark or rotate answers or spoilers.
Spelling flames considered harmful.
Don't overdo signatures.
Limit line length and avoid control characters.
Please do not use Usenet as a resource for homework assignments.
Please do not use Usenet as an advertising medium.
Avoid posting to multiple news groups.

Fig 7-7: Primer for Usenet users by Chuq Von Rospach, posted to the news.answers news group. The primer stands as rules of network news etiquette, or netiquette, for people who post to news groups.

Because the conversations on news groups are always ongoing, you should summarize the remarks to which you are responding (if your news reader permits). Also, refer specifically to the points in an original message to which you are responding. Many people will not have read the original; or, if they have, they may have forgotten the information to which you are reacting. Finally, because most news groups support several different discussions simultaneously, you want to be very clear in your subject line. It is very annoying for people to waste time reading articles about subjects in which they are not interested.

Applying Usenet to academic tasks

Most Usenet groups fall into two general categories. Either they are informal gatherings of people with a common interest who wish to communicate about that issue, or they are groups of people who are doing similar tasks and come together to share insights and expertise. The first type of news group is similar to a group of friends at a favorite hangout. The conversation is often loose and relaxed. People make outrageous remarks to see the reactions they provoke.

The second type is more serious. Many times people need information for a research-related task. Misinformation can have serious consequences.

For students, Usenet is a wonderful recreational activity. You can interact with like-minded or unlike-minded people. Some say that conversation is a dying art. Well, it is alive and well in hundreds of Usenet Newsgroups.

Using Usenet Newsgroups for academic tasks is a trickier matter. One discussion list warning (Chapter 3) holds true for news groups. While many people are willing to be helpful, Usenet members are not interested in doing your homework for you. Moreover, just because a person is involved in a news group does not mean he or she has expertise in a given subject. Most participants are not authoritative sources.

Still, given an appropriate assignment, interacting with a relevant Usenet Newsgroup can lead you to more information and a deeper understanding than perhaps would be possible using only traditional means.

Finding the right news group

If you want to participate in news groups because you think it will be fun and interesting, the best strategy is to begin to monitor those that seem interesting to you. But if you have an assignment, your first task is to identify the news group that may be able to help you.

On some systems, if you enter the command "news group" you will open a file that contains a one-line description of the purpose of each news group. Some local systems also have a file that contains the charter—the purpose and contents—of each news group.

If your local system does not support those files, you can access descriptions of widely circulated news groups in the news.lists news group. The relevant postings are
- List_of_Active_NewsGroups,_Part_I.
- List_of_Active_NewsGroups,_Part_II.
- Alternative_NewsGroup_Hierarchies,_Part_I.
- Alternative_NewsGroup_Hierarchies,_Part_II.

The first two describe news groups in the comp, humanities, misc, news, rec, soc, sci, and talk hierarchies, also known as the Big 8 hierarchies. The second two files describe news groups in the alt, bionet, bit, biz, clarinet, gnu, hepnet, ieee, inet, and other alternative hierarchies. These files are also archived and available via FTP (described in Chapter 6) at rtfm.mit.edu:/pub/usenet/news-lists. Unfortunately, the site at MIT is extremely busy. Other sites that mirror the same information are

N. America:	ftp.uu.net	/usenet/news.answers
	mirrors.aol.com	/pub/rtfm/usenet
	ftp.seas.gwu.edu	/pub/rtfm
Europe:	ftp.uni-paderborn.de	/pub/faq
	ftp.Germany.eu.net	/pub/newsarchive/news.answers
	ftp.sunet.se	/pub/usenet
Asia:	nctuccca.edu.tw	/usenet/faq
	hwarang.postech.ac.kr	/pub/usenet/news.answers
	ftp.hk.super.net	/mirror/faqs

Getting the FAQs

As you learned in Chapter 6, after you ftp to a site, you first log in. You use "anonymous" for your username and your e-mail address for your password.

When you find a news group in which you think you are interested, you can start by reading the FAQ, or Frequently Asked Questions posting, which generally describes the news group and its charter. The FAQ also often contains other valuable information and leads about the topic in question. Most news groups repeatedly post their FAQs at regular intervals.

You can often locate an FAQ by using one of the search tools for the World Wide Web or Gopher. An FAQ is simply a file stored on the Internet and is accessible via the general Internet tools. You can access many FAQs on the World Wide Web at http://www.smartpages.com/faq. One Gopher site for FAQs is gopher.win.tue.nl.

Most FAQs are also available via FTP at the sites listed above. They generally consist of multiple files. Consequently, you will want to run the list command (ls) and the name of the news group in which you are interested. For example, if you are interested in the FAQ for the news group alt.baldspot, enter the command "ls alt.baldspot."

This will list all the FAQ files associated with that news group. Once you see the individual files, you can retrieve the one you want using standard FTP commands.

Because of the amount of information contained in the FAQ archives, some of the FAQs may be compressed. If they are, the file name may end with a .Z. Some FTP servers will automatically decompress files if you omit the .Z when you ask for a file in the retrieval process. If the archive is busy, however, the decompress function may be disabled. Other file compression schemes and how to deal with them are described in Chapter 6.

Another alternative for retrieving any FAQ is to request it from the e-mail server at MIT. To find out how to use the server to get what you want, send mail to mail-server@rtfm.mit.edu. In the body of your message include the word "help." The server will return a mail message to you explaining how to get the document you want.

Archived Usenet information

Most news readers retain Usenet Newsgroup messages for a limited period of time. The quantity of messages being posted daily makes it impossible to save everything. Consequently, when you read a news group, you will only be able to read the messages that have been posted within that specified period.

Old news group messages are generally not saved anywhere. There are often good reasons for this. First, to save all Usenet Newsgroup messages would be similar to saving a record of all telephone conversations. It represents a lot of data. Second, as the Usenet FAQ puts it, the signal-to-noise ratio, i.e., the amount of useful information compared to the amount of useless information on many news groups, is very low. In other words, the information is not worth saving in many cases.

Keyword searches and news filtering

Negotiating Usenet Newsgroups for a particular assignment can be a stressful process, and the payoff in good, solid leads or usable information is uncertain. A useful alternative for students is a filtering service for network news provided by the Database Group at Stanford University. You send keywords in an e-mail message to a server at Stanford University. A search is conducted overnight, and results consisting of several lines from each matching message are returned by e-mail. You send the message to netnews@db.stanford.edu. In the body of the message, type "subscribe" followed by the keywords for which you wish to search.

In addition to the subscribe command, the service has several other commands to manage your subscription. The first three are period, expire, and threshold. They can be included as additional lines in the initial subscribe message. These additional commands must begin on new lines in the message with no initial indentations or spaces. Period determines the number of days between notifications of matches. If you do not include a period command, you will receive notification every day. Expire sets the number of days for which your subscription is active. If you do not specify an expiration date, the subscription will run for 9,999 days. The threshold command determines how closely matched what the news filter finds must be to your keywords for the information to be returned to you. As with WAIS, information is scored according to how well it fits to what you said you were looking for. If you do not specify a threshold score, it will return anything that has a score of 60.

Let's say you are working on a paper about Mark Twain's *Huckleberry Finn.* You have some ideas and hope to find an interested news group in which you can discuss them. But you only have about a week to finish the assignment.

Your subscription message to the news filter service could look like this:

```
$mail send
To: IN%"netnews@db.stanford.edu"
Subject: subscribe Mark Twain
period 1
expire 5
threshold 60
end
```

The results will be a list of articles with about 20 lines each that scored 50 or more in the matching process. The results will be sent to you every day, and your subscription will expire in five days.

After receiving notifications of articles that may be relevant to your interests, you may decide to see an article in its entirety. You can get the whole article with the get command. You will get the articles that are specified by their article IDs. For example,

```
get news.announce.conferences.3670
```

Once you have received several articles, you can fine tune your search using the feedback command to tell the service to look for articles like others that you have received. A feedback message could look like the following:

```
feedback 1
like news.announce.conferences.3670
```

The 1 after the feedback command is your subscription number, a number assigned when you send the original subscribe message to the Stanford server. Following the like command on the second line is the article that you want the service to use as a model for future searches.

You can update your subscription, changing the period, expiration or threshold number, using the update command. Enter "update" and the subscription identification number on the first line. On the following lines you then must enter the parameters you want updated. You can also change the keywords associated with the subscription by using the update command. On the second line you enter the command "profile" followed by the new keywords.

To cancel your subscription, you type "cancel" followed by your subscription ID number. The list command reports all the subscriptions you have.

The news filtering service is geared to finding contemporary messages. It can also search recent archives of Usenet Newsgroup messages using the search command. The body of your message reads "search," followed by the keywords for which you are looking. You may want to include a threshold command on the second line. You should end every series of commands with the end command, particularly if a signature file is routinely appended to your e-mail.

While not 100 percent efficient or inclusive, this service is a helpful way to identify network news groups that may be discussing issues relevant to stories on which you are working. It is also a good method to receive appropriate articles without having to read a host of news groups regularly.

Starting a news group

If you have a topic that you wish to discuss and cannot find an appropriate news group, in general it is not a good idea to start your own. Typically, new news groups begin as subtopics of larger news groups. If you are determined to start a new group, however, you can find guidelines in news.announce.newgroups: How_To_Create_a_New_Usenet_NewsGroup and in news.groups: Usenet_NewsGroup_Creation_Companion. If you wish to start a new news group in the alt hierarchy, in which the discussion is usually the most free-wheeling, you should look at alt.config: So_You_Want_To_Create_an_Alt_NewsGroup.

More commonly, rather than creating a news group for distribution throughout the Usenet network, you may want to create a news group for a class, club or interest group on campus. If that is the case, you should consult with your system administrator. Many campuses already have their own hierarchy name, and within that area there is a great deal of flexibility.

A tour of social news groups

One of the most interesting aspects of Usenet is that the interaction in the news group can be very focused. There are often several news groups clustered around a similar topic.

A common purpose of Usenet is to allow people to interact socially—for men and women, men and men, and women and women to communicate about issues of interest. Among the news groups concerned with this topic of interest to most college students are

- alt.personal: Ads from people who seek e-mail or in-person romantic or personal relationships.
- alt.romance: People who wish to be romantic or talk about romance.
- alt.sex: Although the amount of interesting information is low, from time to time conversations relating to various aspects of sex from birth control to bad relationships take place.

- soc.couples: Discussions about the merits and demerits of being in long- or short-term relationships.
- soc.feminism: A moderated news group for the discussion of feminist issues.
- soc.men: Debates about issues like child support and custody from a male perspective.
- soc.women: Debates about issues like child support and custody from a female perspective.
- soc.single: The common thread is the trials and joys of being single. Many people involved in relationships also join in. It is not appropriate to post personal ads or troll for pen pals here.
- soc.motss: This is a forum primarily for gays and lesbians to interact.
- soc.penpals: People here are looking for pen pals of either the electronic or traditional type.

Conclusion

Over the years, Usenet has maintained a lot of the original frontier atmosphere of the Internet. News groups are created and disappear daily. Discussions on them can be passionate or purposeless, insightful or idiotic. For people who like to interact with like-minded people, news groups can be a lot of fun. And if a news group stops being fun, just don't read the postings.

Unless a Usenet group has been established for a class of yours or a club to which you belong, you may not find that Usenet Newsgroups have a direct bearing on your academic work. Like discussion groups, however, they are a fine window onto the real world of people working in areas which you may be studying. If you are studying the Civil War and want to interact with Civil War buffs, you may wish to look into soc.history.war.us-civil-war. Or if you want more insight into the research of molecular biologists you could become involved in bionet.molec-model. Who knows, you could make some useful contacts for the future.

And if you start early enough, you may be able to use a news group to point you to information on the Internet that can enrich an academic project on which you may be working. In most cases you will not want to use the information you find on postings directly. It is hard to cite and you often cannot be sure of its reliability. But by reading and judiciously asking questions of the group, you may be pointed in directions you didn't know existed.

8

MUDs, IRC, other connections

By the summer of 1995, Jeff Collett, a junior majoring in theater, was a demigod. He was immortal. He could cast powerful spells; he could lead tribes. He would not and could not stoop to help lesser mortals.

How did he achieve such an exalted status? Not through years of religious meditation, apprenticeships to wizards or military training. He became a demigod by spending more than 500 hours in the MadROM MUD, a fantasy role-playing game that runs on servers through the Internet.

In the spring semester of her freshman year, Rebecca Ericson was studying elementary education at Texas Tech University when her brother introduced her to Internet Relay Chat. Soon she found herself at her computer terminal as much as 20 hours a week *chatting* with friends on IRC channels aimed at people sharing some of the same interests she has. "It was fun," she said, "like having a phone conversation with people and not having to pay for it." But she wasn't using a telephone to chat, she was using the Internet.

MUDs and Internet Relay Chat are two real-time (synchronous) communications applications on the Internet. People using these applications are at their keyboards at the same time. Consequently, the interaction and feedback are immediate. The immediacy of the interactions makes MUDs and IRC quite different from e-mail and other Internet applications. People use them because they are fun. And because they are fun, some pioneering professors and students are using these applications to create virtual classrooms in which students and faculty can interact in real time without physically having to be in the same place.

In this chapter, the online student will learn

- The major characteristics of MUDs and related software.
- The workings of Internet Relay Chat.

Some students will want to be able to access the Internet or the campus network from their homes or places of business. Or you may be interested in online information that is not part of the Internet. With that in mind, in this chapter, you will also learn about

- The joys and dangers of accessing your campus computer from home.
- Unique opportunities offered through local bulletin board services (BBSes).
- The offerings of commercial hybrids such as America Online, Prodigy and CompuServe.

The development of MUDs

In the late 1970s, Roy Trubshaw was an undergraduate at Essex University (England). He wanted to make a multiplayer adventure game and to write an interpreter for a database definition language. Richard Bartle was more interested in the game aspect and making the program usable. Together over a period of about a year, Trubshaw and Bartle wrote the first MUD software.

MUD is an acronym for Multi-User Dungeon (or Multi-User Dimension), which can be best described as a virtual, real-time, online environment in which people across the Internet can participate. Since the first such program was written by Trubshaw and Bartle in England, several variations on the MUD have been developed. MOO is an acronym for Mud Object Oriented. MOOs generally use an object-oriented programming language, and the players in a MOO game can create objects and programs within the game. There are other variations on the original MUD program. They include MUSHes, MUCKs, LpMUDs and DikuMUDs. All are multiuser, real-time, interactive programs creating some kind of virtual reality. For the purposes of our discussion, we are including all under the title of MUD.

Trubshaw and Bartle's MUD software permitted several students to simultaneously interact with one another. The software was used to structure an online fantasy game. Primitive at first, many MUDs have evolved into

Fig. 8-1: The log-in screen of a typical MUD offers announcements after you sign in and give your password.

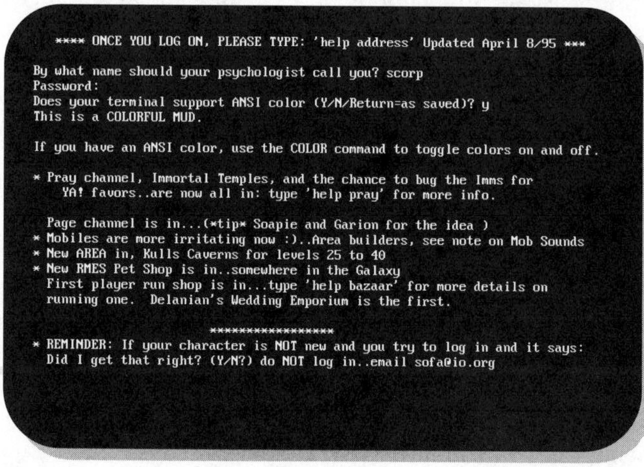

```
**** ONCE YOU LOG ON, PLEASE TYPE: 'help address' Updated April 8/95 ***

By what name should your psychologist call you? scorp
Password:
Does your terminal support ANSI color (Y/N/Return=as saved)? y
This is a COLORFUL MUD.

If you have an ANSI color, use the COLOR command to toggle colors on and off.

* Pray channel, Immortal Temples, and the chance to bug the Imms for
   YA! favors..are now all in: type 'help pray' for more info.

  Page channel is in...(*tip* Soapie and Garion for the idea )
* Mobiles are more irritating now :)..Area builders, see note on Mob Sounds
* New AREA in, Kulls Caverns for levels 25 to 40
* New RMES Pet Shop is in..somewhere in the Galaxy
  First player run shop is in...type 'help bazaar' for more details on
  running one.  Delanian's Wedding Emporium is the first.

              ******************
* REMINDER: If your character is NOT new and you try to log in and it says:
  Did I get that right? (Y/N?) do NOT log in..email sofa@io.org
```

Public-Access MUDs		
Name	**Address**	**Port**
AlexMUD	mud.stacken.kth.se	4000
Ancient Anguish	dancer.ethz.ch	2222
AnimeMUCK	tcp.com	2035
BatMUD	bat.cs.hut.fi	23
CaveMUCK	cave.tcp.com	2283
ChibaMOO	chiba.picosof.com	7777
Conservatorium	crs.cl.msu.edu	6000
Crossed Swords	shsibm.shh.fi	3000
Dark Saga	cobber.cord.edu	5555
Delusions	iglou.com	4999
DragonFire	typo.umsl.edu	3000
Dragonsfire	moo.eskimo.com	7777
Dshores	kcbbs.gen.nz	6000
Enigma	kcbbs.gen.nz	6000
EverDark	atomic.com	3000
Final Realms	kark.hiof.no	2001
GateWay	idiot.alfred.edu	6969
Genocide	pip.shsu.edu	2222
Gilgamesh	shiner.st.usm.edu	3742
Hall of Fame	marvin.df.lth.se	2000
HariMUD	tc0.chem.tue.nl	6997
Haven	idrz07.ethz.ch	1999
Imperial2	hp.ecs.rpi.edu	3141
Kerovnia	atlantis.edu	1984
LambdaMOO	lambda.xerox.com	8888
Last Outpost	lo.millcomm.com	4000
Loch Ness	indigo.imp.ch	2222
Lost Souls	ronin.bchs.uh.edu	3000
Metaverse	metaverse.io.com	7777
Moonstar	pulsar.hsc.edu	4321
MuMOO	chestnut.enmu.edu	7777
Newmoon	jove.cs.pdx.edu	7680
Nirvana IV	elof.acc.iit.edu	3500
OutWorld	tanelorn.king.ac.uk	7777
Paradox	adl.uncc.edu	10478
Phoenix	albert.bu.edu	3500
Prime Time	prime.mdata.fi	3000
Pyromud	elektra.cc.edu	2222
RealmsMUCK	tcp.com	7765
Realmsmud	donal.dorsai.org	1501
SplitSecond	lestat.shv.hb.se	3000
StickMUD	kalikka.jyu.fi	7680
SWmud	kitten.mcs.net	6666
Timewarp	quark.gmi.edu	5150
V-MUCK	mserv.wizvax.com	5201

Table 8-1: A short listing of MUDs, their addresses, and Telnet ports for accessing them. In all, there are more than 320 MUDs available on the Internet.

full-fledged adventure games. The players have goals to accomplish, points are scored (giving players power and status), and objects (not just players) move around through the various regions in the MUD. But MUD technology is not restricted to being used for online role playing. Some MUDs have taken on some richness as virtual reality environments in which many people can simultaneously interact in many different ways.

Jumping into a MUD

You will generally connect to a MUD through Telnet (Chapter 6). Table 8-1 lists the addresses of a few MUDs available on the Internet using the Telnet protocol.

But making the connection may be a little trickier than a standard Telnet usage. Each Internet application has its own port of entry to a computer. The standard port for Gopher, for example, is 70. When an application is supposed to call on that

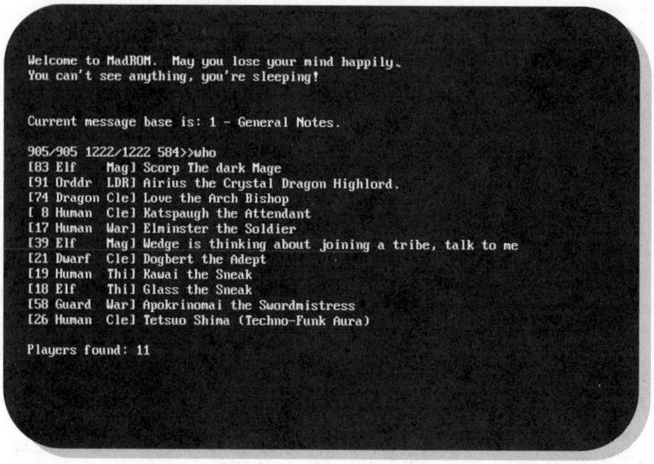

Fig. 8-2: The who command for a MUD reports back the players who are currently logged into the game. The report tells the level the character has attained, the class of being, as well as the rank and the person's assumed identity.

standard port you do not have to include the port number in the URL. The standard Telnet access port is 23. But because MUDs are usually located at other ports, you must specify the port number when you open the location in Telnet. For example, to access MIT's MediaMOO from a VMS Telnet client, one might enter the command "Telnet purple-crayon.media.mit.edu / port=8888." In other clients you may specify the port in other ways. QVT Net's terminal (Telnet) client has a box labeled "port" in which you can specify nonstandard ports. In still other packages you might designate the port by simply adding a space and the port number to the end of the address. You should ask your instructor what method is appropriate for your situation.

Playing in a MUD

When you do connect to the MediaMOO, the welcome screen (Figure 8-4) gives enough information to get you started. After you log into a MUD,

Fig. 8-3: A MUD meeting between characters Scorp and Airius. Commands used during this exchange are tell, wake (Scorp had been sleeping), and look.

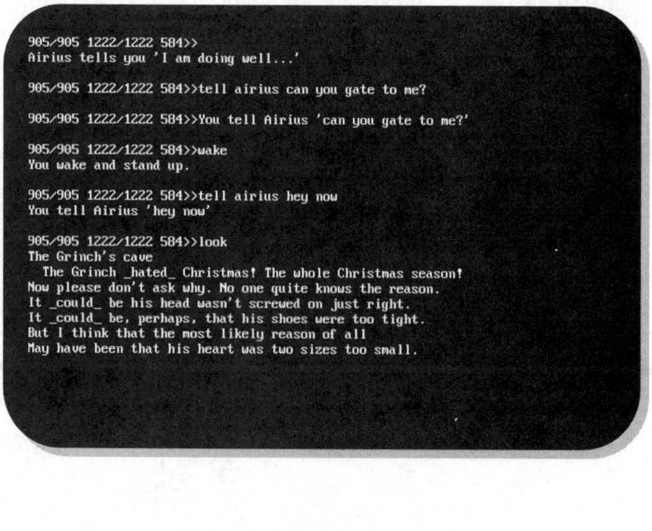

Fig. 8-4: The welcome screen at MIT's MediaMOO briefly describes the background and the rules of behavior in the MOO. Visitors are given the option of signing on as a guest or getting help to establish their own characters or to learn the commands of the MOO.

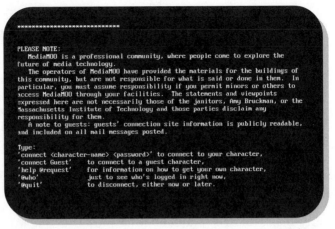

```
*****************************

PLEASE NOTE:
   MediaMOO is a professional community, where people come to explore the
future of media technology.
   The operators of MediaMOO have provided the materials for the buildings of
this community, but are not responsible for what is said or done in them.  In
particular, you must assume responsibility if you permit minors or others to
access MediaMOO through your facilities.  The statements and viewpoints
expressed here are not necessarily those of the janitors, Amy Bruckman, or the
Massachusetts Institute of Technology and those parties disclaim any
responsibility for them.
   A note to guests: guests' connection site information is publicly readable,
and included on all mail messages posted.

Type:
'connect <character-name> <password>' to connect to your character,
'connect Guest'      to connect to a guest character,
'help @request'      for information on how to get your own character,
'@who'               just to see who's logged in right now,
'@quit'              to disconnect, either now or later.
```

typically you are taken to a *reception room* where there may be many other people. If others are there and they are carrying on a conversation you will see the text of their chatter. This can be confusing at first. Most MUD veterans are friendly and tolerant toward newcomers.

Each MUD will have something of its own personality, and among the various MUDs is a variety of different command dialects. Some commands might have to be preceded by the @ sign; others require no special formatting. Table 8-2 lists some common MOO commands. You can generally get help in MUDs by typing "help."

Table 8-2: Some of the more common commands for functioning in a MOO are generally logical. You can get a list of commands currently available to you by typing "help."

Basic MOO Commands

Command	Result of Command
create	you create an object
drop [object]	you drop whatever is named
examine [object]	describes an object to you
get [object]	you pick up an object
help	lists commands available and syntax
look	describes your surroundings
north	∧
east	>
south	move in direction named
west	<
out	∨
"[comment]	you say what follows quotation mark
:[action]	you do what follows colon
@go [location]	transports you to location
@join [person]	carries you to location of person
@quit	exits the MOO
@who	lists people connected to MOO

Thousands of people from all parts of the globe log into more than three hundred MUDs to carry on conversations, to work in shared environments, and to play games interactively. When you join a MUD, you generally assume a character and within limits choose your character traits (text in Figure 8-2 suggests some of the character traits). You then move from place to place in the MUD where you may look around, pick up and take objects with you, buy and sell things, or engage in conversation and/or battle (see Figure 8-3 for an encounter between two characters in one MUD). In some role-playing MUDs you may join tribes and unite with other characters inhabiting the MUD.

In practice, each site takes on its own personality. Until recently, all were text-based. More MUDs are becoming accessible through the World Wide Web, and some experiments are already underway with graphically based MUDs. Current information about MUDs may be found in the FAQ document posted regularly to the news group (Chapter 7) rec.games.mud.announce. This will often include a complete listing of MUDs. The news group rec.games.mud.misc also carries active discussions about MUDs. You can also retrieve the FAQ by Anonymous FTP (Chapter 6) from ftp.math.okstate.edu:/pub/muds/misc/mud-faq. Keyword searches in Veronica (Chapter 5) or any of the World Wide Web search engines (Chapter 4) will also reveal a wealth of material on MUDs. A Gopher site with help information, the FAQ, and links to several MUDs can be found at gopher:// actlab.rtf.utexas.edu. Choose item 10, Virtual Environments. You definitely should read the MUD FAQ before you begin to play.

MUD in the classroom

At the same time Jeff Collett and his friends were using MUD software for role-playing games (RPGs), professors on his and other campuses were using related MOO software to help teach composition and creative writing. The fun, creative nature of real-time interaction that MUDs encourage has captured the imaginations of some college professors, especially those in English departments.

Tari Lin Fanderclai at the University of Florida is one of many composition professors who use MUDs as teaching tools. In her classes, students from several universities interact with each other. They build characters and workspaces using MUD software. In assuming the roles of the characters they create, the students have opportunities to express themselves in new ways, to articulate ideas they might not have tried elsewhere. Fanderclai has found that individuals "who hesitate to speak up in class use their MUD characters to talk about their ideas."

For similar reasons, creative-writing teachers have found MUDs to be useful adjuncts to the classroom. An extensive array of writing-focused MOO resources is available on the World Wide Web at the University of Missouri: http://www.missouri.edu/~moo/. The Missouri Web site contains Telnet links to a number of MOOs. The MediaMOO (purple-crayon.media.mit.edu 8888) mentioned earlier is one of several that have distinguished themselves as educational and/or professional MOOs. Others include "Diversity University" at erau.db.erau.edu 8888, the Post Modern Culture MOO at hero.village.virginia.edu 7777, WriteMUSH at palmer.sacc.colostate.edu 6250, Brown Hypertext Hotel at 128.148.37.8 8888, and the Bio MOO at bioinformatics.weizmann.ac.il 8888.

Because MUDs are just as easily inhabited by students from Maricaibo, Milan or Madrid as they are by students from Minneapolis or Miami, they have unique potential for foreign language classes, classes dealing with international affairs, and certain anthropology and sociology classes.

Internet Relay Chat

In 1994 Northridge, California suffered from disastrous earthquakes. The epicenter of the quake was very close to California State University, Northridge. Normal communications were cut off throughout the Los Angeles area. Still, the earthquake-shaken folks could communicate with the outside world in real time through Internet Relay Chat, sometimes called the *CB Radio of the Internet.*

People who use citizen's band (CB) radio use *handles,* or fabricated nicknames, instead of their real names, and so do people using IRC. CB radio is organized into clearly defined channels where people *hang out.* IRC is also organized into channels. In both environments, you hold two-way, real-time conversations.

In short, Internet Relay Chat is an application that provides live, real-time conversation. Originally written by Jarkko Oikarinen in Finland in 1988, IRC is a multiuser chat system where people convene on *channels* to talk in groups, publicly or privately. Channels are generally defined by the topics that are being discussed at that moment.

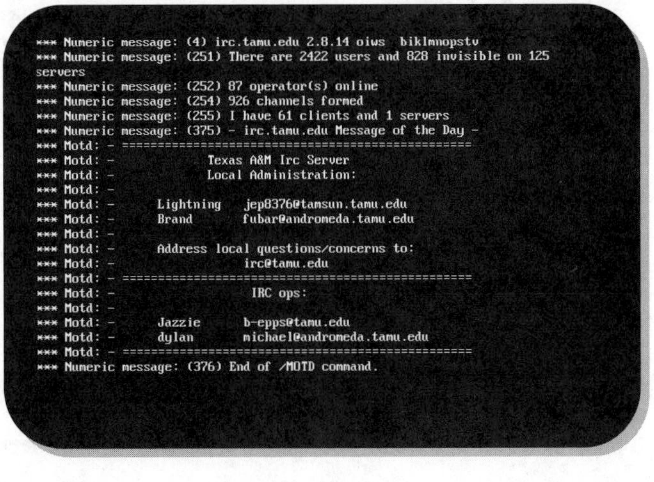

Fig. 8-5: The MOTD screen on the IRC server at Texas A&M reports traffic on IRC.

```
*** Numeric message: (4) irc.tamu.edu 2.8.14 oiws  biklmnopstv
*** Numeric message: (251) There are 2422 users and 828 invisible on 125
servers
*** Numeric message: (252) 87 operator(s) online
*** Numeric message: (254) 926 channels formed
*** Numeric message: (255) I have 61 clients and 1 servers
*** Numeric message: (375) - irc.tamu.edu Message of the Day -
*** Motd: - =================================================
*** Motd: -           Texas A&M Irc Server
*** Motd: -           Local Administration:
*** Motd: -
*** Motd: -    Lightning    jep8376@tamsun.tamu.edu
*** Motd: -    Brand        fubar@andromeda.tamu.edu
*** Motd: -
*** Motd: -    Address local questions/concerns to:
*** Motd: -               irc@tamu.edu
*** Motd: - =================================================
*** Motd: -                IRC ops:
*** Motd: -
*** Motd: -    Jazzie       b-epps@tamu.edu
*** Motd: -    dylan        michael@andromeda.tamu.edu
*** Motd: - =================================================
*** Numeric message: (376) End of /MOTD command.
```

For example, during the police freeway pursuit and subsequent arrest of football great O.J. Simpson, Los Angeles residents, joined by Simpson fans and other interested folks, gathered in IRC channels like #OJ set up spontaneously to discuss the matter.

Internet Relay Chat has a few shortcomings. IRC clients are not as widely distributed as some other Internet tools. Conversation can be difficult to follow, especially in active channels when many people are chatting simultaneously. IRC forces people to communicate under assumed nicknames, which encourages artificial conversation and the use of jargon that can be discouraging to newcomers.

IRC access

As with other Internet services, users of IRC run a client program that connects to a server somewhere in the Internet. IRC is most convenient if you have a local client. To see if you do, type

IRC <CR>

at the system prompt. If you do not have a local client installed, you should try to cajole your systems people into installing one. As with many Internet client programs, software for the client is available on the Internet.

There are several public-access sites for IRC, but they tend to be crowded and can be unreliable from time to time. To reach a public-access IRC client, you telnet to the address. You must include the port number in the Telnet address. If you don't, you will not be able to log onto the remote computer. Table 8-3 lists addresses of some public-access clients. The last entries in Table 8-3 are Free-Net sites. To use the

Table 8-3: Many Telnet sites make IRC software available to the public. In the case of Free-Nets, you generally become a member, then pick IRC from a menu.

Address	Port
sci.dixie.edu	6677
obeliz.wu-wien.ac.at	6996
irc.tuzvo.sk	6668
irc.nysu.edu.tw	6668
telnet.undernet.org	6677
telnet1.us.undernet.org	6677
telnet2.us.undernet.org	6677
telnet3.us.undernet.org	6677
telnet4.us.undernet.org	6677
telnet5.us.undernet.org	6677
telnet6.us.undernet.org	6677
telnet7.us.undernet.org	6677
telnet8.us.undernet.org	6677
telnet1.eu.undernet.org	6677
telnet1.eu.undernet.org	6969
telnet2.eu.undernet.org	6677
wildcat.ecn.uoknor.edu	6677
wildcat.ecn.uoknor.edu	7766
skywarrior.ecn.uoknor.edu	7766
skyhawk.ecn.uoknor.edu	7766
skyraider.ecn.uoknor.edu	7766
intruder.ecn.uoknor.edu	7766
telnet.dal.net	12345
204.94.8.3 / login: irc	
Free-Nets:	
freenet3.afn.org	
prairienet.org	
freenet.grfn.org	
slc9.ins.cwru.edu	
lafn.org	
freenet.hut.fi	
freenet-a.fim.uni-erlangen.de	

Fig. 8-6: Visitors to the Chatzone at WebGenesis' The Globe choose facial icons to go along with their nicknames.

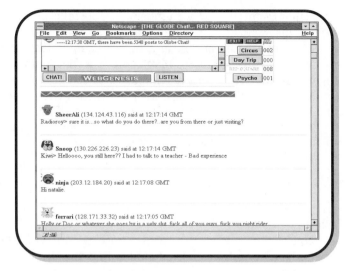

Free-Net IRC client you will have to wind your way through menus at each site. Free-Nets often require you to be a registered member of the site before permitting you to use client software. Public-access sites allow a limited number of users. Just as most other Internet applications are finding their way onto the World Wide Web, so is IRC and its cousins. Visitors to the Chatzone on the WebGenesis server (http:www.webgenesis.com/theglobe/onlinechat/onlinechat.html) select cartoon facial icons to represent their online characters (Figure 8-6).

Using IRC

When you launch Internet Relay Chat in a textual interface, you are greeted by your site's Message of the Day, which in IRC jargon is abbreviated simply MOTD. The MOTD usually provides information about the site as well as current IRC traffic throughout the network. Figure 8-5 shows the MOTD at Texas A&M University's IRC client site. You are asked for a nickname or handle you want to be known as while you are using IRC. If you have a local client, you can make your nickname permanent so you don't have to fill it in each time.

Once you log onto an IRC client and enter a nickname, you may automatically start on an active channel called #chatzone or you simply may be staring at an inactive screen. All IRC channel names start with the # sign. All IRC commands are initiated with a slash mark. Most of the commands are logical.

To become a part of a chat session, you need to know the name of the channel. You can get a list of the different channels that are in use at that particular moment and the number of people talking on them. You do this by typing "/list."

Don't do this if you are in a hurry. The greeting screen in Figure 8-5 reports 926 active channels. If you enter the /list command with no qualifying description, hundreds of channels will scroll past your screen. You can pause the scrolling by typing Ctrl-S and restart the scrolling by typing Ctrl-Q, but you are going to have a long scroll regardless.

Instead, you could do a search for channels on your topic by using a keyword and wild card marks. If the topic is movies, you could give the command

/list *movie* <CR>

and hope to turn up the channel. You might try other combinations to find a relevant channel.

You join a conversation by issuing the command "/join" followed by "#*channel name.*" For example, if you found a channel called movie, you would type the command

/join movie <CR>

When you first join a channel, IRC announces that you have joined to everyone else on the channel and gives you a list of the nicknames of all those currently in the channel.

IRC can support both public and private conversations. When you are participating in a public conversation, everything you write is seen immediately by everybody who is participating on that channel. The action can be fast and furious if a lot of people have something to say at the same time.

The conversation on most IRC channels is pretty mundane, not the stuff to write home about. Several people typically are online getting to know each other. In many ways it is like a party-line telephone conversation without the $2-a-minute charge and frequently with an international flavor. So in most cases, the IRC emphasis is on fun.

When a major event takes place, IRC can be very useful. In the same way that people run to the telephone to spread information about breaking news, some people now log onto IRC to chat about current events. The Internet was designed to withstand physical disruptions to any one part of the network and still continue to function. Therefore, even if the long distance telephone network is overburdened with calls or down for some other reason, IRC may still be functioning. That was the case on January 17, 1994, when the Northridge, California earthquake hit. The command to join the #earthquake discussion on that day was

/join #earthquake <CR>

One hundred sixty people were listed as participants in the #earthquake channel. If all 160 people who had joined #earthquake tried to chat at once, the resulting cacophony would have defeated all human communication processes. Less than a dozen—generally affiliated with news organizations—had posting privileges.

As it was, much of the discussion was interrupted by reports of channel traffic—people entering and leaving the channel, trying to find out some news of the quake. The conversation was dominated by Newswire reporting on the insurance uncertainties quake victims would be facing. The two or three paragraphs of the Newswire statement are interrupted repeatedly both by channel traffic reporting and by others authorized to use the channel for chat.

Most students use IRC for keeping in touch with friends, just as one might use the telephone. Following the telephone comparison, IRC conversation is much like a large party line, with many people listening in. Still, IRC channels can be easily created and controlled. IRC channels could be used for class discussions the way MUDs are used; but IRC, as a newer technology, has not enjoyed the same kind of popularity as MUDs have.

For more information about IRC, on the World Wide Web you can check http://www.fnet.fi/~irc/ or http://www.enst.fr/~pioch/IRC/IRC.html. News groups concerned with IRC include alt.irc, alt.irc.questions and alt.irc.recovery. An IRC primer is available via FTP (see Chapter 6) at cs-ftp.bu.edu /irc/support.

Connecting to the Internet from home

Much of the discussion in this book has assumed that you access the Internet from computers on campus—computers hard wired to the Internet. But what if you want to connect from home? Most campuses have some sort of provision for dial-up access. There are two kinds of dial-up access, and which you have will govern the kinds of things you do from home. The two kinds are simple dial-up and network protocol (SLIP or PPP) dial-up access.

In either case, you are using telephone lines and modems to access the campus computer system. In simple dial-up access, you are dependent on the campus computer for your client software. If your campus system has SLIP (Serial Line Internet Protocol) or PPP (Point to Point Protocol) access, you may run your favorite client software on your own machine at home.

Modems may be *internal* (they are inserted into an expansion slot inside your machine) or *external* (they plug into a serial port at the back of your computer). Internal modems have the advantage of costing less (generally about $20 to $30 less) and of being a part of your machine wherever you take it. External modems have the advantage of being able to be connected to any computer; the same external modem works for a Macintosh or an IBM compatible, or just about anything else. The main difference is in the cabling from the modem to the computer. The other difference is in the software; you need communications software that runs on your computer. You will want to buy the fastest modem you can afford. The minimum speed you will want is 14,400 bps (bits per second).

Simple dial-up access

Most modems sold today can double as fax machines and are sold with communications software that allows you to use telephone lines for connecting to your campus system or to local bulletin boards or commercial services. Some popular communications programs include White Knight and Microphone for the Macintosh; ProComm Plus, QuickLink, WinComm, Smartcom, and MTEZ for DOS and/or Windows machines. Your campus computing services may have shareware or public domain communications software they can provide to you. On the Macintosh side, Red Ryder is a serviceable shareware program. For DOS, ProComm 2.43 is a full-featured program. Windows comes with a simple, small communications application called Terminal. Additionally, popular *works* programs like Microsoft Works and Claris Works contain communications programs within them.

Using any of these communications packages, you access the campus computer by way of a simple dial-up connection. The communications software implements what is known as *terminal emulation* to make your computer behave as though it were a dumb terminal (as opposed to a smart computer capable of doing its own *thinking*) connected to the computer at the end of the telephone lines. You can tell your software what kind of terminal to emulate. Until or unless you know better, you should set your emulation at "VT 100" (or "VT 102") or at "TTY." Many bulletin boards (discussed later in this chapter) and some Telnet sites implement simple color and graphics through what is known as the ANSI standard. You may want to experiment with this option if your software permits it.

When your computer is emulating a terminal, the host computer to which you attach is calling all the shots. In this case, you have a text-only interface (the way most of the screen images in this book look) with the possibility of some ANSI *graphics* if your software supports ANSI. The client software you are using resides on the host. Keyboard commands produce whatever result the software running on the host dictates. An exception to this is that your communications program may intercept some keyboard combinations and not send them to the host (see the discussion on Gopher commands).

You need to find out from your campus computing service the phone number to access the system and the communications settings necessary. Those settings include the baud rate, parity, data bits and stop bits. The two most common settings are 1) even parity, seven data bits, one stop bit; and 2) no parity, eight data bits and one stop bit. These would translate into 1) E-7-1 and 2) N-8-1 in communications software shorthand. In your communications program you set up dialing directories or small parameter files that include these settings as well as the name, the phone number and the baud rate for each site.

One of the great advantages of simple dial-up access is that the least powerful, least expensive computer using a comparatively slow modem will get you access to much of what the Internet has to offer. The reason for this is that all the computing work is being done by your remote host, which then sends to you only text. The disadvantage is first that you cannot choose your client software, and you cannot use graphical World Wide Web browsers like Netscape and Mosaic. A second potential disadvantage is that other people also will be accessing your host computer; if many people are using your host to run programs, you may witness delays and visible slowdowns.

Network protocol (SLIP, PPP) dial-up access

If your campus offers SLIP or PPP access, you will have a couple of great benefits. First, you are not dependent on the host computer to do work for you. Instead, your computer does the computing, and you are not subject to traffic jams on your host except for those times when you are retrieving your mail. Second, you may choose to use client software that appeals to you because you are free from dependence on the host. Finally, if you have a powerful enough computer and a fast enough modem, you may take advantage of your network dial-up access to run the newer graphical World Wide Web browsers that put so much of the Internet into point-and-click access.

When you are using SLIP or PPP access, in place of your communications software you have a small program called a *dialer* whose sole purpose it is to set up and maintain a connection with your access provider. The connection it maintains is the connection that allows you to run your own software. You first have to install and set up your dialer in much the same way you set up a dialing directory for other communications software. You tell the dialer the phone number to call, the bits-per-second rate of your modem, and so forth. Your campus computing specialists should have handouts that tell you how to set up your dialer.

After your dialer is set up, you have to do the same thing with each of your client programs: Web and Gopher browsers, Telnet, FTP, Usenet news reader, and your e-mail client. The discussion of each of these protocols names some client software. There are also a few programs like Minuet and QVT Net that incorporate several of these functions under one umbrella. World Wide Web browsers (Chapter 4) may also permit access to Gopher, FTP, Telnet, Usenet News and at least the sending of mail.

Local bulletin board systems (BBSes)

If you have your own computer, a modem and communications software, you can tap into a range of online communities that go beyond the Internet. If you have left your home town to go to college, local bulletin board systems (BBSes) are good places to get in touch with some of the new community happenings and resources beyond the campus boundaries. Some campus information systems will include community calendars for the benefit of students, but they probably won't have the flavor of a local BBS.

A community of sixty thousand should have a half-dozen or more local computer bulletin board systems. A larger community will have more. You find out their phone numbers in one of several ways.

Visit a local computer store or Radio Shack and ask them for some of the phone numbers. *Computer Shopper* magazine carries a list of BBS numbers by area code each month. The list changes constantly. Your campus computing specialists may be able to point you to one board or another. If you get the number of a couple of BBS systems, they often have more extensive lists for their areas. You have only to log into one or two boards and look for the local site list.

Connecting to a BBS is much like connecting to a Telnet site or to your campus system. You will be asked to log in as a visitor or to give your name and password. Then you will see a series of menus to access message sections, software, calendar, announcements, and so on. The software (files) section frequently has a file that lists all the software available for download and another file that lists other local bulletin boards. Some bulletin boards charge limited fees for access. Many are free. Many bulletin boards have some kind of thematic focus. Each board has a name that often suggests what its focus is. There are religion-oriented boards, community-oriented boards, computer-centered boards, and others.

Some local bulletin boards provide e-mail gateways to the Internet and/or Usenet news feeds. Some BBSes are interconnected and form their own small internetworked systems. FidoNet, ILink, VBBSnet, WWIV, and RAnet are some of the BBSes that maintain their own networks from one community to the next.

Commercial hybrid systems

On a larger scale are commercial hybrid computer systems with familiar names like CompuServe, America Online, Prodigy, Delphi, and GEnie. Newer systems like the Microsoft Network and AT&T Interchange are likely to compete with the more established systems.

These systems are often called commercial hybrids first because they are commercial—for profit—enterprises, and second because they offer a blend of services resembling your local neighborhood BBS on one hand and access to high-priced databases on the other. Typically they charge a monthly fee of about $10, for which you get access either to a set of basic services or to a certain number of hours online. Beyond the basic services or the base time allotment, you are assessed an hourly access charge.

All these systems give you e-mail accounts and e-mail access to the Internet. They also have their own gateways to other Internet services. One of the advantages of memberships with the commercial hybrids is that they have local telephone access over a wide geographical area. CompuServe is the largest in this regard, with local nodes throughout the United States, Europe, Latin America, Asia and other places. Thus, wherever you might travel you can have access to your account. If you would like to establish an account with one of the commercial hybrids, each of the *Big Five* can be reached at a toll-free telephone number. America Online is reached at 800-827-6364; CompuServe at 800-848-8199; Delphi, 800-695-4005; GEnie, 800-638-9636; Prodigy, 800-776-3449. Some offer a free *test drive* period before you sign up.

Conclusion

The Internet and other online services are not all big, heavy libraries or all work. They contain programs that allow students (and others) away from home to communicate with other people, anywhere in the world. Furthermore, programs like MUDs and Internet Relay Chat permit synchronous—or real time—conversation online. With its origins as a role-playing game, MUD technology underscores the recreational possibilites of internetworking. And the same technology that permits the game can enable intercontinental classroom instruction.

Further good news is found in the realization that you do not have to be on campus to enjoy access to the rest of the world. Simple dial-up connections, SLIP and PPP access, local bulletin boards, and commercial hybrids all provide some degree of connection to others in the rest of the world.

Finding it: Research strategies

The professor in the public policy class always smiled when he gave the juniors and seniors their semester-long assignment. Their objective: to learn all there is to know about an issue of public concern and to write a comprehensive report, including all the policy options under consideration, the supporters of each option, the likely policy choice, and the prospective impact of the choice. In addition to the report, the professor also required the students to turn in an extensive bibliography of sources consulted and copies of any reports, materials or information they gathered.

Every semester, the students reacted in the same way. How would they know when they knew all there was to know? How would they know when they were the experts? "You'll know," the professor would reply, enigmatically.

And they did. At the end of each term students turned in long reports about issues as diverse as the ethical treatment of animals in laboratory research to efforts to control violence on television to the economic impact of professional sports on host cities. The reports were usually accompanied by transcripts of legislative hearings, copies of articles from obscure scholarly journals, little-known studies by little-known public interest research groups, quotes from activists, comprehensive listings of newspaper articles written on the topic, and a lot of other hard-to-find information stored in out-of-the-way places.

And each semester many students succeeded in becoming, for the first time, experts on a difficult subject. The most successful achieved that status by effectively combining traditional research techniques and the resources available via the Internet with perseverance, creativity and hard work. Along the road they learned that Thomas Edison's dictum that genius consists of 2 percent inspiration, 98 percent perspiration is still true, particularly if you wish to enrich your educational experience using the Internet. You must work hard, perhaps harder than before; but the payoff can be great.

This chapter will discuss
- Strategies for integrating the Internet into your research efforts.
- Other ways in which the Internet can be used to enhance your academic experience.
- How to avoid potential pitfalls associated with using the Internet.

Developing a research strategy

A bit of folk wisdom holds that if you don't know where you are going, any road will get you there. For students who wish to integrate the Internet into their research efforts, that saying has deep implications. Before you set out to do research, you must first have some idea of what you want to learn. Your destination may change as you as you move forward, but to keep your bearings you must have a goal in mind.

If you don't know where you are going when you begin to use the Internet, you are never going to get there. The Internet is just too large, with too many pathways and distractions for the naive Net novice to accomplish anything of much use. Just as you would not walk into a huge, multifaceted library with no book in mind and expect to find what you want to read, you cannot blindly begin to use Gopher, access the World Wide Web or subscribe to a host of discussion lists and find the information you want.

Before you begin to use the Internet for your research, you must develop a systematic research strategy. The specific strategy will depend on several factors, including your topic, the required length of the project, your interests and the amount of time you have to complete the assignment. The Internet opens up a vast new storehouse of information to you. But it will take time for you to explore that storehouse.

At the core, all research projects have the same five steps. First, you must define your topic. Second, you determine the range of material available and gather general information. Third, you look for the answers to more specific questions suggested by your preliminary research. Fourth, you weigh your findings and draw conclusions. Last, you write and submit your project.

The Internet supplies tools that can help you at several points in this process.

Step One: Finding a topic

In most cases, the best way to determine a specific topic for a research paper or project is to consult with your professor. The most common objective professors have when they assign long-term projects is to have you apply the strategic thinking skills and insights you have learned inside the classroom to fresh material in an unstructured setting.

Consequently, you need to identify a topic that will meet that educational objective as well as be interesting to you. One method for identifying a topic is to focus on the aspects of the class that have been most interesting to you. From that section of the course, you should then ask yourself a set of simple questions:

- Based on what I have learned, what else would I like to know about this subject?
- Can those questions be answered within the framework of this assignment?
- Can I find the materials I need to answer the question in a timely fashion?
- Will this topic be acceptable to the professor?

If the answer to the last three questions is yes, you should develop a search plan. In their book *The Search*, Lauren Kessler and Duncan MacDonald suggest a checklist to determine if you have created an effective plan. The key questions:

- Have you outlined what you want to know?
- Do you have specific questions that you want to answer?
- Do you have an idea of potentially appropriate sources?
- Can you find the information you need?

As you develop your search plan for material on your topic, you should create a list of synonyms for your topic. For example, you may want to do research on "child abuse" and not find much material. That's because librarians filed the material under a near synonym, "domestic violence," which also incorporates related topics like "spousal abuse." A resource to help you second-guess how librarians might file material is the *Library of Congress Subject Headings*, a reference book in almost every university library. A version of the *Library of Congress Subject Headings* is available online by Telnet at locis.loc.gov (140.147.256.3). You will need to ask for "help" to get a document that describes how to use the QuickSearch Guide. Once you use it two or three times, it becomes fairly easy.

Armed with appropriate subject headings, you can develop your search plan. Once you have a search plan, you can start working.

Finding potential online consultants

After you have selected a topic, you should begin your research immediately. The standard approach of waiting until a week before the project is due, running to the library to check out four books on the topic, and then pulling an all-nighter to write up your findings won't work if you want to make the best use of Internet resources.

If you are using the Internet, before you actually start gathering material you should identify the online discussion lists (Chapter 3) and the Usenet Newsgroups (Chapter 7) appropriate to your topic and begin to monitor them.

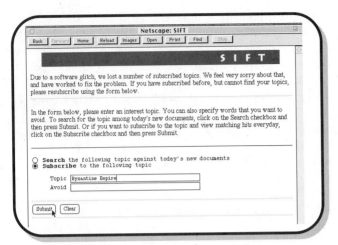

Fig. 9-1: The SIFT service at Stanford University permits searching of news group archives and subscribing to an ongoing search.

To locate the relevant Usenet Newsgroups, you have two options. The most straightforward way is to simply scroll through the lists of news groups for which your university has a news feed. Most schools carry between 3,000 and 5,000 news groups. But because the groups are arranged in a hierarchical manner, you will not have to scroll through all 4,000 to find the ones in which you may be interested. For example, if you are working on a topic in history, it is unlikely that you will find any appropriate group in the .comp or the .sci categories.

This method of finding news groups is analogous to browsing the shelf in a library. Alternatively, you could use the World Wide Web search engines (described later in this chapter) that will search news group archives.

The result will be a list of available news groups related to that keyword.

Once you have identified the news groups you wish to monitor, you subscribe using the commands associated with the news reader you are using. In NN you use the u command to both subscribe and unsubscribe to news groups. In VMS News you use sub and unsub to subscribe and unsubscribe. In many Macintosh and Windows readers and the reader associated with Netscape, you simply click on the appropriate box.

You also have two options for identifying potentially helpful electronic discussion lists. Perhaps the easiest is to send an e-mail message to listserv@listserv.net. Leave the subject line blank and in the body of the message type "list global/keyword." The keyword describes your topic. For example, if you are doing a report on the Shoemaker-Levy comet, which crashed into Jupiter in 1994, you may wish to use astronomy, Jupiter, comet or the comet's name as a keyword.

Alternatively, you can review the Web pages of Listserv, Listproc and Majordomo, the dominant software for running electronic discussion groups, on the World Wide Web to locate groups with which you may wish to interact

in the future. Sites that can help you to find appropriate discussion lists
include

- http://www.clark.net/pub/listserv/listserv.html.
- http://www.cc.utexas.edu/psycgrad/majordomo.html.
- http://www.tile.net/.
- http://www.neosoft.com/internet/paml/bysubj.html.
- http://www.nova.edu/Inter-Links/cgi-bin/lists.

A third approach to identifying useful news groups and discussion lists
is to search through the e-mail archives to see who is discussing the topics in
which you are interested. Stanford University's SIFT (Stanford Information
Filtering Tool) News Service digs through both e-mail discussion lists and
Usenet news archives to find postings containing keywords or combinations
of keywords that you specify. SIFT finds appropriate references and sends
you an e-mail message that describes, in digest form, what SIFT found. SIFT
is accessed at http://sift.stanford.edu. A way to use the service via e-mail is
described in Chapter 3. A similar service is provided by Indiana University's
UCS Support Center at http://www.ucssc.indiana.edu/mlarchive. The service also tells you how to set your e-mail subscription parameters (including
turning off your mail while you are on vacation) and other useful information about managing e-mail.

After you have identified appropriate news groups and discussion lists
you can then subscribe to them using the procedures described in Chapter 3.
The next step is to monitor the online discussions to see if the participants
are discussing issues appropriate to your topic and if they seem generally
knowledgeable about your subject. At this point you should just *lurk* in the
background to ascertain the relevance and quality of the list.

You should not jump right into the fray of discussion. And you should
definitely not ask the participants in the group to suggest research topics to
you. That is for you and your professor to determine.

Your objective at this point should simply be to identify the list or news
group to which you can turn later should you need to. Used the right way,
participants in discussion lists and news groups can serve as online consultants. Used incorrectly, at best your questions or comments will be ignored; or
you may face harsh criticism from others in the group.

Your first selections may not be appropriate and you will have to subscribe and unsubscribe to several before finding the two or three best. Usually you will want to participate in only two or three discussion lists or news
groups. Reviewing the messages takes time, and interacting with online discussion groups will probably represent only a small fraction of your total
research effort.

Also remember to unsubscribe if an online discussion group is not appropriate or you have finished your project. If you don't, you will cause the discussion
list moderator (the person responsible for administering the list) serious problems at the end of the semester or whenever your e-mail account is closed.

Step Two: Finding general information at your library

After you have begun to identify the discussion lists that you will want to use later, your next step should be your campus library. You can use your library both to find resources available there and as a gateway to resources around the world.

In many research projects, you will want to find books that have been written on your topic. Use the card catalog to find the books on your campus and then, if your library uses the CARL system, be sure to check out the catalogs at other Public Access Catalog Systems, particularly the library catalogs at large state university systems such as the University of Maryland and the University of California. In most cases, especially if you are at a relatively small school, you will find many more books and other materials at the larger systems. Through CARL you may also be able to survey the holdings of the local public library systems such as the city of Los Angeles. The free library systems in many cities and states have huge repositories of holdings.

You must do your library search early in your research, however; for if you find a book that looks appropriate and is not in your library, you will need to work with the interlibrary loan department of your school to get the material. It can take several days to several weeks to receive books via interlibrary loan.

Most libraries also provide access to other catalogs of information for you to search. *Periodicals Abstracts* is an excellent database that catalogs articles in hundreds of magazines. Many provide access to databases for business and other specialized areas as well.

If your campus is not on the CARL system or one like it, you can easily telnet (see Chapter 6) to a library which is. For example, you can telnet to the University of Maryland library at victor.umd.edu. Though it is not part of the CARL system (although you can get there through CARL), the University of California has extensive holdings. Its library system is called Melvyl and you can telnet to it at melvyl.ucop.edu. You can access CARL directly by Telnet at pac.carl.org. CARL is also on the Web at www.carl.org.

You can review a list of libraries you can access via Telnet by using Gopher (Chapter 5). The address is libgopher.yale.edu. If you wish to access the Gopher site using your World Wide Web browser, the URL is gopher://libgopher.yale.edu. Finally, you can browse some of the holding of the Library of Congress, the most comprehensive library in the United States, via Gopher at marvel.loc.gov. The Web URL is gopher://marvel.loc.gov.

Because most libraries are connected to larger systems like CARL, you can now use your library to find information well beyond its walls. You are no longer limited to searching for material in your own library, but you must start this process early. Once you have identified books and other material outside your campus that you wish to use, it will take some time for them to arrive via interlibrary loan. A few services, like CARL's UnCover, will fax articles to you if you have a fax machine and a credit card, but this can be expensive.

Step Three: Accessing online information

The objective of the library research is to help you refine your objective. In most cases, by casting your net wide enough, you will locate much of what you need to carry out your project in libraries—yours and others. Traditionally that is all a student could do.

But with access to the Internet, you can now go beyond what was once possible. You can take the next step and find information that may not yet have made its way to library catalogs. You can locate and retrieve the very latest data on your subject.

To locate and access online information, you use the search engines and subject directories associated with Gopher, WAIS and the World Wide Web. Veronica and Jughead, the search engines for Gopher, are described in Chapter 5. Some of the search engines for the World Wide Web are described in Chapter 4, as are the subject directories. (Archie, which is a search engine to locate software retrievable via FTP, is described in Chapter 6.)

For several reasons, the World Wide Web generally is the easiest and most comprehensive tool to locate information. Remember, the Web was designed to incorporate the other Internet applications like Gopher. And because of the attention it has received, fresh information is being made available on the Web every day. It is the most dynamic Internet information service.

Web-based tools for finding information

The Web has emerged as a vast, virtual library stretched around the world. The range of information is staggering. Finding what you need for your research project would be like trying to find the proverbial needle in a hay stack were it not for the availability of sophisticated searching and retrieving tools.

Unfortunately, these tools are capable both of uncovering exactly what you need and of flooding you with torrents of irrelevant, useless documents through which it will take you hours to wade. Their effectiveness depends on how wisely you pick your tools and how well you use the tools you have chosen.

You were first introduced to Web searching tools in Chapter 3. In this section you will get a closer look at the different kinds of searching tools and the different methods they use to find information. You will also learn tactics you can use to customize your search results.

When you want to find information the Internet holds on a particular topic, your typical first move is to visit a network site that offers to you either a subject-oriented catalog or a keyword search engine. Some sites offer both. A few Web-based catalogs reach beyond the World Wide Web to offer indices or catalogs of GopherSpace, Telnet sites, Usenet news archives, e-mail discussion lists, or FTP software archives.

All search sites have one thing in common: Each operates from some kind of an index. How that index is generated—by robot or human—determines the difference between two large classes of network indices.

Robot-generated indices

Some indices on the World Wide Web are created by computer programs (called spiders or crawlers) that work by automatically visiting Web sites looking for new documents and building an index of them. Some index-generating programs read only titles of documents. Some read document links, and some read every word in the document. The strengths of robot-generated indices are twofold.

First, the robot programs can catalog vast numbers of sites and links. A site in Canada called OpenText, for example, had cataloged some 15 million links by the summer of 1995. The Webcrawler—owned by America Online—at the same time had cataloged more than 1.5 million Web pages.

The second strength of crawlers or spiders is that they are sensitive to changes in the World Wide Web. As new sites or pages are put up on the Internet, they find these new documents during the robot's routine rounds. As old sites or pages are moved or removed from public access, the robot notes those changes also.

Robot-generated indices include (all URLs start with http://)
- Aliweb—Web.nexor.co.uk/public/aliWeb/aliWeb.html.
- DejaNews—www.dejanews.com.
- Harvest Broker—town.hall.org/Harvest/brokers/www-home-pages/.
- Infoseek—www.infoseek.com/.
- Lycos—lycos.cs.cmu.edu/.
- OpenText—www.opentext.com:8080/omw.html.
- Webcrawler—webcrawler.com/.
- World Wide Web Worm—www.cs.colorado.edu/home/mcbryan/WWWW.html.

The comprehensive nature of the robot-generated indices is also their weakness. Because anyone with an account on a Web server can put up pages on the Web, a lot of frivolous material is served. By automatically generating indices of everything that is out there, robots are not very discriminating. So when you ask for a list of documents on a given topic, you often get a lot of hits that are totally irrelevant to your search. You may find yourself wading through hundreds of Web pages without coming across anything useful.

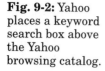

Fig. 9-2: Yahoo places a keyword search box above the Yahoo browsing catalog.

Moreover, some search engines only return a subset of the pages with matching keywords. The page with the information you need may not be included in that subset.

Human-edited indices

To address that problem, some search engine providers employ human beings who are trained in library or information sciences to manually build the indices or to edit the indices created by robots. The intent of human-edited indices is to minimize the amount of irrelevant material reported when someone asks for information on a given topic. Editors of a number of Web indices solicit input from experts in various fields as they build catalogs of topic-oriented resources and other indices for locating information on the Web. If a prospective site passes the editors' scrutiny, it is added to the index.

Among the edited indices (all URLs start with http://) are
- Clearinghouse for Subject-Oriented Internet Resource Guides www.lib.umich.edu/chhome.html.
- Gopher Jewels—galaxy.einet.net/GJ/.
- Internet Public Library—ipl.sils.umich.edu/.
- Riceinfo—riceinfo.rice.edu/RiceInfo/Subject.html.
- TradeWave Galaxy—galaxy.einet.net/.
- Whole Internet Catalog—gnn.com/wic/.
- Yahoo—www.yahoo.com/.

Both the TradeWave Galaxy and Yahoo combine two information-gathering interfaces. Each site offers a keyword search engine to its edited index. Like the rest of the sites in the edited index list, Galaxy and Yahoo also present a subject-oriented catalog for browsing.

At browsing sites, information is ordered in hierarchies. To find what you want, you have to have a sense of how the human indexers might classify information. For example, if you were interested in movie animation, at Yahoo you would select first Entertainment, then Movies and Films, and finally Animation. At Galaxy, which is organized a little more like university studies, you would pick first Humanities, then Arts, followed by Motion Pictures and finally Animation.

The weakness of subject-oriented catalogs for many students is that students don't want to have to guess how some specific information might be cataloged. The strength is that the observant browser might find a good deal of closely related material that would be overlooked in keyword searching.

Web-based indices to non-Web material

Because World Wide Web browsers such as Mosaic and Netscape strive to be all-encompassing Internet navigating tools, they can be used to access Gopher sites, Telnet sites, read Usenet news postings, and move files by FTP. One of the recent developments on the World Wide Web is the creation of sites that catalog or index resources found in each of these areas. The TradeWave Galaxy and Yahoo, described above, offer both subject-oriented browsing and keyword searching. At the Galaxy site, you can specify that you want Galaxy to search Gopher indices and/or the Hytelnet database of Telnet sites.

Several sites on the Web specialize in providing access to search engines that do the finding for you. Some of these sites will allow you to conduct a keyword search using several tools at once. A few of the meta search sites are

- scwww.ucs.indiana.edu/metasrch/—Indiana University.
- www.albany.net/~wcross/all1srch.html—the All-in-one Search Page.
- www.iquest.net/iq/reference.html—Super Searcher.
- www.supernet.net/search.htm—SuperNet Search Page.
- Web.nexor.co.uk/cusi/cusi.html—the main CUSI site.
- www.qdeck.com/cusi.html.
- www.tenn.com/cusi/cusi.html.
- www.ulysses.net/cusi/cusi.html.
- www.ptd.net/cusi/cusi.html.

Each of these sites permits searching of indices (using tools) previously described as well as providing access to others.

Effective searching

The lack of a consistent method to index sites across the Web leads to an interesting phenomenon. If you submit the same keywords to different search engines, you will get dramatically different results. So, if you want the best information and/or want to do a thorough job of research for a school project, you will want to use more than one search site.

Fig. 9-3: Some keyword search sites, such as the TradeWave Galaxy, permit you to specify a number of search parameters.

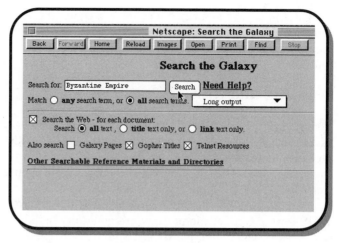

Most keyword search sites permit you to define search parameters. By placing restrictive parameters on your search, you can make your network searches more efficient through eliminating a lot of hits on irrelevant material. In other words, you get reports on what you want without getting a lot of extraneous material. Two kinds of parameters facilitate search narrowing.

In the first case, you can choose the database(s) you want to search. CUSI sites give you several options for doing this. At the TradeWave Galaxy, remember, we were able to ask Galaxy to search the Hytelnet database and Gopher sites for relevant material. You could also restrict your search to Galaxy pages if you want.

The second kind of search restriction is achieved by using keyword qualifiers in Boolean logic statements (and, or, not). If you performed a search of the Internet for all references to the word Clinton, you could get thousands of documents. If you are interested in the Clinton Health Care Plan, and your search site supports Boolean logic, you could ask for Clinton AND health AND plan. The result would be a report of documents containing all three words.

In Figure 9-3, for example, we have specified that we want Galaxy to find documents containing both the word Byzantine and Empire and that we are going to search the entire text of Web documents. We have also checked boxes to search beyond the Web into titles of Gopher documents and into Telnet resources.

As you become familiar with each search site, be sensitive to the tools available for narrowing your search. Most sites have help files that show how to do custom searches at the site. You might want to practice making similar searches with different restrictive qualifiers, just so you can get the feel for the ways you can control your searches.

Once you have identified a set of search engine sites that you like, you should add them to your list of bookmarks, which will make it easier to call them up in the future.

Retrieving with WAIS

Though the most dynamic, the World Wide Web is not the only vehicle for finding information through the Internet. WAIS (Wide Area Information Servers) is also a powerful searching tool. If your Internet host has a WAIS client available, you may launch the program by typing "wais" or "swais" from the system prompt. If you do not have a WAIS client on your personal computer or your Internet host, you will have to borrow one. You might choose WAIS from a Gopher menu (they are generally listed under other Internet resources) or you might use Telnet (Chapter 6) to get to a WAIS site and then log in as "wais" or "swais." Publicly available (Telnet) WAIS servers may be found at

- sunsite.unc.edu, log in as "swais."
- wais.nis.garr.it, log in as "wais."
- wais.funet.fi, log in as "wais."
- 192.216.46.98, log in as "wais."
- 192.31.181.1, log in as "wais."
- 193.63.76.2, no log in, choose "c."

WAIS searches information that volunteers have indexed around predefined topics. WAIS information is organized into database libraries and you have to preselect the library (subject area) you want to search. At this writing there are hundreds of WAIS libraries. You tell WAIS what databases to search (from a list of more than 600) and then give it the word(s) or phrase you are trying to locate. With great speed, WAIS scours documents in the databases you designate and gives you a report of hits that are ranked in order of the closeness to your search terms. Each hit is given a score from 1 to 1,000. Theoretically, a perfect match is 1,000. However, WAIS will give 1,000 to the best match and score others in comparison.

For example, let's say you start your WAIS search by telnetting to sunsite.unc.edu. You log in as "swais." You have to tell the sunsite server what terminal you have; the default is VT 100. The screen in Figure 9-4 shows that we have taken the first steps toward launching a simple search. The top of the screen says there are 597 sources (database libraries) to choose from. When you are at the sources screen in WAIS, you move a highlight bar down through the sources listing until the bar rests on the desired source. To mark a database for searching, you hit the spacebar.

For the purpose of demonstrating a simple search, four database sources (aarnet-resource-guide, AAS_jobs, academic_email_conf, and agricultural-market-news) located at four different servers were marked. Having marked the databases, you type "w" (for word) to give WAIS a keyword for which to

Fig. 9-4: You start a WAIS search at many sites by choosing the databases you want WAIS to investigate. Here we have checked three databases and typed "Texas" as our keyword.

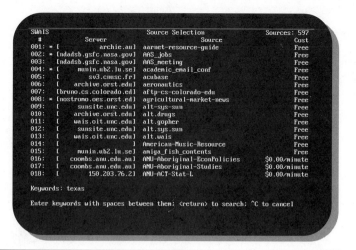

```
SWAIS                             Source Selection              Sources: 597
   #            Server                     Source                    Cost
001: * [          archie.au]  aarnet-resource-guide                  Free
002: * [ndadsb.gsfc.nasa.gov]  AAS_jobs                              Free
003:   [ndadsb.gsfc.nasa.gov]  AAS_meeting                           Free
004: * [      munin.ub2.lu.se]  academic_email_conf                  Free
005:   [       sv3.cnusc.fr]  acubase                                Free
006:   [    archive.orst.edu]  aeronautics                           Free
007:   [bruno.cs.colorado.ed]  aftp-cs-colorado-edu                  Free
008: * [nostromo.oes.orst.ed]  agricultural-market-news              Free
009:   [       sunsite.unc.edu]  alt-sys-sun                         Free
010:   [    archive.orst.edu]  alt.drugs                             Free
011:   [   wais.oit.unc.edu]  alt.gopher                             Free
012:   [       sunsite.unc.edu]  alt.sys.sun                         Free
013:   [   wais.oit.unc.edu]  alt.wais                               Free
014:   [                    ]  American-Music-Resource               Free
015:   [      munin.ub2.lu.se]  amiga_fish_contents                  Free
016:   [    coombs.anu.edu.au]  ANU-Aboriginal-EconPolicies   $0.00/minute
017:   [    coombs.anu.edu.au]  ANU-Aboriginal-Studies        $0.00/minute
018:   [      150.203.76.2]  ANU-ACT-Stat-L                   $0.00/minute

Keywords: texas

Enter keywords with spaces between them; <return> to search; ^C to cancel
```

search. You then type in the keyword and press the Return key. In the example, "Texas" was entered as the keyword.

Once a search is started, WAIS attempts to connect to each of the server sites and retrieve the documents. If it cannot make a connection, it tells you so. When the search is ended, WAIS tells you how many items it found, listing them together with the scores each item tallied. Our search for Texas produced 10 hits. Figure 9-5 shows the results of the search. Each located source is given a score. The top two items scored perfect 1,000 marks. WAIS reports scores, the name of the source, the title of the document containing the match, and the length of the document in lines.

In the sample search, WAIS found matching documents from news group archives, Bitnet mail lists, agricultural databases and others. You can view the documents WAIS uncovers, you can save them to the machine on which

```
SWAIS                             Search Results               Items: 10
   #    Score    Source              Title                        Lines
001: [1000] (academic_email_)  Copyright 1994 by Diane K. Kovacs, The D 21763
002: [ 462] (academic_email_)  tx-firearms        Contact: tx-firearms-re   10
003: [ 385] (academic_email_)  BIRDEAST×ARIZVM1.BITNET@CORNELLC.CIT.COR  106
004: [ 385] (academic_email_)  CADUCEUS@Beach.Gal.UTexas                  15
005: [ 385] (academic_email_)  FedTax-L@SHSU.BITNET                       41
006: [ 385] (academic_email_)  FICTION on LISTSERV@PSUVM.PSU.EDU          28
007: [ 385] (academic_email_)  INFO-TI-EXPLORER@SUMEX-AIM.STANFORD        19
008: [ 385] (academic_email_)  comp.sys.ti        Discussion about Texas I
009: [ 385] (academic_email_)  comp.sys.ti.explorer   The Texas Instrumen
010: [   0] (ANU-Demography-)  Search produced no result. Here's the Ca  105

<space> selects, arrows move, w for keywords, s for sources, ? for help
```

Fig. 9-5: Results of a WAIS search are displayed in a listing ranked by relevancy scores.

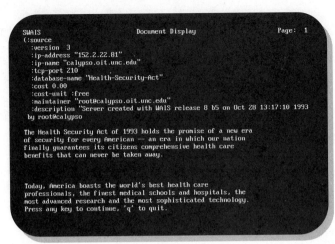

Fig. 9-6: One of the replies to a WAIS search on information about health care produced a document on the Health Security Act of 1993.

your client software resides (if it is your personal computer or the host site where you have an account), or you can have the document mailed to you. WAIS most often turns up text files, but it may just as well find video or audio segments. If your document is text, you may view it by positioning the highlight bar over the item in question and hitting the Enter key. Figure 9-6 shows a portion of one such document, retrieved during a WAIS search for health care information.

If you like the document WAIS found the first time and want more like it, you can mark it with a "u" (use) and ask WAIS to search again. This time WAIS will take the marked document as its example and look for other documents that use a lot of the same words.

Like Gopher and some Web clients, WAIS clients offer minimal help commands on screen continuously. A full list of commands, such as those given in Figure 9-7, is available by typing "h." Probably the most difficult part of using WAIS is that first step. Traditionally there has been no convenient way to browse for information by topic or to know whether any given database has information of use to you. What you must do is read through screen after screen of alphabetical database listings (more than 600 if you want to get all of them) and mark (with the spacebar) the ones you think might pertain to your topic.

To address the problem, some sites present WAIS users with only one source: the directory of servers. The welcome message reads in part:

```
To find additional sources, just select the directory-
of-server.src source, and ask it a question. If you know
the name of the source you want, use it for the keywords,
and you should get that source as one of the results. If you
don't know what source you want, then just ask a question
```

Fig. 9-7: WAIS keyboard commands are case sensitive. If any of these commands do not work, try asking for help by typing a question mark or an "h."

WAIS Keyboard Commands

j, ^N	Move Down one item
k, ^P	Move Up one item
J	Move Down one screen
K	Move Up one screen
R	Show relevant documents
S	Save current item to a file
m	Mail current item to an address
##	Position to item number ##
/sss	Position to item beginning sss
	Display current item
	Display current item
|	Pipe current item into a unix command
v	View current item information
r	Make current item a relevant document
s	Specify new sources to search
u	Use it; add it to the list of sources
w	Make another search with new keywords
o	Set and show swais options
h	Show this help display
H	Display program history
q	Leave this program

that has something to do with what you're looking for, and see what you get.

What this means is that instead of getting a list of 600 potential sources to browse through and mark, you get one. Give it something to search for and if it turns up sources you like, you can mark them for use.

A WAIS review

The WAIS search involves several steps:

1. Select the databases you want to search.
2. Tell WAIS the keywords you want to locate.
3. WAIS goes out to all the databases you have selected and searches for matching documents.
4. WAIS scores matching documents and displays a list of them on the screen with their scores, the name of the server, the title of the matching document and its relative size.
5. You may view documents thus listed, mail them, or use them as starting points for new searches.

The WAIS interface is nowhere near as clear and easy to understand or to use as the Gopher menuing system so it scores lower than Gopher in that regard. Nor is WAIS nearly so accessible. Though there are clients available for personal computers, the number of WAIS clients available by Telnet can be counted on your fingers.

The power of WAIS is threefold. First, WAIS will find many things other network finders do not. Second, WAIS has the ability to handle phrases, which can greatly assist you in finding what you seek. Third, by using documents returned in one search as new sources, you can do recursive searching that may produce extremely beneficial results.

Search GopherSpace with Veronica and Jughead

After you have completed your searches on the World Wide Web and WAIS, you may wish to search through GopherSpace to identify information available via Gopher. The procedure for searching Gopher databases is fully described in Chapter 5.

Most general Gopher sites (such as marvel.loc.gov; gopher.tc.umn.edu) will offer Veronica and/or Jughead searches under such menu choices as Internet Resources or The World. A few specific URLs for accessing Veronica and/or Jughead are at

- gopher://veronica.scs.unr.edu.:70/11/veronica.
- gopher://marvel.loc.gov:70/11/internet/veronica.
- gopher://riceinfo.rice.edu:70/11/OtherGophers.
- gopher://liberty.uc.wlu.edu:70/11/gophers.

Step Four: Weigh your findings

At this point in your project, you will have collected a mass of material. You may have read and noted books and journal articles. You should have been able to find reports, studies and other documents online. You may have found some of the online discussion that you monitored particularly relevant.

At this point, the challenge is to winnow your material and clarify the points you want to make. As you work through the material, it may be time for you to begin to participate in the online discussion that you have monitored.

For students researching projects, it is appropriate to interact with discussion groups in two ways. First, you may wish to ask a very specific question you have, based on your research. For example, a student doing a report on health care could not find what HCFA stood for. She posted a message to a group and discovered they were the initials for a little-publicized federal agency involved in health care.

The second acceptable task is to bounce off the group an idea you may have developed doing your research. For example, let's say you were looking at the history of liberalism in America for a political science class. Based on your research, you get the idea that liberalism has always been a minority position in America. You may want to suggest that idea, with some support or documentation for your argument, to an online discussion group concerned with Democratic Party issues.

The guiding rule is to treat your colleagues in the discussion groups with respect. They participate because the interaction on the list is interesting.

They are not there to do your homework. You should only use the lists to get answers to questions as a last resort. If you really can't get the information elsewhere, you can turn to them. And you should use the list to discuss ideas only if you think you truly have an interesting idea to discuss.

In addition to the discussion lists you have monitored, while searching the Web and elsewhere, you may have come across the e-mail addresses of experts in your field with whom you would like to correspond about your topic. In those cases you should first send them an e-mail message (see Chapter 3) describing your project and asking if they would mind answering questions. You can then move forward based on their responses.

Step Five: Preparing the report

As you prepare your final report, there are three issues that you should keep in mind. First, if you have diligently searched the Web for information, there is a strong possibility that you have come across images that you may want to use to illustrate your project. Remember, you must treat images you find on the Web as copyrighted material. Under copyright law, you can use small amounts of copyrighted material in research. But you should use only modest amounts of information.

Second, much of the material you find via the Internet you will save in an electronic format. That makes it easy to cut and paste blocks of information into your report. You should not do that. Copying electronic material into a report without proper citation is plagiarism and a significant violation of the academic code at all schools and universities.

Finally, you must cite where you found your information. If you discovered an electronic version of information that has initially appeared in print, you can simply cite the printed version. If the information exists only online, you should use the citation format described in Chapter 4.

Other academic uses for the Internet

While the Internet is a dynamic tool for finding information and expert help for research, it can be used in many other ways to enhance your educational experience. Perhaps the most obvious are the possibilities of using the Internet to collaborate with your classmates and to interact with students having similar interests around the world. For example, let's say you have to do a group project. Instead of trying to meet with each member of the group face to face, after your organizational meeting you can keep in touch via e-mail. In this way you can also see the work each group member has prepared, comment on it and edit it. The assignment truly becomes collaborative.

Many different student groups have formed their own discussion lists or created their own home pages on the World Wide Web. There are discussion lists for undergraduate and graduate students in different disciplines;

for students from different ethnic and racial backgrounds; and for students involved with different aspects of campus life such as athletics, student government, the student newspaper and clubs. Many students participate in online chat rooms and other real-time interactive services described in Chapter 8.

By searching out these possibilities, you can broaden your horizon well beyond your local campus. You can find and interact with your peers around the world.

On the other hand, many professors are beginning to incorporate these tools into their course offerings. It is not difficult to establish an online discussion list or Usenet Newsgroup for a single course. Professors are also establishing Web pages both to distribute information and for students to share their work. Along the same lines, many schools have set up electronic forums for students. Clearly, the Internet can allow for heightened interaction both inside and outside the classroom.

Finally, the Internet is a great vehicle for identifying software in the public domain and shareware (software that you can try before you decide to purchase it) that you may like to use. To locate software, you can use Archie '95 (http://www.pvv.unit.no/archie) which puts a graphical interface on the Archie FTP file-locating engine (Chapter 6). You provide the search string and other search-defining parameters, and Archie '95 reports to you the appropriate files and their locations.

The Virtual Shareware Library (http://vsl.cnet.com/) takes Archie a step further. VSL will let you find software by not only file names but file descriptions and other parameters. You then download the software using FTP (Chapter 6).

Pitfalls to avoid

The Internet is a seductive tool for research and academic work. However, it is very easy to misuse it. The most common mistake people make is not starting at the beginning. You must first think through your topic before you actively begin to pursue information. Since you have access to so much more information, you have to have a more focused approach to find what you need than you have had to have in the past.

And you cannot depend on others to help you do your work. In most cases, unless you are very well known and well liked on the list, the folks on a discussion list or in a news group are not going to want to select your research topic or do your searching for you.

Second, while using the Internet should make your research better, it will not make it easier to complete. In most cases, the library used to be the first and last stop for research. It should still be your first stop. But you have many other places to go once you have finished there. It takes time to explore all the possibilities.

Finally, because the information you find on the Net is in electronic form, you may be tempted to act in unethical ways. You must resist that temptation.

In essence, the Internet frees you from the physical constraints of your campus and plunges you into a new, information-rich, interactionally intense environment. But it is still up to you to realize the maximum benefits.

Chapter 10

The rules of Net behavior

The fall of 1995 was not a good time for America Online (AOL), at that time the country's largest and fastest growing online service. Early in September the *San Francisco Chronicle* reported that hackers had stolen the passwords of several AOL employees, including the chief executive officer's. Many employees then had to change their passwords for fear their accounts had been compromised. Shortly thereafter a two-year FBI investigation into child pornography on AOL led to raids on 120 homes and dozens of arrests. Then Arnold Bowker, a resort owner in the Dutch Antilles, sued the information service for the name and address of one of its members, who, he claimed, had libeled him in one of its travel forums.

These events helped focus attention on the rules, regulations and restraints that are and should be imposed upon online communications. Like AOL, the Internet has opened a vast new channel of communication for students. It allows students and professors to share information in ways that they never could before. Users of the Internet have an unprecedented opportunity to learn and to communicate in new ways and with large, international communities of colleagues.

But with this opportunity comes serious responsibility. When you begin to use the Internet, you become a part of several different and significant communities, including the users of computing resources on campus, the academic and intellectual community at your school, the worldwide network of Internet users, and society itself in the broadest sense of the word. Participation in each has its own set of obligations.

This chapter will discuss

- Responsibilities Internet users have to their home campuses.
- Academic ethics and the Internet.
- General rules of behavior for Internet users.
- Legal and free-speech issues and the Internet.

Your school, their computers

Freedom. Escape from parental control. Autonomy. For many students, college is the first time they are truly on their own. They can make independent decisions without consulting their parents or other adults. They can choose what to do and when to do it.

And to a certain extent that is true. Most colleges and universities do not view themselves as serving in the role of parents away from home. College students can control the course of their college careers.

And though your primary responsibility when you attend college is to yourself, you also have a responsibility to others around you. This responsibility is keenly felt when you use resources that are also used by the entire college community. In the same way that you should not steal a library book, tear an article out of a journal or disrupt a class, you should not misuse the campus computer network and campus access to the Internet.

Using the campus computer network and campus access to the Internet involves two sets of obligations. First, you must use the network in a way that will enable others to use it efficiently after you and will lessen the burden on the academic computing professionals whose responsibility it is to keep the network up and running. Second, you must be careful that your actions do not violate the rules and obligations by which your campus must abide, including the restrictions on an educational license for using the Internet.

Generally, you access the campus computer network in one of two ways. Either you work at a computer in a lab that provides public access to a community of users, or you dial into the network and work on a computer on which you have an account. Under the first scenario, you should follow a defined procedure to help assure that the facility can be efficiently used by all.

When you begin work at a lab, you should first close any application programs that the person before you left open. As you work, if you don't have a reserved storage area on the system, you should save your work on your own diskette, which you can take with you when you finish.

As you work, if a sequence of key strokes or mouse clicks does not perform a task as expected, you should not simply keep re-entering the same sequence. If the sequence doesn't work once, it won't work the second, third, fourth or fifth time either. Continually re-entering a mistake could freeze the machine. If you are not sure what you are doing and you are in a public lab, it is usually safer to ask for advice than to just repeat the same mistake again and again. Most schools have technology help desks that you can call via intercampus telephone. You should not hesitate to use this resource.

On the other hand, because the Internet is not bulletproof yet, from time to time when you are using an Internet application your screen will freeze, you may be knocked off the network, or the client software may inexplicably bomb. If that happens, in most cases you should not worry about simply exiting and restarting the program even if you are logged onto a host computer elsewhere. Most hosts are programmed to cut off access if you do not enter a key stroke within a specified period of time, so you will do no harm.

As you know from Chapter 6, you can easily find and download software from the Internet. In most cases, this is not a good idea if you are using a public-access computer. Software can be infected by computer viruses, computer programs that attach to other programs and cause the infected computer to malfunction in some way.

Many campuses provide anti-virus software on their public-access computers. If yours does, you should use it whenever you put a floppy disk into the machine. But even if you can scan for viruses, it is not the role of students to load public domain and shareware software onto public-access computers. In some larger schools such as the University of Michigan, for example, it is impossible for users to load software onto public-access computers anyway. In those schools, authorized software is reloaded at specific intervals and unauthorized programs are erased.

You should also not steal software from public-access computers. Once again, many schools have built-in protection against students just downloading software from a hard drive. But even if your school does not, stealing software is wrong.

When you complete your activities for a session—surfing the Web, telnetting to another computer, or using a non-Internet-related application—you should close all the applications that you have used. But don't turn off the computer. Once again, allow those responsible for the lab to take care of tasks like that.

If you are working on a central computer on which you have an account, your primary responsibility is to use the account in the way in which you were authorized. For example, you have been allocated a specific amount of disk storage; you should not exceed your limit. Second, you may have access only to certain application programs or other files. You should not trespass where you do not belong.

Your campus and the Internet

Some people consider the Internet an elaborate telephone system for computers. While there is some merit to the analogy, there are many significant differences as well. The telephone network is considered a common carrier. In exchange for being granted an operating monopoly in the early part of the century, American Telephone & Telegraph gave up the right to control the content of what was being carried over the telephone lines. In giving up control of the content, it also was freed from legal responsibility for that content. In essence, if people misused the telephone, the abusers were responsible, not the telephone company.

This is not entirely the case with the Internet. If you misuse the Internet, your college could be responsible. For example, a stock market analyst writing on the Prodigy online computer service (see Chapter 8) blasted a company call Stratton Oakmont. In response, Stratton Oakmont sued Prodigy for libel. A judge allowed the case to proceed, arguing that because Prodigy admitted to monitoring messages (a procedure it had initiated to curtail hate speech on the service) it also had a legal responsibility for the content of the material.

If you access the Internet through your school, school officials may share responsibility for the information you send and receive. Nine states have already passed online censorship laws, some of which ban "indecent" speech and speech that "harasses, annoys and alarms" users. If you are sending and receiving e-mail or other computer files that fall into these categories, your college or university may be at risk. Some of the laws even require companies and universities to monitor e-mail and other computer uses to make sure the laws are not violated.

Unfortunately, some of the most questionable material on the Internet, particularly on the World Wide Web, is found on public-access pages set up by students. Posting obscene material, hate speech and other kinds of communication can put you and your school at risk.

In fact, it is not yet clear exactly how the First Amendment's free-speech rights will be applied to computer-mediated campus-based speech. (The First Amendment will be fully explored later in this chapter.) An early test came in the fall of 1994. A journalism professor at Santa Rosa (California) Junior College had established men-only and women-only computer bulletin boards. Some men posted derogatory remarks about some women on the men-only board. The messages were then made public and the women sued, charging that the single-sex conferences violated a federal law that prohibits sex discrimination in schools that receive federal funds. They contended that the derogatory comments were a form of sexual harassment creating a hostile educational environment.

The U.S. Department of Education's Office of Civil Rights argued that computer bulletin boards are an educational activity and do not enjoy the same level First Amendment protection as the campus newspaper. In fact, the office has proposed banning comments that harass or denigrate people on the basis of sex or race. Although the Santa Rosa College's lawyer suggested that the online conference should have been protected by the First Amendment, the college agreed to pay three students $15,000 to settle the charges.

Your school also works within another set of constraints. What an organization can and can't do on the Internet depends on the type of organization it is, which is designated by the last three letters in the organization's domain name (see Chapter 2). Schools and universities are in the educational domain (.edu). That means the school has promised to use the Internet for educational and research activities and not for commercial activities. In return, the school receives certain licensing and pricing considerations.

Therefore, ethically and legally, the school may not use its Internet access for tasks unrelated to its educational and research mission. For example, it cannot sell Internet access to users. Nor can it establish for-profit businesses on the World Wide Web. And neither can you. Although the Internet, and particularly the World Wide Web, are still by and large self-policing, it is part of your responsibility to stay within the rules that govern your institution.

Academic rights and responsibilities

Although the Internet represents an important new technology, it does not alter fundamental values, among them academic responsibility. At the core of the honor code at most campuses is the simple obligation of students to do their own work within the framework and conditions specified by their instructors. The Internet does not change that obligation.

Because of its utility, the Internet may tempt students to take unethical shortcuts. You should resist that temptation. For example, e-mail makes it very easy for students to get unauthorized help from friends and colleagues around the country. Indeed, online discussion lists facilitate finding people who have similar interests who can assist you with difficult problems or long-term projects. Some classes will establish their own online discussion lists. And personal e-mail makes it very easy for students within a class to work together and ask each other questions.

The Internet fosters collaboration, and collaboration is generally good. But you must still do your own work. If you have others do it for you, no matter how convenient or covert it is, you are cheating. You must restrict your collaboration to the confines of the assignment.

Along the same lines, through the World Wide Web, Gopher and WAIS you will be able to access many documents in an electronic format. It is very simple to cut and paste material from those documents into your projects and reports. Unless you quote that material and properly cite it, you are committing plagiarism, one of the principle violations of most honor codes. In fact, many schools expel students who plagiarize other people's work.

If you do use information you found on the Internet, you should cite the source. Citation formats are discussed in Chapter 4. Citations for information on the Internet are important for three reasons. First, all academic knowledge is built on a foundation of knowledge that comes before it. As you write a report, you should show that foundation. Second, because the Internet allows you access to much fresher and a wider range of sources than you are likely to find in your library, your professor or teacher may want to access some of the information you use in your paper. Finally, citing information from the Internet still carries with it a certain amount of panache.

As a student (or professor), you have an obligation to help create a learning environment that is conducive to the learning of all. For some reason, some students believe e-mail and other Internet applications give them license to harass and intimidate classmates and colleagues. As you become more comfortable with these new tools, you have an academic obligation to be gracious to those who are not yet as far along the road as you.

Cyberspace citizenship

When you use the Internet, you enter a worldwide community. During the past several years, the community has developed its own culture and rules of behavior. Most of these rules are not law; if you don't follow them you will not be arrested. Nevertheless, for people who wish to be polite and to behave in an appropriate manner, they are important to keep in mind.

Lists of rules—commonly called netiquette—are posted on various parts of the Internet itself. One of the best known is Arlene Rinaldi's "Netiquette," available at http://www.fau.edu/rinaldi/net. But there is no single Emily Post of the Internet. The Internet is a community in development, and those who were there first should not necessarily be the ones to dictate to everybody else how to behave. The pioneers have their own agendas that do not necessarily account for the interests of newcomers. Moreover, in face-to-face human interaction the rules of etiquette are continually in flux. And that is how it should be on the Net as well.

Nevertheless, if you keep five basic principles in mind while you use Internet applications you will be a good citizen of cyberspace.
- At the final destination, there is a person.
- When you use the Internet, you are in public.
- Your actions have unanticipated impact.
- Nobody enjoys having his or her time wasted.
- Tools work better when used appropriately.

A network of people

Although the Internet is regularly described as a network of computer networks, in reality it consists of people using a network of computer networks. Virtually all the information flowing through the Net is intended for use by other humans.

Chuq Von Rospach has pointed out in his primer on how to work with the Usenet community, which is available in the news.announce.newusers news group (see Chapter 4), that because the computer is the instrument through which you interact with others on the network, it is easy to forget that there are people involved.

In Usenet Newsgroups and online discussion lists, too often people respond rashly, without taking into account the feelings of others. In one case, a person signed onto a list of a group of scientists who intended to collaborate on a joint project. They were still working out ground rules when the person opined that for the sake of moving the project forward, they could not hope to achieve consensus on every issue. Another person promptly responded that the first person's attitude was fascist and disgusting. The first promptly withdrew from the project.

In the early days of the widespread use of Usenet and online discussion lists, the arguments would get so hot that the word flame was used to describe when one person in the discussion would attack another. As more people have begun to be involved in online discussion, flaming has become increasingly frowned upon. As with most intemperate debate, flaming generally sheds more heat than light on a subject.

But the subject of discussion is not the only issue. Usenet groups and discussion lists thrive when thoughtful, knowledgeable people participate. After the initial thrill of voyeurism—observers, or lurkers as they are called in Net jargon, in essence witness a personal argument—flaming is dull. Moreover, it discourages people from participating. Who knows? Perhaps the person you discouraged with your flame is the person who could most help you on your project.

In addition to avoiding personal attacks, you must take time to understand the nature of the discussion before you plunge in. Over time most discussion lists and news groups take on a certain character or personality of their own. They discuss certain topics in certain ways. They defer other related issues to other groups. You should be sensitive to the character of the group. In the same way that you would not insist that the fan club for the Baltimore Orioles discuss bowling scores, even though they are both sports, you cannot insist on a news group discussing issues outside of its charter as decided by the participants.

Humor is also usually very personal. What is very funny to some is simply offensive to others. Furthermore, some people simply have no capacity for recognizing when somebody is being ironic or sardonic—or the difference between the two. Subtle humor can easily be lost.

With that in mind, an array of different types of symbols has developed to try to indicate the emotional stance of the writer. A little smiley face denotes an attempt at humor. (Nobody has yet determined why it is okay to include a little smiley face in electronic correspondence but not in traditional material :-) .) For people working in text only, they may type in the emotion they are trying to convey like this: <grin>.

In any case, when you get involved with a news group you should lurk before you leap into a fray. You are joining a group of strangers. Get to know them first before you begin to share your opinions.

Public behavior

In 1993, David Gelernte, a Yale University computer science professor, was the victim of an attack by the Unabomber. Severely injured, he did not wish to talk to the media about the attack. He did, however, send an e-mail message to a colleague. Somehow that letter was eventually circulated onto discussion lists on the Internet and eventually made its way to the pages of the *Washington Post*. Gelernte was not happy to see his private thoughts made public without his permission, but they were.

In fact, although many students get the idea that because they can access the Internet at 2 o'clock in the morning when nobody is physically around they are acting privately, nothing could be further from the truth. You must conduct yourself on the Internet as if everything you do will be subject to public scrutiny, because it probably will be.

Clearly, when you participate in a public discussion list or news group, your remarks will be available to the other people on the list. Ill-conceived, poorly argued, flimsy excuses reflect poorly on you. In addition, from time to time people forward remarks from one list to another. Theoretically, anything you post to a discussion list could circulate to millions of people in many places around the world even if that was not your intention. Furthermore, people engaged in research can frequently access your remarks from databases in which they have been stored.

But public discussion lists are only the tip of the iceberg. Not long ago a newspaper cartoon portrayed a computer user accidentally sending a private message to everybody on a mailing list. Mistakes like that frequently happen. And even person-to-person e-mail is not private. Recently a supervisor who surveyed the e-mail of employees at his company found that two employees were exchanging derogatory e-mail about him. He took exception to their remarks. They have sued him for invasion of privacy. Until now the courts have ruled that companies (and presumably colleges) have the right to monitor employee e-mail. Indeed, as noted earlier, some anti-online censorship laws may even require monitoring.

The World Wide Web is also a huge public space. Many schools are allowing students to put up personal Web pages. Many of the pages reflect a great deal of immaturity. If you are in the position to create a Web page, try to project an image by which you want several million people to know you.

Unanticipated impact

Robert Morris was a student at Cornell University when he released a computer virus onto the Internet as an experiment. He thought the virus was relatively harmless, that it would disrupt some operations but do no actual or permanent damage.

He was wrong. The virus proliferated wildly and at one point it appeared that some important computer sites at major national defense installations might be affected. For his action—which Morris himself saw as an experiment gone awry—Robert Morris was sentenced to prison.

As part of the vast network of people using the Internet, your actions have impact in ways you often cannot anticipate. For example, earlier you learned that when you set up an e-mail account on a centralized computer on your campus, a specific amount of storage space is reserved for you. You were advised not to exceed your quota.

But let's say you subscribe to several mailing lists and then go home for vacation and your e-mailbox fills up. What happens? In many cases your system will have been programmed to send back any new messages to the sender, even if the sender is a discussion list program. The returned mail may be sent to everybody on the discussion list. Eventually the list owner or moderator will have to take the time to unsubscribe you from the list.

Or let's say you do not unsubscribe to the discussion lists before you return home for summer vacation or graduate from school. In many cases, each spring, or certainly after graduation, student e-mail accounts are discontinued. When that happens the list moderator will get an "unknown user" message for virtually every message sent through the list. Even though discussion lists seem to work automatically, remember that at the final destination there is a person. Try to make that person's job easier.

Discussion lists and Internet applications that involve interpersonal communications are not the only venues that can generate unanticipated consequences. As people create their own personal pages on the World Wide Web they should keep in mind that they are sharing the ability to send graphics, video, audio and other data—that is, the bandwidth of the network—with the other users on their local system as well as with the general Internet community.

While the idea of establishing a personal page is to generate attention, you have to operate with the needs of others in mind as well. From time to time people have posted risqué photographs on their pages and then bragged about the traffic they have generated and the bandwidth they have consumed. But heavy traffic generated by one site often means slower operation for others on the network. In many cases system administrators force people to remove nonessential pictures from heavily used sites. And it is well within the administrators' rights to do so.

Nobody enjoys having his/her time wasted

A question was posed on a list of journalism historians. A student was doing research on early West Virginia newspapers and wanted to know where good archives were located. Another student responded that he didn't believe that his colleague would find much before 1920 because that was when the daily newspaper was invented.

The respondent also admitted that he had slept through his journalism history class. Indeed, he had. And his answer to the query reflected it—it was wrong.

Perhaps it is the apparent anonymity of the Net that prompts people who would never think to raise their hands in a class if they didn't know the answer to feel free to volunteer all sorts of false and faulty information on the Net. When they do they waste everybody's time.

Now many people find the Internet a great way to waste time in general. And it is. But people like to waste time on their own and do not need your help. That means that they don't need you to continually reiterate your position in an ongoing discussion if you are not clarifying your position or making a new point. They do not need to know that you agree with somebody else or that you liked a message that somebody else disliked. They don't need you to ask silly questions that could be answered by reading an FAQ. And they don't need you to send a test message to see if your subscription is working or if you have mastered the send procedure.

People who have set up discussion lists want to have interesting online conversations. Because of the nature of online discussions, people are often coming into the middle of a conversation. It is helpful, therefore, if you include in your comments a summary of previous comments to which you are responding. On the other hand, there is usually no need to completely copy a previous posting to make your point.

In most cases people do not like to read long messages. (If you must write a long message, you may want to break it up using subheadings.) Nor do they want to read messages in which they are totally uninterested. So in the subject line of your e-mail you should include a succinct description of the content and a warning if the message is lengthy.

If somebody posts a question that calls for a specific answer, as opposed to a comment in a discussion, in most cases you should provide the answer via private e-mail. Reading 20 answers to the same question can get tedious.

Respect for the time of others is also the basis of the strong antipathy against mass e-mailing, called *spamming* in Net argot. In 1995 two lawyers sent a message to hundreds of Usenet groups soliciting business for their legal practice. Most of the lists were completely inappropriate for the message. Although the lawyers received some positive responses, they set off a fire storm of hostility as well. Eventually their system administrator had to close their e-mail account.

On the other hand, from time to time you may have a message that is appropriate for several different groups. In that case you should indicate in the subject line that the message is cross-posted or forwarded from elsewhere.

Like discussion lists and news groups, the World Wide Web offers many opportunities to waste time, some more enjoyable than others. For example, large and complex graphics, audio and video can take a long time to download. Many times, people do not have the time, patience or interest for the download. So, if you have made a large file available on your Web page, you should let viewers know the length (in kilobytes), giving them the option to skip the file. You should try to keep most of the graphics on the pages fairly small (in terms of data).

There are other ways to make your Web pages friendlier to busy people too. For example, posting the date of the last revision and including a What's New section helps Web surfers determine whether new information has been posted since their last visit. Including text links for people who do not have a graphical browser or who do not wish to wait for graphics to load can also be helpful.

Use the right tool appropriately

One key to good citizenship in cyberspace is to use each Internet application in an appropriate way. If you join a discussion list or news group, interact in the same way you would with any group. Be polite. Respect others. Take time to learn and to understand the character of the group. Don't be manipulative.

If you create a Web page, treat it as if you were creating a work that could be seen by millions of people. If you are surfing the Web, act in the same way that you would in any library—with respect for the rights of the creators of the information you are accessing.

Antisocial, immature behavior is as unbecoming on the Internet as it is in face-to-face interactions.

The law, free speech and the Net

The principles outlined above define a code of conduct that can be violated without legal sanction. But even impolite, ill- mannered users of the Internet must operate within the law. Legal constraints on the Internet operate in at least two distinct areas—property rights and free speech.

In 1993, Steve Jackson, who ran a computer bulletin board in Texas, had his computer equipment confiscated by the police, effectively shutting down his service and his business. The charge—stolen telephone credit card numbers had been stored on his bulletin board.

Computer information—software and data—is property. You cannot take it without permission. That is stealing. You cannot use it in unauthorized ways. If you do, and you store the information on a computer at your university, not only are you putting yourself at risk, you could be putting your school at risk as well. Law enforcement officials are not delicate when they find stolen merchandise. They usually do not simply download the information; they take the hardware as well.

In addition to the police, the software industry itself is working hard to prevent software piracy. Large users who violate software licenses face fines and other sanctions. As a user, you have to respect the legal constraints within which your school operates.

And although the Internet is an international network of computer networks, minimally the same restrictions on speech apply to it as apply to general speech in the United States. Students generally have to be concerned primarily with four categories of speech: libel, copyright, speech codes and obscenity.

Libel laws specify when a person can be punished for publishing false information about somebody else. Because posting information on the Internet can be considered publishing, you should be careful about what you say about other people. If what you post is both false and harmful to somebody's reputation, you could open yourself to a libel suit should the person get angry enough to file a lawsuit against you. Opinion is no defense against libel. The best safeguard is to avoid spreading untrue, harmful information about people.

Copyright is generally poorly understood—if understood at all—by students. In essence, copyright gives control of the use of information to the creator of that information in most cases. While you can use small sections of information in your school reports—this is called fair use—you may not copy or appropriate the work of another. While it is hard to imagine a situation in which somebody would sue a student for copyright violation, it is important to remember that information on the Internet is copyrighted even if it is not marked with a copyright symbol.

Speech codes are among the hottest issues on campus right now. Not recently, a student at the University of Pennsylvania was suspended from school for calling a group of students water buffaloes. He was charged with creating an atmosphere not conducive to learning, in violation of campus codes of behavior. Though he was eventually reinstated, the furor surrounding the issue has not diminished.

The legality and appropriateness of codes governing speech on the campus computer network is much clearer than the appropriateness of campus speech codes in general. Students have no right of access to computers and have no right of access to the Internet. Students must abide by the policies established by their institutions.

The final issue is *obscenity*. You cannot post obscene material on the Internet without incurring risk. While obscenity has specific legal definitions in each state, even material that does not meet those strict definitions may be banned from the Internet. Certainly your university has the ability to ban it from its computers.

Cyberspace: The new frontier

In the final analysis, the Internet is a new frontier in the sense that people are coming together on the Internet to interact in new ways. As with other frontiers, the rules of behavior have not yet been fixed. But three principles have been clearly established. First, the law of the land is the law of the land. The laws of libel, obscenity and copyright apply equally to the Internet as elsewhere, if not more so. Second, the owner of the computer system—in this case your university—has the right to establish policies to govern its use. You have no right of access. Other university regulations such as the honor code also remain in force. And finally, people like to interact more with people who behave appropriately, taking into account the needs of others as well as their own needs.

Chapter 11

Making the humanities grade

If you have ever delighted in a great movie or listened again and again to a favorite song, then you have enjoyed the fruits of what scholars study in their probing of humanities. If you have ever admired the works of notable men and women—Joan of Arc, Socrates, Martin Luther, Michelangelo, Emily Bronte, Mark Twain—then you have cherished the essence of humanities. If you are a deep thinker, marveling at the place of mankind in the universe, then you are engaged in one of the humanities disciplines.

Do you like to paint? Perhaps you have written a poem or two. Humanities.

Humanities is a term that has come to be applied to those areas of human activity that separate humankind from the rest of the animal world. It involves the creative spirit that leads men and women to produce works of art—paintings, music, theater and literature. Humanities encompasses profound and noble thinking of people, as expressed in the works of philosophy. Humanities considers the very language by which people express themselves. Humanities comprehends the stories of people's accomplishments as individuals and as groups—the building of cities, universities, cathedrals and other great institutions and architectural monuments.

What is it that man hath wrought? That is the stuff of humanities.

Though you may never take a class called Humanities, you almost certainly will be asked to study some subjects within the humanities disciplines before you graduate. This chapter will help you to explore online resources for

- Mastering English language and literature.
- Delighting in the fine and performing arts.
- Sounding the depths of philosophy.
- Coming to grips with history.
- Delving into the richness of foreign languages and cultures.

Your goals at college—conscious or not—should include the desire to learn as much as possible about something that already interests you. In that process, you may be assigned to do research reports on any number of topics. As you approach your research and writing assignments, you may find yourself knowing exactly what you want to study and to write about on some occasions, and on others you can't for the life of you come up with a topic. Several information *catalog* sites on the Internet are uniquely suited for helping students find topics. They may also be good starting points if you have a more defined sense of your topic. Chapter 9 outlines some basic research principles that will help you with any research topic.

General humanities catalogs

A few sites in GopherSpace and on the World Wide Web have positioned themselves as general humanities catalogs, providing links to resources in a broad range of humanities subjects. One of these is Oxford University's The HUMBUL Gateway at http://info.ox.ac.uk/departments/humanities/international.html. Others include

- The University of California at Santa Cruz's InfoSlug Gopher at gopher://scilibx.ucsc.edu/11/The%20Researcher/Arts%20and%20Humanities.
- The University of California at Santa Barbara's Humanities Computing Facilities Gopher at gopher://ucsbuxa.ucsb.edu:3000/.
- The University of California at Santa Barbara's *Voice of the Shuttle* at http://humanitas.ucsb.edu/.
- Michigan University Humanities Computing Gopher at gopher://una.hh.lib.umich.edu/11/humanities/genhumres.
- Norwegian Computing Center for the Humanities at gopher://nora.hd.uib.no/.
- Washington and Lee University Humanities Collection at gopher://liberty.uc.wlu.edu/11/library/human.
- The University of California at Riverside's Infomime at http://lib-www.ucr.edu/rivera/.
- The World Wide Web Virtual Library humanities section at http://www.hum.gu.se/w3vl/w3vl.html.
- Cycor's Humanities Links at http://www.peinet.pe.ca:2080/Chorus/links.html.
- The Carnegie Mellon University English Server at http://english-www.hss.cmu.edu/.

English language and literature

English departments at colleges and universities divide their discipline into three areas: language, composition and literature. Language, as the name suggests, studies the structure of the English language. Under this guise, we study words and their meanings (semantics), as well as grammar, which includes the rules for putting words together to make sentences and how those sentences should be punctuated when they are written.

Composition takes language a step further and deals with the manner in which sentences are combined to make paragraphs, essays, and the like to convey more complex messages. Many schools offer classes in technical writing and/or creative writing under the umbrella of composition.

Literature treats the larger body of written expression. It encompasses the study of poetry, drama, novels, short stories and other creative expressions. You will find a fair number of resources online.

Language resources online

The English Language & Culture page at Ohio University is topped by an index to subgroupings of many language and writing resources. Included are texts, online communities, tourism in English-speaking countries, references, and other resources. The page is located at http://WWW.tcom.ohiou.edu/OU_Language/lang-english.html.

Human-Languages Page is something of a gathering place for information about languages of the world. It includes job announcements and links to many foreign language resources and is located at http://www.willamette.edu:80/~tjones/Language-Page.html.

The Linguist Network contains archives and resources for discussion of linguistics in an academic setting. The network is located at http://engserve.tamu.edu/files/linguistics/linguist/linguist.html.

English Server at Carnegie-Mellon University (http://english-www.hss.cmu.edu/) includes links to many English-related resources including extensive links to Languages and Linguistics resources on the Internet.

You may join e-mail discussion lists for the English language by sending the message "Subscribe *LISTNAME your name*" to a machine, typically using the address scheme "listserv@*host.domain*." More detailed instructions are given in Chapter 3. Some lists of interest to students of the English language include

- ENG-GRAD (for English graduate students)
  listserv@cfrvm.cfr.usf.edu.
- English Language Discussion Group, WORDS-L,
  listserv@uga.cc.uga.edu.
- Assembly for the Teaching of English Grammar, ATEG,
  listserv@miamiu.muohio.edu.

Literature resources online

The boundaries between disciplines within the humanities can be very thin. Witness literature versus philosophy. We study the works of Shakespeare as

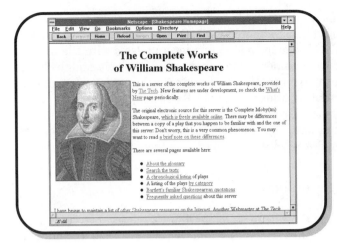

Fig. 11-1: The Complete Works of William Shakespeare page is one of the rich literature resources available on the World Wide Web.

examples of great literature. But one of the reasons Shakespeare's works have enjoyed four centuries of continued popularity is that the playwright's characters give such eloquent expression to profoundly philosophical ideas. On the subject of man's place in the universe, consider these varying estimates:

- "What a piece of work is man! how noble in reason!" Hamlet muses.
- "Life's but a walking shadow, a poor player that struts and frets his hour upon the stage and then is heard no more," Macbeth laments.
- "How beauteous mankind is! Oh, brave new world, that has such people in 't!" Miranda marvels in *The Tempest*.

The reach of expression in Shakespeare's characters is so great and captures so much of the variety of life that scholar Alfred Harbage described the maturing of Shakespeare's art as the development of "infinite variety." One might also consider the Internet as a place of infinite variety.

One of the notable enterprises on the Internet is Project Gutenberg, an initiative to place works of literature online in a publicly accessible format. Project Gutenberg began in 1971 when Michael Hart found himself with $100,000,000 worth of computer time at a University of Illinois computing center. Hart decided that the greatest value created by computers would not be computing, but the storage, retrieval, and searching of what was stored in our libraries. He conceived of a project that employs volunteers and donations to enter and store electronic texts.

The Project Gutenberg Library is divided into three sections:

- "Light Literature" such as Lewis Carroll's *Alice in Wonderland,* and *Through the Looking-Glass,* Aesop's *Fables,* and J.M. Barrie's *Peter Pan.*

- "Heavy Literature" such as the Bible and other religious documents, Shakespeare's works, Melville's *Moby Dick,* and Milton's *Paradise Lost.*
- "References" such as *Roget's Thesaurus,* almanacs, encyclopedias, and dictionaries.

All texts are in the public domain and are available in ASCII format readable by nearly every word processor. The Internet home of Project Gutenberg is at http://jg.cso.uiuc.edu/pg/pg_home.html. The files are also available by Anonymous FTP at ftp mrcnext.cso.uiuc.edu. An index of available texts can be retrieved from the /extext/articles directory. The file name is 01INDEX.GUT.

Several other sites also house the Project Gutenberg Library or portions of it. Sites will list available texts by author and by title. At least one subject index is available: http://www.w3.org/hypertext/DataSources/bySubject/Literature/Gutenberg/.

Similar in some respects to Project Gutenberg is Project Bartleby at Columbia University. The Bartleby project started much later than the Gutenberg project (it began in 1994) and has focused on classics of literature. So far, it has included collections of poetry as well as the 1901 edition of Bartlett's *Familiar Quotations* and the 1918 edition of William Strunk's Elements of Style. Bartleby may be accessed at http://www.cc.columbia.edu/acis/bartleby/index.html.

Students and faculty create literary resources

Elsewhere, students and faculty at colleges and universities worldwide have taken pride in building online literary resources. A major Web resource for English literature is maintained by the University of California at Santa Barbara. The address is http://humanitas.ucsb.edu/shuttle/english.html. The UCSB site has a mirror (duplicate site) at Oxford University in England, http://info.ox.ac.uk/~enginfo/shuttle/ENGLISH.HTML.

At Duke University Michael Shumate has created a resource called Hyperizons dedicated to hypertext fiction. Located at http://www.duke.edu/~mshumate/hyperfic.html, the site has links to several other similarly predisposed network resources.

At MIT graduate student Jeremy Hylton maintains The Shakespeare Homepage at http://the-tech.mit.edu/Shakespeare/works.html. The site is searchable and contains links to the Web version of Bartlett's *Familiar Quotations* at Columbia University, a glossary, chronological and alphabetical listings of the plays, and links to other Shakespearean sources on the Internet.

Also at MIT physics major Daniel Stevenson has created a server for classical Greek and Roman literature at http://the-tech.mit.edu/Classics. The site contains nearly four hundred texts, is searchable, and contains links to other sites of similar interest.

David Phillips at Yale University has compiled extensive lists of links to American Studies (including literature) resources at http://pantheon.cis.yale.edu/~davidp/lit.html. Texas Tech University English Department (http://english.ttu.edu/home.html) maintains a creative writing resource online called Prairie Island Literary Review, accessible from the department server, which also provides links to other literary and cultural sources.

At the University of Pennsylvania the English Department maintains both Gopher and World Wide Web resources. The English Gopher server is at gopher.english.upenn.edu and contains both departmental information and extensive links to the rest of the world of literature. The department also maintains an electronic journal for contemporary art and writing, called *CrossConnect* at http://tech1.dccs.upenn.edu/~xconnect.

Other electronic journals available on the Internet include the Bryn Mawr Medieval Review (gopher://gopher.lib.virginia.edu/11/alpha/bmmr), the Bryn Mawr Classical Review (gopher://gopher.lib.virginia.edu/11/alpha/bmcr), the Mississippi Review Web (http://sushi.st.usm.edu/~barthelm/index.html), and The Boston Book Review (http://www.bookwire.com/bbr/bbr-home.html).

You may join e-mail discussion lists for English language literature by sending the message "Subscribe *LISTNAME your name*" to a machine, typically using the address scheme "listserv@*host.domain*." More detailed instructions are given in Chapter 3. Some lists of interest to students of English language literature include

- English and American Literature Section, EALSL, listserv@gwuvm.gwu.edu.
- Medieval English Literature Discussion List, MEDEVLIT, listserv%siucvmb.bitnet@listserv.net.
- American Literature Discussion Group, AMLIT-L, listserv@mizzou1.missouri.edu.
- Discussion of American Literature from 1880–present, AMLIT2-L, listserv@tamvm1.tamu.edu.
- Modern British and Irish Literature, MODBRITS, listserv@kentvm.kent.edu.
- Society for Literature and Science, LITSCI-L, listserv@vmd.cso.uiuc.edu.

Writing and composition

Creative writing, technical writing, basic composition, fiction writing and similar courses will come within the scope of this part of the English student's study. Network resources include sites that specialize in writing tools, discussions of people's work, and even writers' MOOs. The links between literature and writing are so intimate that the student with a focus on writing should be familiar with the literature resources described earlier. Some other Internet sites concentrate more directly on writing tools and resources.

Part of the World Wide Web Virtual Library, Writers' Resources on the Web is a site accessed at http://www.interlog.com/~ohi/www/writesource.html. The site, maintained by Debbie Ridpath Ohi, provides links to resources in twelve different genres as well as groups resources into such tool areas as workshops, marketing of compositions, and networking with other writers.

The Writers Page is an alphabetized list of network resources aimed at writers. It is available at http://www.texas.net/~stevelar/writers.html. A large collection of links to network resources for writers resides at http://www.dfw.net/~cnichols/writing.html.

The Computer Writing and Research Labs at the University of Texas at Austin operate computer-assisted classes in writing for the Division of Rhetoric and Composition and the Department of English. At the CWRL Web site (http://www.en.utexas.edu:80/) one can find links to many research and teaching materials as well as extensive links to materials on text-based virtual environments (MUCKs, MOOs, Chapter 8).

Michigan Tech University operates a Writing Center for "anybody who wants to improve their reading, writing, and language skills." The Writing Center has a home page at http://www.hu.mtu.edu/wc/welcome.html that has links to writing labs and centers throughout the United States.

The Children's Writing Resource Center (http://www.mindspring.com/~cbi/) offers resources for children's writers. The site features special reports, market tips, the latest children's bestsellers, the *Children's Book Insider* newsletter, and links to other sites.

Missouri University maintains A Virtual Place for Writers at http://www.missouri.edu/~wleric/writery.html that, among other things, provides access to a MOO where students can find tutors.

You may join e-mail discussion lists for writing and composition by sending the message "Subscribe *LISTNAME your name*" to a machine, typically using the address scheme "listserv@*host.domain*." More detailed instructions are given in Chapter 3. Some lists of interest to students of composition include

- Writers list, WRITERS, listserv@mitvma.mit.edu.
- Writing Workshop Discussion List, WRITING, listserv@psuvm.psu.edu.
- Fiction Writing Workshop, FICTION, listserv@psuvm.psu.edu.
- Non-Fiction Writers Workshop, NFICTION, listserv@psuvm.psu.edu.
- Rhetoric, Language, Prof Writing, PURTOPOI, listserv@vm.cc.purdue.edu.
- Poetry Writing Workshop, POETRY-W, listserv@psuvm.psu.edu.
- Novel Writing Workshop, NOVELS-L, listserv@psuvm.psu.edu.

Fine and performing arts

Beyond literature, the creative spirit of humankind expresses itself in the related fields of art and architecture. The art in architecture is clearly evident in the design of buildings as well as monuments, towers, bridges and many highway structures.

Painting and other visual arts

The graphics-handling capabilities of World Wide Web browsers is nowhere more helpful than in the realm of visual arts. Museums, art collections, research material and much more are available.

The World Wide Arts Resources Corporation maintains a site that offers links to galleries, museums, art publications and more. The site has both English and German language options at http://www.concourse.com/wwar/default.html. Furthermore, the museum links represent countries from more than two dozen nations throughout the world. Besides being organized topically and geographically, the WWAR site offers a keyword search engine.

Keyword searching is also available at another large art resource—the Smithsonian Institution's National Museum of American Art. Located at http://www.nmaa.si.edu/, the site offers tours of art galleries, art history documents, educational programs and more.

A site especially rich in art history resources is maintained at http://arth.concordia.ca/AHRC/intro.htm, the online home of the Art History Research Centre in Canada. The site offers listings of mail lists, news groups and other network resources having an artistic bent. Included are research archives, indices of articles in academic journals, library and bookstore catalogs and more.

The WebMuseum (formerly Le WebLouvre) in Paris is the project of Nicolas Pioch. The collection of paintings, music and other art resources has attracted so much interest that it has mirror sites all over the world. The home of the WebMuseum is at http://mistral.enst.fr/wm/. The welcome page gives a listing of dozens of mirror sites, organized by geographical region.

Other notable art resources include the Getty Art History Information Program (http://www.ahip.getty.edu:80/ahip/home.html), the Rice University RiceArts resources (http://riceinfo.rice.edu:80/projects/depts/arts/), the Australian National University ArtServe collection (http://rubens.anu.edu.au:80/), and the Piero Project at Princeton University (http://mondrian.princeton.edu:80/art430/art430.html). Several of these sites have searchable databases.

Photographic exhibits abound on the World Wide Web. You might try

- http://cmp1.ucr.edu/exhibitions/cmphome2.html, the California Museum of Photography at University of California, Riverside.
- http://math.liu.se:80/~behal/photo/, an extensive collection of photographic resources gathered by Bengt Hallinger, a graduate student at Linkoping University in Linkoping, Sweden.
- http://sunsite.unc.edu/nppa/, home of the National Press Photographers Association.
- http:/www.i3tele.com/photo_perspectives_museum/faces/perspectives.home.html, the Photo Perspectives home.

Fig. 11-2: Australian National University provides a focus on Mediterranean art and architecture in its Web site called Art Serve.

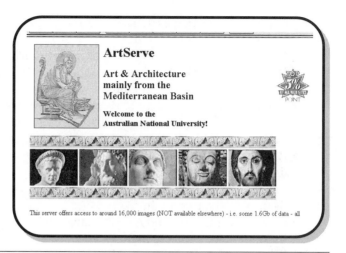

Architecture

Architectural studies are advanced curriculum not available to college freshmen and sophomores. However, many arts and humanities classes consider architecture as part of their lessons. And network resources can give the student a flavor of the broader reach of architecture as well.

One of the premier Internet architectural resources began as a University of Michigan Gopher server dedicated to the dissemination of architectural knowledge (libra.arch.umich.edu). In 1995 ArchiGopher moved to a Web site at http://libra.caup.umich.edu/ArchiGopher/ where it serves up images of paintings, computer-aided design models, as well as more traditional architectural material.

Architects need to deal with more down-to-earth zoning and planning requirements beyond the more artistic design concerns. Dan Tasman of the University at Buffalo maintains the Planning and Architecture Internet Resource Center at http://www.arch.buffalo.edu/pairc/, which includes links to extensive resources on planning, zoning, economic development, design competitions, journals and many other areas of interest to architects.

The Architecture Virtual Library similarly includes a wide range of resource links as well as a topic search capability from http://www.clr.toronto.edu:1080//VIRTUALLIB/arch.html. Another general architectural resource site with links to a wide range of resources is maintained by Nick Birchall at http://www.u-net.com/~birchall/arch.htm.

You may join e-mail discussion lists dealing with fine arts and architecture by sending the message "Subscribe *LISTNAME your name*" to a machine, typically using the address scheme "listserv@*host.domain*." More detailed instructions are given in Chapter 3. Some lists of interest include

- Student Artist Discussions, ARTIST-L, listserv@uafsysb.uark.edu.
- Fine-Art Forum, FINE-ART, listserv@rutvm1.rutgers.edu.
- Discuss Issues Relevant to Contemporary Art, ARTLIST, listserv@listserv.arizona.edu.
- Basic and applied design (Art and Architecture), DESIGN-L, listserv@psuvm.psu.edu.
- Ceramic Arts Discussion List, CLAYART, listserv@ukcc.uky.edu.
- RLG Art and Architecture, RLGART-L, listserv@yalevm.cis.yale.edu.
- Landscape Architecture Electronic Forum, LARCH-L, listserv@listserv.syr.edu.
- Consortium for Art and Architectural Historians, CAAH, listserv@pucc.princeton.edu.
- Beginning Photographers, BEGIN-PHOTO, listserv@listserv.arizona.edu.

Performing arts

Those expressive arts that take place within a clearly defined time frame and often require a stage are generally grouped under the title of performing arts. Included are music, drama and dance. Internet resources tend to be longer on the traditional music variety, including digitized recordings of music of all kinds, sheet music and historical documents.

Dance

Sites specializing in dance resources sometimes single out a particular style of dance or focus on a geographical area or one dance company's schedule. General dance resources on the Net include Internet Dance Information Sources at http://www.webspace.com/~wingrove/links.htm, the World Wide Web Virtual Library dance resources at http://www.tmn.com/Artswire/www/dance/dance.html, James S. White Ballet's Dance Links at http://bohr.physics.purdue.edu/~jswhite/dance_links.html, Marv Vandehey's Dance Directory at http://www.cyberspace.com/vandehey/dance.html, and Steve Allen's Dance Index Page (specializing in folk dance) at http://ucowww.ucsc.edu/~sla/dance/dance.html.

Dance resources allied with particular companies include the San Francisco Ballet at http://www-leland.stanford.edu/~rbeal/sfb.html, Ohio State University Department of Dance at http://www.dance.ohio-state.edu/, Butler University Department of Dance at http://www.butler.edu/~laurent/dance_homepage.html, the Southern California Dance and Directory pages at http://www.usc.edu/dept/dance/, and American Dance Festival pages at http://www.nando.net/events/dance/dance.html.

Theater or drama

One extensive guide to drama or theater resources on the network is maintained by Deborah Torres and Martha Vander Kolk of the University of Michigan School of Information and Library Studies, available at http://www.ircam.fr/divers/theatre-e.html. This is a broad index of resources organized by Internet tool and by subjects, which include such things as medieval drama, historical costumes, and modern performance studies. An index to professional commercial theater production worldwide is maintained at http://www.fleethouse.com/fhcanada/western/bc/van/entertan/hqe/net-link.htm.

Intuitons, a student-run experimental theater company at the University of Pennsylvania maintains a guide to resources for the collegiate theater community. The guide is located at http://dolphin.upenn.edu/~intuiton/guide.html. The UCSB English server listed under literature (and mirrored at Oxford University) has a strong complement of dramatic literature links at http://humanitas.ucsb.edu/shuttle/english2.html#drama. Links to Net resources of several dozen theater companies may be found at http://www.yahoo.com/Arts/Drama/Theater_Companies/.

Online journals treating the drama landscape include *The Drama Review* at http://www-mitpress.mit.edu/jrnls-catalog/tdr.html and *Theater Insight* at http://www.utexas.edu/students/ti/.

Theatre Central is maintained by Andrew Kraft of MIT. Visitors to the site at http://www.mit.edu:8001/people/quijote/theatre-central.html are greeted with a table of contents for resources that include links to sites devoted to Broadway shows, Shakespeare, acting schools, theater calendars, and playwriting.

Buzz Communications' Casting Notice Bulletin Board is aimed at actors, producers and directors of stage and screen. Los Angeles and New York casting calls are posted as well as a few from other parts of the country. The Casting Notice Bulletin Board is accessible at http://www.buzznyc.com/casting/bb.home.html.

For those who aspire to write for the theater, the Screenwriters' and Playwrights' Home Page offers primers and guides; sample scripts; tips; discussion groups; addresses for e-mail lists; interviews; and articles on stagecraft, writing, and plot development. The page is situated at http://www.teleport.com/~cdeemer/scrwriter.html.

A theater site focused on musical productions may be found in Gopher format at gopher://gopher.etext.org/11/Quartz/theater. The site includes lyrics of many productions, FAQs, and other resources. The site suggests another of the performing arts, music.

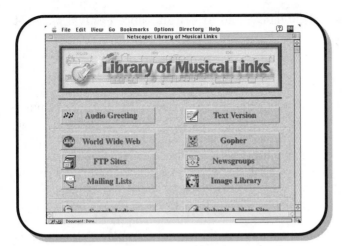

Fig. 11-3: Jason Rush, a student, created and maintains an extensive Library of Musical Links on the Internet.

Music

Music resources on the Net include digital recordings, the software to play those recordings, sheet music, lyrics, papers on music theory and composition, magazines, journals, discussion lists, news groups, individual band home pages, and even live radio broadcasts.

An exhaustive index of musical resources on the Net is maintained by the Sibelius Academy, the only music university in Finland. The list of resources and links is divided into stylistic categories ranging from Church Music to Composers to MIDI to Ethnomusicology. Music Resources occupies net space at http://www.siba.fi/Kulttuuripalvelut/music.html. The University of Washington Music Library in a similar fashion maintains a reference desk of Internet resources at http://www.lib.washington.edu:80/libinfo/libunits/soc-hum/music/resource.html.

Music theory and history resources available on the Internet include Music Theory Online at http://boethius.music.ucsb.edu/mto/mtohome.html, the Early Music Web at http://www.sirius.com/~justinr/em2.html, and a Renaissance music notation site at http://q.continuum.net/~raybro/phpl.cgi?index1.html.

For musicians Scott Lehman maintains a collection of links to musicians' resources on the Internet. The site has a keyword search facility and is grouped by subject areas including New Products, Guitar, Keyboards and Synthesizers, MIDI, Bands, Software and Services. Called Harmony Central, the site is located at http://harmony-central.mit.edu/.

Indiana University Music Library people maintain a major site providing links to other Web sites, Gopher sites and more. The index gives a virtual visitor the opportunity to browse by academic sites or not, by geography, by artist, and by using other major network music indices. There is even an area set up by users with alphabetized listings. The Music Resources on the

Internet site is just about as exhaustive a network music resource as one might find on the Internet. It is located at http://www.music.indiana.edu/misc/music_resources.html.

For those who have an interest in Johann Sebastian Bach, his music and his life, the J.S. Bach Home Page at http://www.tile.net/bach/ provides links to resources treating all. Lists of recordings of Bach's music are organized along several lines. There are also links to archives of MIDI (Musical Instrument Digital Interface) files containing Bach music.

Another major listing of musical resources is the creation of Jason Rush, a student at the University of Southern California. His Library of Musical Links is organized on the basis of Internet protocol (FTP, Gopher, Web, mail, Usenet) but also provides a search engine. Rush invites visitors who know of sites he has not included in his library to suggest them for inclusion. The site is found at http://www-scf.usc.edu/~jrush/music/.

Some other sites catering to more popular music are The Lyrics Page at http://vivarin.pc.cc.cmu.edu/lyrics.html; Musical Places on the Net at http://www.crl.com/~djconn/music.html; and The Ultimate Band List, which calls itself the "web's largest interactive list of music links where" visitors can add links to their favorite bands. You can browse the bands alphabetically, by genre, or by network protocol. The Ultimate Band List is housed at http://american.recordings.com/wwwofmusic/ubl/ubl.shtml.

The MIDI Home Page at http://www.eeb.ele.tue.nl/midi/ contains a good deal of information on the MIDI digital music standard. Several places on the Internet contain music archives in MIDI and other formats.

- The Internet Underground Music Archive at http://www.iuma.com/, which includes listings according to band name and recording label, links to online magazines, and news of the music industry.
- The Classical MIDI Archives at http://198.68.188.62/midi.html (classical music stored in MIDI format).
- The DannySoft MIDI Archive, with digital recordings of classical music, TV themes, seasonal material, and a "miscellaneous" category, accessed at http://www.xensei.com/users/savilon/midi/.

You may join e-mail discussion lists dealing with performing arts by sending the message "Subscribe *LISTNAME your name*" to a machine, typically using the address scheme "listserv@*host.domain*." More detailed instructions are given in Chapter 3. Some lists of interest include

- The Theatre Discussion List, THEATRE, listserv@pucc.princeton.edu.
- Theatre History Discussion List, ASTR-L, listserv@vmd.cso.uiuc.edu.
- The Women and Theatre Program Discussion List, WTP-L, listserv@uhccvm.uhcc.hawaii.edu.
- Theatre and musical artists, composers, COLLAB-L, listserv@psuvm.psu.edu.

- Medieval Performing Arts, PERFORM,
  listserv@iubvm.ucs.indiana.edu.
- Records of Early English Drama Discussion, REED-L,
  listserv%utoronto.bitnet@listserv.net.
- Music History, MUS330A, listserv@listserv.arizona.edu.
- University of Buffalo Music Theory List, UBMUT-L,
  listserv@ubvm.cc.buffalo.edu.
- Discussions on all forms of music, ALLMUSIC,
  listserv@american.edu.
- Academic Discussion of Popular Music, ROCKLIST,
  listserv@kentvm.kent.edu.
- Electronic Music Discussion List, EMUSIC-L,
  listserv@american.edu.
- Bluegrass music discussion, BGRASS-L, listserv@ukcc.uky.edu.
- Folk music presenters, FOLKVENU, listserv@psuvm.psu.edu.
- Music Education, MUSIC-ED, listserv@vm1.spcs.umn.edu.
- Classical Music List, CLASSM-L, listserv@brownvm.brown.edu.
- International folkdance and traditional dance list, DANCE-L,
  listserv@nic.surfnet.nl.
- Dance Heritage Coalition List, DANCE-HC,
  listserv@cunyvm.cuny.edu.
- Renaissance Dance Mailing List, RENDANCE,
  listserv@morgan.ucs.mun.ca.
- Morris Dancing Discussion List, MORRIS,
  listserv@indycms.iupui.edu.
- Discussion of Any Aspect of Ballroom and Swing Dancing,
  BALLROOM, listserv@mitvma.mit.edu.

Philosophy

Historically, philosophy encompasses much of the knowledge, wisdom and understanding of humankind. The study of philosophy used to embrace such subjects as astronomy, biology, chemistry, ethics, government, logic, mathematics, music, physics, psychology and sociology. To this very day, the highest academic degree in all of these fields is the Ph.D., or Doctor of Philosophy. And while we today break these areas of study into separate fields, philosophy still touches on all learning and intellectual pursuits. The very word philosophy comes to us from ancient Greek terms meaning "love of wisdom," and it is free from discipline area boundaries.

If you become a philosophy student today, you will find that the study of philosophy tends to be divided into five major categories:

- Metaphysics deals with the principles, substances and meanings that underlie all tangible reality. It encompasses speculation upon the nature of being, of the cause, substance, and purpose of everything. It deals with questions of space and time, distinctions

Fig. 11-4: Bjorn Christensson's Guide to Philosophy page permits keyword searching on terms contained in the writings of many philosophers.

between things and ideas, and whether there is a first cause, or God, that has made everything and put it into motion.

- Epistemology ponders the limits of human knowledge. It ponders such questions as whether the world is really as we perceive it, or do people perceive only appearances that conceal the true substance of reality. It asks how we know things and what is the nature of knowledge.
- Logic is the science of thinking. It concerns methods for testing rational arguments and standards for assessing the validity of those arguments and the conclusions drawn from them. Logic is related to scientific hypotheses and to mathematics.
- Ethics concerns itself with questions of moral behavior and the responsibilities people have to each other and to society as a whole. As ethicists debate whether there are absolute standards of behavior or only situational standards, they come very close to religion as a discipline.
- Aesthetics deals with the nature of beauty, the arts, and taste. Aesthetics deals with the question of how humans judge what is beautiful. Is it a rational process, or is it merely an emotional preference?

The scope of philosophy remains so broad in the topics upon which it touches that it seems to comprehend all of the humanities and perhaps a few other areas as well. Still, sticking with the areas we have defined here, one might try the following locations.

Net resources on philosophy

On general philosophy, the American Philosophical Association maintains both Gopher resources (gopher://apa.oxy.edu/) and Web access (http://

www.oxy.edu/apa/apa.html). The Gopher server is home to a bulletin board service as well. Both sites provide not only pertinent local documents but also links to many other Internet resources. Valdosta State University in Georgia hosts a Resources in Philosophy site with extensive links to philosophical resources at http://www.valdosta.peachnet.edu/~rbarnett/phi/resource.html.

McGill University maintains a philosophy Web server at http://www.philo.mcgill.ca/. Boston University provides an annotated catalog of philosophy and religion sites available on the Net at http://web.bu.edu/LIBRARY/Religion/contents.html; http://www.ed.ac.uk/~ejua35/phillink.htm.

Other general resources include Bjorn's Guide to Philosophy, with links to the works and biographies of philosophers as well as to many other Web resources in philosophy. Bjorn Christensson's guide may be found at http://www-und.ida.liu.se/~y92bjoch/. The Philosophers Page permits keyword searching for terms contained in the writings of many philosophers, whose works are accessible through a pull-down menu. Links to a few other sites are included. The resource is accessed at http://129.101.39.86/Philosophy/default.htm. Sean Cearley has created Sean's One Stop Philosophy Shop, accessible at http://www.rpi.edu/~cearls/phil.html, an encyclopedic gathering of links to network resources in philosophy.

On metaphysics, Michael Heim maintains a collection of resources at http://www.jovanet.com/~mheim/index.html; Metaphysical Review can be found at http://einstein.unh.edu:1905/MetaphysicalReview/MetaphysicalReview.html; and the Metaphysics Research Lab at Stanford University may be reached at http://mally.stanford.edu:80/.

Those interested in epistemology have as a dedicated network resource, the work of Onar Am, whose Origins of Knowledge page may be accessed at http://www.hsr.no/~onar/.

For logic, Marco Hollenberg maintains a collection of document preprints on a server at the Univeristy of Utrecht in Holland, http://www.phil.ruu.nl:80/home/marco/preprints.html.

Ethicists have journals online, including The Ethical Spectacle at http://www.spectacle.org/ and the Journal of Buddhist Ethics at http://www.cac.psu.edu/jbe/jbe.html. On a practical note, the Institute for Business & Professional Ethics maintains a web site at DePaul University, http://www.depaul.edu:80/ethics/.

A school of philosophy known as objectivism, born from the writings of Ayn Rand, has inspired many resources on the Internet, including a site called Objectivism on the WWW maintained by Diana Mertz Brickell at http://avocado.wustl.edu/~diana/objectivism/ and the Objectivism WWW Service at http://www.vix.com:80/pub/objectivism/.

Similarly, German philosopher Friedrich Nietzsche has enough of a network following that he has a home page at http://www.usc.edu/dept/annenberg/thomas/nietsche.html. The site provides bibliographies in German and English, links to several Nietzsche societies and to Nietzsche scholarship. Adherents to New Age metaphysics have created a site called the School of Wisdom at http://www.webcom.com/~metanoic/wisdom/, and Steven A. Brown has provided a collection of links to Chinese philosophy at http://www.monash.edu.au/cc/staff/sas/sab/WWW/index.html.

You may join e-mail discussion lists dealing with philosophy by sending the message "Subscribe *LISTNAME your name*" to a machine, typically using the address scheme "listserv@*host.domain*." More detailed instructions are given in Chapter 3. Some lists of interest include

- The Electronic Journal of Analytic Philosophy, EJAP, listserv@iubvm.ucs.indiana.edu.
- Forum for Discussion of the History of the Philosophy of Science, HOPOS-L, listserv@ukcc.uky.edu.
- Moderated Discussion of Objectivist Philosophy _ Technical, AYN-TECH, listserv@iubvm.ucs.indiana.edu.
- Moderated Discussion of Objectivist Philosophy, AYN-RAND, listserv@iubvm.ucs.indiana.edu.
- Society for Women in Philosophy Information and Discussion List, SWIP-L, listserv@cfrvm.cfr.usf.edu.
- Medieval Philosophy and Political Thought List, MDVLPHIL, listserv@lsuvm.sncc.lsu.edu.
- American Philosophical Association, APACIC-L, listserv@cmsa.berkeley.edu.

History

Systematic reconstruction of societies' pasts leads to the building of history. Histories in turn shed light on the present and suggest possibilities for the future of societies. The recording of history and its discussion represent other ways that humankind sets itself apart from the rest of the animal kingdom and seeks to bring meaning and order to life. History helps people understand events of the past and their relationships to them. The Athenian historian Thucydides suggested that history provides us with the only introduction we have to our own futures.

Historians traditionally have organized the story of man into ages or epochs delineated by major events, significant inventions, great wars, or the leadership of remarkable rulers. Many of those divisions are arbitrary. Thus historians of Western Europe have generally lighted upon Columbus' discovery of the New World as the beginning of the Renaissance and the end of the Dark Ages. But many elements of the Renaissance had begun to express themselves long before Columbus set sail.

The divisions historians affix to the story of humankind almost always includes geopolitical boundaries (Western Europe in the previous example). Historical resources archived on the Internet similarly are divided by geopolitical boundaries as well as arbitrary divisions in time. The number of

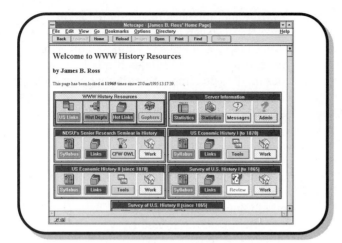

Fig. 11-5: The WWW History Resources site maintained by James B. Ross provides a series of icons to activate links to history resources.

documents, collections and resources is almost as numerous as the number of events in all of history. What follows is only a small sampling.

The University of Southern California and the Los Angeles City Historical Society have combined to create the History Computerization Project. The project's Web site, at http://www.directnet.com/history/, includes a massive directory of historical resources on the Internet. The directory is arranged alphabetically by sponsoring or hosting organization (university, historical society or other group). There is no keyword searching engine. Thus unless you know who has charge of the information you seek, the sheer size of the directory could make it difficult to find what you want in a hurry.

The World History Archives at Central Connecticut State University are home to "documents that support an understanding of world history and the struggle for social progress," and are housed at http://neal.ctstateu.edu:80/history/world_history/archives/archives.html. Archive resources are organized around issues and by large global regions such as The Americas and the Pacific Region. The archives site is associated with another project called The Gateway to World History at http://neal.ctstateu.edu:80/history/world_history/world_history.html. The Gateway project offers search tools, reference works and links to a wide range of academic resources for the study and understanding of history.

The University of Kansas is home to the World Wide Web Virtual Library History resources at http://history.cc.ukans.edu:80/history/WWW_history_main.html. At Kansas, history resources on the Internet are indexed in four schemes: alphabetically by resource name, by era, by region, and by subject.

The Institute of Historical Research at the University of London provides a simple and direct interface to many resources at http://ihr.sas.ac.uk:8080/.

The number of special collections—historical documents on some narrow area of focus—accessible through the Internet is staggering. They range from collections on individual nations to collections on individual wars to focuses on movements and even on single events.

For example, James B. Ross at North Dakota State University maintains an extensive list of resources on U.S. History at http://134.129.87.200/jrhome.htm. Yahoo (http://www.yahoo.com) lists 21 sites with U.S. Civil War collections. Another interesting U.S. History resource is the Library of Congress American Memory collection. It is composed of primary source and archival material relating to American culture and history. Billed as the Library of Congress' key contribution to the national digital library, it resides at http://rs6.loc.gov/amhome.html.

Julia Hayden maintains a major resource called The Ancient World Web at http://atlantic.evsc.virginia.edu/julia/AW.html. The hundreds of resources indexed at the site are organized in three ways: geographically, by subject, and in a meta index (alphabetical listing of all resources). Another ancient history site goes by the name of Diogenes' Links To The Ancient World at http://www.snider.net/lyceum/.

The EuroDocs page at Brigham Young University focuses on primary historical documents from Western Europe and can be accessed at http://library.byu.edu/~rdh/eurodocs/. There is a special collection of medieval and Renaissance articles, texts and manuscripts maintained at Indiana University at http://www.honors.indiana.edu/~atrium/atrium.html. The Cybrary of the Holocaust may be accessed at http://www.best.com/~mddunn/cybrary/. And Texas A&M University maintains a Soviet Archives collection at gopher://gopher.tamu.edu:70/11/.dir/soviet.archives.dir.

This last resource illustrates an important principle. A good many historical resources are served up in Gopher format. They include

- The University of Heidelberg (Germany) History Gopher at gopher://gopher.urz.uni-heidelberg.de:70/11/subject/hd/fak7/hist.
- Tennessee Tech's History Gopher at gopher://gopher.tntech.edu:70/11gopher_root%3a%5bcampus.as.hist%5d.
- The National Archives and Records Administration Gopher at gopher://gopher.nara.gov/.
- The Mountain Net Gopher has a fair collection of historical documents linked at gopher://gopher.mountain.net:70/11/History.
- Texas A&M University Gopher lists many historical resources at gopher://gopher.tamu.edu:70/11/.dir/history.dir.
- A special collection of historical documents resides on the Cornell University Law School Gopher at gopher://fatty.law.cornell.edu:70/11/foreign/historical/.
- The Wiretap Gopher keeps an archive of U.S. historical documents at gopher://wiretap.spies.com/11/Gov/US-History.

Whole libraries of historical documents, papers and other historical resources are available through the Internet. The possibilities for doing historical research are limited only by the student's imagination.

You may join e-mail discussion lists dealing with history by sending the message "Subscribe *LISTNAME your name*" to a machine, typically using the address scheme "listserv@*host.domain*." More detailed instructions are given in Chapter 3. Some lists of interest include

- History–Peer Distribution List, HISTORY, listserv@ukanvm.cc.ukans.edu.
- H-Net List for World History, H-WORLD, listserv@msu.edu.
- Historians' Newsletter, HISTNEWS, listserv@ukanvm.cc.ukans.edu.
- H-Net Western History List, H-WEST, listserv@msu.edu.
- Forum on non-Eurocentric world history, WORLD-L, listserv@ubvm.cc.buffalo.edu.
- Medieval History List, MEDIEV-L, listserv@ukanvm.cc.ukans.edu.
- H-Net List for Women's History, H-WOMEN, listserv@msu.edu.
- Early Modern History Forum, EMHIST-L, listserv@rutvm1.rutgers.edu.
- H-Net and ASLH Legal History Discussion list, H-LAW, listserv@msu.edu.
- Early Modern History – Renaissance List, RENAIS-L, listserv@ulkyvm.louisville.edu.
- H-Net Western History List, H-WEST, listserv@uicvm.uic.edu.
- H-Net History Graduate Students discussion list, H-GRAD, listserv@uicvm.uic.edu.

Foreign language

Among the secrets of mastering a foreign language are the activities of using the language as much as you can and of coming to understand the culture(s) in which the language is used. In the first case, using the language refers not to translating but to engaging in activities where you are encouraged to actually think in the language in question. Listen to radio programs using the language, attend operas if appropriate, read books and stories in the language in question, converse and correspond with others using the language you are learning. In the second case, more governments and government agencies are coming online each month. Their offerings include cultural ministries, tourism bureaus, and others that provide information— sometimes in multilingual offerings.

The Internet can be a powerful ally for learning foreign language and culture. The Net is global in its scope. It is as easy to send e-mail to the Ukraine as it is to send it across town. It is as easy to connect to a network site in Egypt or Australia as it is to one in Arizona or Alberta. And this suggests a pair of strategies available to the Net-connected foreign language student that can really accelerate mastery of any foreign language. First, read online newspapers that employ your language. Second, join discussion groups (e-mail lists) that address the cultural concerns of people who use your language. Third, search out network sites that incorporate the language you are studying.

Foreign language mass media

Newspapers and other mass media organizations worldwide have set up shop on the World Wide Web. Their offerings represent for the foreign language student wonderful opportunities to use the language and to gain cultural, political and historical insights that can only help in the quest to master the language. A few Web sites serve as clearinghouses from which you can select newspapers and/or other media presentations from a wide variety of sources. Some may be found at

- http://www.newslink.org/menu.html.
- http://www.algonet.se/~nikos/broadeuro.html.
- http://www.yahoo.com/Business_and_Economy/
  Business_Directory/ Companies/ Media/Newspapers/.

In addition to using these general sites, you might want to try a few specific ones. If you are studying Russian, you may find the Russian newspaper *Izvestia* online at http://www.online.ru/mlists/izvestia/izvestia-izvestia/. Information on several Eastern European countries can be found at http://www.itaiep.doc.gov/eebic/ceebic.html.

Media organizations from the Czech Republic have material in Czech, English, French, German, and Spanish at http://www.columbia.edu/~js322/czech.html.

Spanish: The Spanish embassy in Canada sponsors a Web site with background information on Spain, traveler's information and access to Spanish newspapers. The site is located at http://www.DocuWeb.ca/SiSpain/media/menu.html. A broad range of Mexican information resources may be accessed at http://condor.dgsca.unam.mx:2500/noticias.html. A few Mexican newspapers on the World Wide Web include *El Norte,* http://www.infosel.com.mx/elnorte/; *Excelsior,* http://worldnews.net/excelsior/excelsior.html; *El Diario de Monterrey,* http://www.pixel.com.mx/diariomty/; *Reforma,* http://www.infosel.com.mx/reforma/; and the bilingual *La Prensa* http://www.hispanic.com/LaPrensa/LaPrensa.html.

French: The Swiss news magazine *L'Hebdo* may be reached at http://www.hebdo.ch; Swiss government, http://www.admin.ch/.

German: Austrian business magazine, *Wirtschafts Woche,* http://www.wirtschaftswoche.co.at/wirtschaftswoche/; Swiss government, http://www.admin.ch/

Italian: Newspaper, *Corriere Della Sera,* http://www.comm2000.it/rcs/; Swiss government, http://www.admin.ch/; Italian Embassy Virtual Newsstand, http://www.italyemb.nw.dc.us/italy/virtnews.htm.

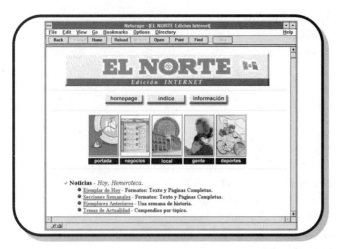

Fig. 11-6: Foreign language media, such as the online version of *El Norte,* shown here, can be helpful in gaining an understanding of a language and the cultures that use it.

Greek: Newspapers *Thessaloniki* and *Makedonia* at http://www.hyper.gr/makthes/.

Swedish: Many resources available from http://www2.e.kth.se/esekt/org/tidningar.html; *Norkopings Tidingss* at http://www.uc.nt.se/nt/; Swedish radio, http://www.sr.se; Swedish television, http://www.svt.se; Nordic News and Media, http://www.algonet.se/~nikos/nordmed.html.

Chinese: From Hong Kong, *Ming Pao Daily News* at http://www.hknet.com/mingpao.

Japanese: Shima Media Network, http://www.smn.co.jp/week/; Asahi News, http://www.asahi.com/.

You may join e-mail discussion lists dealing with foreign languages by sending the message "Subscribe *LISTNAME your name*" to a machine, typically using the address scheme "listserv@*host.domain*." More detailed instructions are given in Chapter 3. Some lists of interest include

- Foreign Language Teaching Forum, FLTEACH, listserv@ubvm.cc.buffalo.edu.
- Japanese Language Discussion List, NIHONGO, listserv@mitvma.mit.edu.
- Latin American Linguistics and Languages Discussion List, LATAMLIN, listserv@mitvma.mit.edu.
- Discussion about Spain and its people, ESPANA-L, listserv@cnsibm.albany.edu.
- Forum de discussio per a catalanoparlants, CATALA, listserv@aliga.cesca.es.
- German News, DE-NEWS, listserv@vm.gmd.de.
- Recherche & discussion entre francophones, surtout du Canada, FRANCO-L, listserv%ualtavm.bitnet@listserv.net.

- Discussion list for Italianists, ITALIA-L, listserv@irlearn.ucd.ie.
- Russian History Forum, RUSHIST, listserv@earn.cvut.cz.
- Russian Club at MIT Discussion List, RAMIT-L, listserv@mitvma.mit.edu.
- Russian History Forum, RUSHIST, listserv@umrvmb.umr.edu.
- Swedish Initiative for a Research and Education Network, SIREN, listserv@searn.sunet.se.

Government and travel sites

Many nations have official or semiofficial national information servers sponsored by government. Travel and tourism interests have been aggressive about putting information on the Internet. A keyword search (Chapter 9) on the country's name should reveal relevant sources. A few sites bear particular mention.

City.Net (http://www.city.net) bills itself as "the most comprehensive international guide to communities around the world." Updated regularly, the site provides information on travel, entertainment and business, plus government and community services for all regions of the world. The site's focus, as the name implies, is on cities. You call up information on a city either through a search engine or through a geographical tree. When you locate the city you want, you may find anything from theater and restaurant listings to historical information. For the traveler, one very useful feature of City.Net is its link to a mass transportation server in France that provides maps of subway systems and will even provide routing information.

Craighead's Business Reports provides information to business travellers, including cultural information at http://www.craighead.com/craighead/#CBR.

The United States Department of State maintains information on many foreign countries accessible from the Library of Congress Gopher at gopher://marvel.loc.gov:70/11/federal/fedinfo/byagency/executive/state/. The State Department is directly accessible at http://dosfan.lib.uic.edu/dosfan.html and at gopher://dosfan.lib.uic.edu/. The Web site is searchable.

The World Factbook of the U.S. Central Intelligence Agency provides information on many nations. It is one of several useful CIA publications available at http://www.odci.gov/cia/publications/pubs.html.

Conclusion

The humanities, as a study of human creativity, encompass a broad range of activities and fields of study. History, philosophy, language, literature and the arts have filled museums and libraries with interesting exhibits. The Internet is also a rich repository of resource material on the humanities. Wise use of the Internet can be a powerful asset to an enriched college experience in the humanities.

Chapter

12

The social sciences grade

The social sciences involve the application of scientific methods to the study of human life including human behavior and activity. Of course, the study of human life and our ways of living is an extremely complex subject. Consequently the social sciences—or the human sciences as they are sometimes called—have been divided into specific categories of activity such as political and economic systems, the feelings and perceptions of individuals, interpersonal and mass communication processes, the way society is organized in general and the way societies conduct everyday business. The last category includes such activities as culture, religion and education.

Social scientists attempt to study human activity in a specific area according to a specific research methodology. Based on the observations they make and the data they collect, social scientists then try to draw generalizations and conclusions that can explain, and sometimes predict, specific types of human behavior. Sociologists, for example, try to understand why industrial societies like the United States are organized in the way they are. Political scientists try to unravel the implications of the different ways nations and societies govern themselves.

As in other scientific activity, social scientists will usually organize their investigations or experiments within the context of a specific theory. In sociology for example, Karl Marx developed a powerful theory of the relationship of the organization of the economy to politics and social life. A lot of the study of society in the twentieth century was strongly influenced by that theory. In psychology, Sigmund Freud developed a theory of the unconscious that dominated research in that area for more than half a century.

Some social sciences also have an applied component as well. That is, professionals try to apply research findings to practical tasks. Psychologists, for example, not only want to understand the way the mind works, they wish to develop theories to help people maintain their mental health. Anthropologists may help corporations build a more productive internal culture.

In this section, you will find Internet resources for five of the major disciplines within the social sciences: psychology, political science, sociology and anthropology, communications, and education. Economics, which is also generally considered a social science, will be included in Chapter 13 on business. In a well-rounded undergraduate education, you will usually be required to take at least two courses in social science. An undergraduate major in social science is often excellent preparation for graduate work in a wide range of professional fields including law, business, the media and psychology.

Psychology

Psychology is the study of the human mind or psyche. The field is divided into a myriad of smaller categories including: human development, which looks at the psychological changes people experience as they grow older; personality, which looks at the processes in which people become who they are; abnormal psychology, which looks at human behavior that flows outside commonly accepted bounds; perception, which tries to understand how people experience the world through their senses; sexual development, which looks at the process of assuming a sexual orientation; cognitive psychology, which includes intelligence and language; behavior, which studies how people act (as opposed to how they say they feel); as well as neuroscience, addiction, and more. Finally, psychology has a long-standing therapeutic tradition that involves counseling.

A good starting point to find resources on the Internet for psychologists is Psychological Resources on the Internet, Sorted by Topic at http://www.gasou.edu/psychweb/resource/bytopic.htm. A little like an index in a book, this site provides links to resources in 18 subdivisions of psychology including the application of psychology within specific areas like health, education, organizations and sports.

Another comprehensive site with links to resources in psychology is the Resources for Psychology and Cognitive Sciences on the Internet at http://sasuke.shinshu-u.ac.jp/psych. Maintained at Shinshu University in Nangano, Japan, this server offers a keyword search for resources and has links to psychology departments around the world as well as many online psychology journals including *Behavior Therapy*, the *American Journal of Psychology* and the *Journal of Artificial Intelligence Research*.

The American Psychological Association is the primary professional organization for more than 132,000 psychologists in North America. It maintains a rich Web resource at http://www.apa.org. Users can access brochures about issues in mental health, read several of the APA's publications and gain insight into a wide range of issues in which psychologists are involved or about which they should be concerned. This site provides an excellent window for students into psychology as it is practiced in the real world.

Fig. 12-1: The New York Psychoanalytic Institute and Society is a leading center of Freudian psychology.

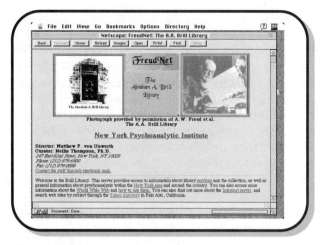

Arc, the country's largest voluntary organization for people with mental retardation, their families, and professionals in the field of mental disabilities and related areas has a site at http://fohnix.metronet.com/~thearc/welcome.html. With more than 1,100 chapters and 140,000 members, Arc has adopted positions on issues that affect people with mental retardation and their families. People involved with developmental psychology might find this an appropriate stopping point.

People interested in addiction should try the home page of the National Center for Alcohol and Drug Information (NCADI) at http://www.health.org. A service of the U.S. Public Health Service, NCADI is the world's largest resource for current information about alcohol and other drugs. It also maintains an electronic network dedicated to exchanging ideas about abuse prevention.

As with other social sciences, there are several seminal thinkers in psychology whose ideas have had a major impact on the field over time. Sigmund Freud is considered the founder of modern psychology. The New York Psychoanalytic Institute and Society, a leading center of orthodox Freudian psychology, maintains a home page at http://plaza.interport.net/nypsan. You can find back issues of the *Journal of Clinical Psychoanalysis* there. An overview of Sigmund Freud himself, including his biography, techniques, insights into his theory of the mind and a bibliography are at http://www.iris.brown.edu/iris/freud/Freud_OV_274.html.

A close associate and disciple of Freud, Carl Jung, eventually broke sharply with him and established his own distinct school of psychological thought. An anthology of Jung's writings is found at http://miso.wwa.com/~nebcargo/Jung. The purpose of the site, according to its creator, is to gather as many of Jung's writings as possible to serve as a primer and refresher about his work.

Swiss psychologist Jean Piaget made major theoretical and empirical contributions to developmental psychology. The Jean Piaget Society has a home page at http://www.wimsey.com/~chrisl/JPS/JPS.html. The site includes information about the society itself; appropriate conferences; links to other developmental psychology Web pages and Internet resources; information about the Piaget Society's online discussion list (to which you can subscribe by sending an e-mail message to "listserv@nic.umass.edu" with the command "subscribe piaget-l *yourname*" in the body of the message); and access to the online journal, the *Genetic Epistemologist*.

Many other journals about psychology are available via the Internet as well. The *Journal of Applied Behavior Analysis*, which reports on experimental research into application of behavior analysis to social problems, is available at http://www.envmed.rochester.edu/wwwrap/behavior/jaba/jabahome.htm. The *Journal of Mind and Behavior* is dedicated to an interdisciplinary approach to psychology and related fields. It can be found at http://kramer.ume.maine.edu/%7Ejmb/Welcome.html. *Psycoloquy* is a refereed electronic journal sponsored by the American Psychological Association. It publishes articles and commentary in all areas of psychology, cognitive science, behavior biology, linguistics, philosophy and more. *Psycoloquy* is accessible via Gopher, FTP or the Web at ftp://ftp.princeton.edu/pub/harnad/Psycoloquy/. It is also a Usenet Newsgroup at sci.psychology.journals.psycoloquy.

Personality assessment is an important aspect of psychology. You can get a demonstration copy of PDQ-4(c), a user-friendly interactive program that identifies personality disorders at http://travel1.travel-net.com/~alphalog/alpha1.html.

There are several electronic discussion lists for people interested in psychology. The quality of the discussion and the activity on the list varies greatly. To subscribe to a list, send a message to "listserv@*location-of-list*" with the message "subscribe *LISTNAME yourname*." Don't forget to unsubscribe when you no longer wish to be on the list. (See Chapter 3 for more detailed instructions.) Some relevant lists are Counpsy@uga.cc.uga.edu (Counseling Psychology Practice and Science), Psycgrad@adadvm1.uottawa.ca (Psychology Graduate Students), Psysts-l@mizzou1.missouri.edu (Psychology Statistics Discussion).

Political science

Political science is the study of the politics of the way societies govern themselves. The field is generally divided into several major areas including political theory, political institutions, political process, public policy, comparative politics and international relations. Most introductory courses in the United States concentrate on American political institutions and processes, although a good grounding in political theory is considered essential.

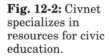

Fig. 12-2: Civnet specializes in resources for civic education.

The American Political Science Association, the primary academic association in the field, maintains a Gopher service at gopher:// apsa.trenton.edu:70/. Its purpose is to provide access to online resources useful for research and teaching in political science. It has links to other Gopher servers and Internet sites governing virtually every major subdivision of the discipline.

A guide to resources about political theory can be found at http:// swift.eng.ox.ac.uk/jdr/index.html. The page has been split into four sections ranging from classical theorists to contemporary political theory. The strongest material is found on modern political theorists from Machiavelli to Marx.

A vast library of resources about civic education including access to summaries of major historical documents ranging from the Magna Carta in 1215, the Virginia Declaration of Rights in 1776 and the French Declaration of Rights in 1789 to the Helsinki Accords in 1975 and Elie Wiesel's Dedication of the Holocaust Museum in 1993 can be found on Civnet at http:// www.infomall.org:80/Showcase/civnet. Resources offered include book-length documents, articles, lesson plans and links to organizations involved with civic education and discourse on civil society.

Political institutions are those structures through which political life is conducted. In the United States, the first locus of study is generally the three branches of the federal government. As befitting the first baby boom presidency, the Clinton administration warmly embraced technology. Following the lead of the White House, both the executive and the legislative branches of government have gone online.

The White House is located at http://www.whitehouse.gov. There you can listen to an audio welcome message from the president or the vice president, tour the mansion, or get information about the operation of the executive branch of government. The White House Web site provides direct links

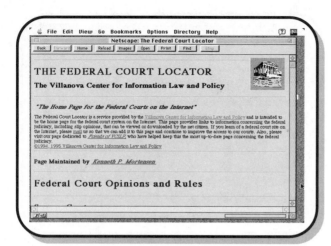

Fig. 12-3: The Federal Court Locator is an online resource housed at Villanova University.

to more than 25 executive agencies ranging from the Central Intelligence Agency to the Voice of America.

Another route into the executive branch of government is through FedWorld at http://www.fedworld.gov. Established in 1992 by the National Technical Information Service (NTIS), FedWorld's mandate is to provide "one-stop shopping" for governmental information. The FedWorld home page has links to 50 other government servers and has sorted information into categories, making it easier to identify the location of the information you want. NTIS receives more than 700 new pieces of information for distribution each week.

The U.S. House of Representatives and the U.S. Senate have also established sites on the Web. The House Web server at http://www.house.gov offers information about bills and resolutions being considered by Congress; information about what is happening on the floor of the House and information about how individual members of Congress voted on measures, the committees on which they serve, and the legislation that they have sponsored. There are links to Web pages and Gopher sites maintained by individual members as well as educational resources, visitor information and selected laws.

Not as tightly tied to the actual, ongoing legislative process, the Senate's Web page at http://www.senate.gov gives a rundown on the members of the Senate and their committee assignments. It also has background material including a brief history, a review of the legislative process, a glossary of terms and a historical bibliography. You can also take a virtual tour of the U.S. Capitol.

The General Accounting Office is Congress' investigative arm. It is responsible for auditing and evaluating government programs and often publishes reports on fraud, corruption and inefficiency in governmental programs.

You can access copies of its reports and testimony it has presented to Congress at http://www.gao.gov.

Given the nature of its deliberations, the U.S. Supreme Court has not embraced Internet technology. However, the Federal Court Locator at http://www.law.vill.edu/Fed-Ct/fedcourt.html is intended to serve as a home page for the federal court system. The page provides links to information about the court system including Supreme Court and Circuit Court of Appeals decisions. Supreme Court decisions from 1990 on are available via a keyword search at http://www.law.cornell.edu/supct/supct.table.html. The site also has some selected decisions from prior to 1990 including Roe v. Wade and decisions concerning school prayer.

Political institutions

The leaders of political institutions are chosen through a political process. In the United States and other participatory governments, elections are at the center of the political process; and political parties are integral players in election campaigns. The Republican National Committee, the organizing arm of the Republican Party at the national level, has a home page at http://www.rnc.org. Called Main Street on the Web, the site contains Republican perspectives on the issues of the day, links to the home pages of Republican candidates for national office, and a wide range of other Republican initiatives. You can also order gifts, clothing, and other paraphernalia with Republican insignia from the site.

The Democratic National Committee's home page is at http://www.democrats.org. You can find the latest remarks by President Clinton on the issues of the day, the Democrats' positions on the major issues of the day and other campaign-related information. You can also listen to a greeting from President Clinton or Mark Fowler, co-chairman of the DNC.

A nonpartisan source of information about candidates running for office is provided by Project Vote Smart at http://www.vote-smart.org. You can find biographies of candidates, summaries of where they stand on the issues and extensive contact information. It does not limit itself to just Democrats or Republicans.

In theory, if not in practice, election campaigns are waged around key issues and public policy proposals. PoliticsUSA at http://www.politicsusa.com/ is a source for nonpartisan news, analysis and information and a platform for multipartisan political dialogue. It contains information about issues like the environmental superfund and health care policy.

The Democratic Leadership Council and Progressive Policy Institute is an important Democratic-oriented think tank that devises public policy solutions to pressing social problems. Examples of its work can be found at http://www.dlcppi.org.

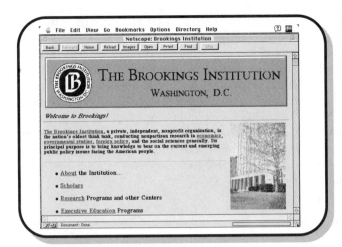

Fig. 12-4: The Brookings Institution is a nonpartisan research organization.

The Heritage Foundation is an important source of ideas for the Republican Party. Its home page is located at http://www.heritage.org. You can find press releases, position papers and copies of its journal, *Policy Review*. The objective of the Web site is to spread the ideas of free enterprise, limited government, individual freedom, a strong national defense and traditional American values. The Town Hall section of the page is intended to develop an interactive community for the discussion of conservative thought.

The Brookings Institution, the nation's oldest think tank, is a private, independent, nonpartisan research organization focusing on economics, foreign policy and the social sciences generally. Its objective is to bridge the gap between social science and policymaking. Its home page is at http://www.brook.edu. In addition to selected articles from *The Brookings Review*, one section of the home page represents a collection of links to home pages used regularly by Brookings researchers. Its *Think Tank Times* has pointers to the major U.S. and international news services.

Congressional Quarterly is an important source of information about the operation of government and the political process read by insiders in Washington. It operates a Gopher service at gopher://gopher.cqalert.com. You can find a selection of articles there.

Public opinion polling is a central feature of contemporary elections. The Gallup Poll is the oldest scientific polling company and one of the most respected. Its home page can be found at http://www.gallup.com. It offers an archive of the monthly Gallup Poll of current events and a statistical database.

Because politics is of deep interest to many people around the world, scores of discussion lists about political issues have emerged. The quality of the discussion and the activity on the list varies greatly. To subscribe to a list, send a message to "listserv@*location-of-list*" with the message "subscribe *LISTNAME yourname*." Don't forget to unsubscribe when you no longer wish to be on the list. (See Chapter 3 for more detailed instructions.) Some relevant lists are C-News@world.std.com (Conservative News Items), Cong-Reform@essential.org (Ralph Nader Congressional Reform), Dem-net@netcom.com (U.S. Democratic Party), ECA-L@gusvme1.gsu.edu (Eastern Europe and the Former Soviet Union Discussion), Femisa@csf.colorado.edu (Feminism and gender), Humanrights-l@acc.wuacc.edu (International Human Rights), Jpol@Israel.nysernet.org (Jewish Politics), Marxism@world.std.com (Marxism); Pofp-l@uga.cc.uga.edu (Public opinion and foreign policy); Polcomm@vm.its.rpi.edu (Political communication), and Psrt-l@mizzou1.missouri.edu (Political science teaching and research).

Sociology and anthropology

Both sociology and anthropology involve the study of people as they conduct their everyday activities. When both disciplines emerged toward the end of the 19th century, sociologists seemed more concerned with societies that had already industrialized—modern or advanced societies, in the words of the period—while anthropologists often studied life in regions of the world that had not yet industrialized. They called those societies premodern, or primitive societies.

One of the central features of an industrialized society is its class structure, in which people are generally grouped into the upper, middle or lower class. Traditionally, social structure has been a central locus of sociology. On the other hand, anthropologists have been interested in belief systems and social practices. Culture was at the center of the work of anthropologists.

Currently, however, the two disciplines have converged. While each has its separate intellectual heritage and theoretical positions as well as traditional research methodologies, both are concerned with a similar set of issues. Both are concerned with the way societies are organized, the way social life is maintained in a stable fashion, and the elements of social change. Both look at issues like social structures and community, organizations, social interaction, deviance and control, inequality and stratification, sex roles and the family, population dynamics, collective behavior and social movements, and social change.

Moreover, anthropologists also often study ancient societies in conjunction with archeologists. Physical anthropologists study social life among animals, search for fossils of early humans and explore population genetics. Anthropological linguistics traces the development of spoken languages.

Sociology has several well-defined subfields as well. Demography looks at the characteristics of human populations. Criminology studies crime, its prevention and punishment.

Both sociology and anthropology make use of different types of data. Quantitative researchers use data that can be represented by numbers and mathematical relationships. Qualitative researchers observe the social processes under study.

Links to many sources for both anthropologists and sociologists can be found at the American Studies Web at http://pantheon.cis.yale.edu/~davidp/soc.html. It has links to the World Wide Web Virtual Library for social sciences, the social science information gateway (which, in turn, has links to 500 social science sites on the Internet and is indexed and searchable), the University of Michigan Museum of Archeology, the Electronic Journal of Sociology, and more.

An excellent starting point for anthropologists can be found at http://sosig.erc.bris.ac.uk. It provides links to the Library of Visual Anthropology, the Institute for Social and Cultural Anthropology at Oxford University, and the Stanford University Anthropology Home Page, among others.

The Anthro-Gopher at Yale University is at gopher://toto.ycc.yale.edu:7000/1. It provides an international directory of scholars working in anthropology and archeology as well as the archives for the Usenet Newsgroups sci.anthropology and sci.archeology.

The Anthropology Collection at the Yale Peabody Museum at gopher://george.peabody.yale.edu:70/11/main/Anthropology is in the process of computerizing its collection. Almost 150,000 records detailing its ethnological holdings from North America, Southeast Asia and Oceania are available.

The Applied Anthropology Computer Network can be accessed via http://www.acs.oakland.edu/~dow/anthap.html. Intended for members of the Society for Applied Anthropology and the National Association of Practicing Anthropologists, it contains a bibliography of current anthropological methods, some full text papers and news on selected subjects.

Cultural studies draw from the field of anthropology, sociology, gender studies, psychology and feminism to discuss contemporary work and cultural practices. A server with links to a wide range of sources to introduce you to the issues and concerns of the field can be found at http://english-server.cmu.edu/theory.html. The sources include links ranging from serious contemporary social theorists such as Foucault and Sarte to more frivolous links such as CourtTV.

The Demography Home Page is located at http://www.ciesin.org/datasets/us-demog/us-demog-home.html. It is part of an initiative to provide simple access to demographic information about the United States. It has links to national data resources including the Census Bureau's current population survey, economic census data and county business patterns, online documentation such as citations and data dictionaries, and data extraction tools. Often the data sets involved can be downloaded via FTP.

The Princeton Office of Population Research at http://opr.princeton.edu/archive/archive.html holds a series of specialized datasets including the American Fertility Series, the European Fertility Series and the World Fertility Series. A good general site for people interested in demography can be found at http://coombs.anu.edu.au/ResFacilities/DemographyPage.html. It

Fig. 12-5: The applied Anthropology Computer Network is constructed for the members of the Society of Applied Anthropology and the National Association of Practicing Anthropologists.

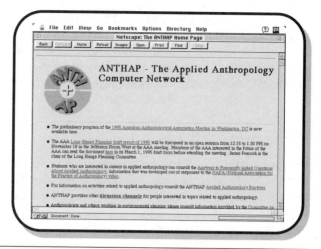

keeps track of leading facilities of value and significance to demographers. It currently has more than 140 links.

Another excellent source for data concerning political and social research can be found at the Inter-university Consortium for Political and Social Research at the University of Michigan. It runs a Gopher service at gopher://gopher.icpsr.umich.edu:70/1. Its mission is to archive and promote the use of social science data sets.

For people who are not comfortable using raw social science data, Jim Jacobs, the data services librarian at the University of California, San Diego, has created a glossary of social science data and computer terms. It can be found at http://odwin.ucsd.edu/glossary.

There have been several major thinkers in sociology. The writings of Marx, Engels, and Leon Trotsky can be found at http://english-www.hss.cmu.edu/marx.html. This holding mirrors the holdings of The Progressive Sociologists Network, which can be accessed at http://csf.Colorado.edu/psn. The writings of Emma Goldman, a major figure in the history of feminism and radicalism, are available at gopher://library.berkeley.edu:70/11/resdbs.soci/goldman.

Symbolic interaction is an important school of sociological thought. Symbolic interaction concentrates on qualitative research, particularly the interaction among people. The Society for the Study of Symbolic Interaction has a home page at http://sun.soci.niu.edu/~sssi.

The Division of Critical Criminology of the American Society of Criminology has a home page at http://sun.soci.niu.edu/~critcrim. It has useful links to a wide range of sources about criminology including the *Journal of Criminal Justice and Popular Culture*.

Online discussion lists about sociology and anthropology have been created. To subscribe to a list, send a message to "listserv@*location-of-list*" with the message "subscribe *LISTNAME yourname*." Don't forget to unsubscribe when you no longer wish to be on the list. (See Chapter 4 for more detailed instructions.) Some relevant lists are sbanth-l@ucsbvm.ucsb.edu (Anthropology graduate students), Ivsa@pdomain.uwindsor.ca (International Visual Sociology Association), russoc-l@ukcc.uky.edu (Rural Sociology Discussion List), and socgrads@uicvm.uic.edu (Sociology graduate students).

Communications

Communications is a relatively new field in social science. It began to be institutionalized as an academic discipline after World War II, drawing on the traditions of journalism, sociology and rhetoric. Currently, the field is divided into several different subdivisions including interpersonal communications, organizational communications and mass communications. Mass communications is often organized along several different lines, including journalism, public relations and advertising, as well as by the type of media technology involved in communicating the message—including television, radio and computer-mediated communications. Free speech is also a central area of concern as is health communication and persuasion.

The American Communication Association, a national association for scholars, students and professionals involved in communication studies, has established an excellent starting point for researchers at http://www.uark.edu/depts/comminfo/www/ACA.html. The page has pointers to resources in every major subdivision of the field, First Amendment, copyright and intellectual property issues and several online books.

The Journalism Periodicals Index is accessible via Gopher at gopher://gopher.uwo.ca/11/publications/ijp. The index is a cross-referenced subject index produced on microfilm at the University of Western Ontario and currently contains more than 14,000 citations to articles from about 40 trade, professional and academic journals related to journalism and mass communication.

The World Wide Web Virtual Library page for journalism is maintained at http://www.cais.com/makulow/vlj.html. Its purpose is to provide a comprehensive starting point for resources in journalism and related fields. Major subsections of the page include pointers to clubs, associations and societies; college and university departments; and news bureaus, organizations and services.

The School of Journalism at the University of Florida maintains a home page with links to communications-oriented Web servers around the world as well as some other interesting resources. Its URL is http://www.jou.ufl.edu/commres/.

Media history is an important, if neglected, subject. The history of communication media technologies is the organizing principle of the site at http://spot.colorado.edu/~rossk/history/histhome.html. The site includes sections on television, movies, comics, journalism, computing, culture, printing and more.

Fig. 12-6: The National Press Club maintains a collection of resources for news reporters, one of many occupations in the communications fields.

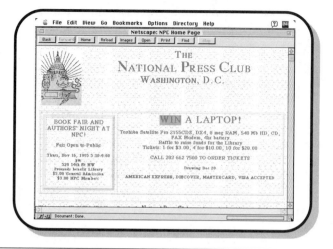

The National Press Club in Washington has been used by leading newsmakers to make comments on the day since it was founded in 1908. It also contains the Eric Friedheim Library and News Information Center and has set up an extensive Web site at http://town.hall.org/places/npc/ with a broad range of links to other organizations including Journalism and Academic WWW sites, Usenet Newsgroups related to journalism, the Society of Professional Journalists and more. The Internet Newsroom contains a description of Internet uses and practices for editors and reporters published by Editors Service.

The Poynter Center, one of the major institutes in journalism, maintains a home page at http://www.nando.net/prof/poynter/hrintro.html. One of the most interesting sections is Hot News/Hot Research. It points to Internet resources for an appropriate news story each week.

More than 500 news-oriented online services are currently being operated or are under development by newspapers worldwide. To survey those efforts, you may want to start at Editor & Publisher's Online Newspaper Services Resource Directory at http://www.mediainfo.com/edpub/e-papers.home.page.html. The site's developer also publishes a five-day-a-week column about newspapers and news media. Editor & Publisher also operates an online job-listing service at the same site.

Many of the major media are experimenting with online services and the Internet. The Raleigh *News & Observer* was one of the first newspapers to jump onto the Internet. Its home page is at http://www.nando.net. Time Inc. has put many of its stable of magazines online. The URL is http://pathfinder.com. And CBS has a Web site at http://www.cbs.com.

The growth of the Internet has sparked the study of computer-mediated communication or CMC. A good starting place for the exploration of CMC is http://www.rpi.edu/Internet/Guides/decemj/icmc/toc3.html. The purpose of the

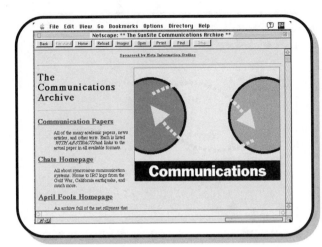

Fig. 12-7: An archive for research papers written on computer-mediated communications is maintained at the University of North Carolina.

page is to collect, organize and offer resources about the Internet and computer-mediated communication technologies, applications and culture. This site includes links to sources of Internet tools as well as research about CMC.

There is an archive for many of the research papers written about CMC at http://sunsite.unc.edu/dbarberi/communications.html. All of the papers, as well as news articles and other texts are listed with an abstract and links to the actual works themselves.

People interested in the legal and regulatory aspects of the growth of the Internet as well as First Amendment law in general may wish to access the *Federal Communications Law Journal* at http://www.law.indiana.edu:80/fclj/fclj.html.

Several very active discussion lists have emerged around the study of communication. To subscribe to a list, send a message to "listserv@*location-of-list*" with the message "subscribe *LISTNAME yourname.*" Don't forget to unsubscribe when you no longer wish to be on the list. (See Chapter 4 for more detailed instructions.) Some relevant lists are Stumedia@uabdpo.dpo.uab.edu (Student journalists list), magazine@vm.its.rpi.edu (Magazine discussion list), Carr-l@ulkyvm.louisville.edu (Computer-assisted research and reporting list), CMC-sig@deakin.edu.au (Computer-mediated communication), Copyediting-l@cornell.edu (Copyeditors list), and Journet@qucdn.queensu.ca (Journalism educators list).

Education

Although education is not considered a social science, it involves many of the same issues, methods and ways of looking at the world. Like psychologists, those studying education are concerned with the individual student. Like sociologists, they need to understand the broader contexts in which education takes place. Like political scientists, they have to take into account the political processes that shape the outlines of the educational system. Consequently, people studying education will be introduced to educational theory and philosophy; they will learn teaching methods and develop curricula; they will develop assessment tools and explore different types of research methodologies. Educational policy is an important consideration.

With its roots in the academic world, the Internet has long been understood as a network of learning and a network for learning about learning. Consequently, there are many well-developed sources of information for educators and those training to be educators at every level from preschool to higher education.

ERIC, the Educational Resources Information Center, may be the most comprehensive source of information for education. It supports 16 subject-specific clearinghouses from adult education to urban education, from preschool to teacher education and reading, science and math, and social studies. Moreover, it has more than 700 lesson plans, access to the ERIC database and full-text ERIC digests. The federally supported project's URL is http://ericir.syr.edu/. You can also find an archive of online discussion groups on educational topics.

The U.S. Department of Education maintains an extensive Web server at http://www.ed.gov. In addition to news, initiatives by the Secretary of Education and funding opportunities, there are guides to resources published by the department for teachers. It is also assembling a collection of links to educational material for parents.

Edweb, available through http://k12.cnidr.org/, is another starting point for those looking for educational resources on the Internet. It provides links to online information about educational policy and information infrastructure and classroom success stories. It is sponsored by the Corporation for Public Broadcasting and The Center for Networked Information Discovery and Retrieval.

Since its founding in 1963, the Learning Research and Development Center has explored the nature of thinking, knowing and understanding inside and outside the classroom. It explores the need for innovation and achievement in education. Its home page at http://www.lrdc.pitt.edu provides access to abstracts of reports and articles about the process of learning, educational policy and learning in the work world.

Student, teacher and school assessment is one of the most significant issues in education. The National Center for Research on Evaluation, Standards and Student Testing (CRESST) at http://www.cse.ucla.edu is intended to supply information leading to productive assessment reform in American schools. It has a clickable map to guide users to the area of information they seek. CRESST is a research unit of the Graduate School of Education and Information Studies at UCLA.

Not long ago a report from the U.S. Department of Education described the United States as a nation at risk because of falling educational

Fig. 12-8: The ERIC site is a major library for education resources.

standards and achievement. It identified groups of young people who were at greater risk of educational failure because of limited English proficiency, poverty, race, geographic location or other disadvantage. The National Institute on the Education of At-Risk Students and the National Research and Development Center is one of the institutes created in 1994 by the Department of Education. Information about it is located at http://www.ed.gov/ prog_info/At-Risk/.

The Educational Policy Analysis Archives is a peer-reviewed scholarly journal published electronically and accessible at http://info.asu.edu/asu-cwis/ epaa/welcome.html. Both abstracts and the full text of articles are available. Published by the College of Education of Arizona State University, EPAA articles deal with educational policy at all levels and in all nations.

Also at Arizona State University, the Measurement, Statistics and Methodological Studies program in the Division of Psychology in the College of Education maintains Web pages with materials thinking about, conducting and teaching research methods in education and applied social sciences. The URL is http://seamonkey.ed.asu.edu/~behrens/home.html.

Since 1964 Educom has been a source of important information for academic policymakers and planners by offering timely insights into educational technology and computing. It offers thrice-weekly, bimonthly and monthly updates on its Web site at http://educom.edu. It also sponsors an electronic discussion group for people interested in instructional technology.

The Virtual Schoolhouse at http://sunsite.unc.edu/cisco/schoolhouse.html is a metalibrary of links for K–12 education. You can search its archives by keyword. It also provides a series of links by subject and maintains an extensive listing of elementary, secondary and international schools on the Internet. In a typical offering, the Art Room provides links to museums, exhibits, virtual field trips and other art-related pages.

Fig. 12-9: The CRESST site at UCLA supplies information leading to productive teaching assessment.

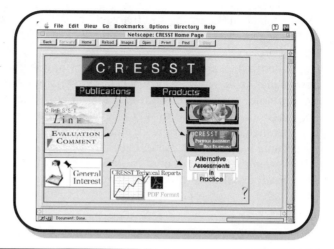

The Eisenhower National Clearinghouse at http://www.enc.org encourages the adoption and use of K–12 curriculum materials in science and mathematics, which create an improved learning environment. To that end, it maintains a collection of multimedia materials. The catalog is searchable through ENC's Resource Finder. Furthermore, the center scours the Internet for interesting new math and science resources. Each month it posts new links; the links from previous months are archived.

Small Planet is a source of ideas for educators. Its home page at http://www.smplanet.com/internet.html provides access to its interdisciplinary lesson plans for upper elementary and middle school classrooms, which incorporate links to other Web sites, as well as a hot list of sites for teachers and students.

The Curriculum Web at http://www.curriculumweb.com/curriculumweb is intended to be a starting point for educators interested in surfing the Web. As part of its offerings it hopes to host distance-learning adventures as well.

The *Chronicle of Higher Education* is the main professional newspaper for higher education. It publishes Academe This week at http://chronicle.merit.edu. It includes notable Internet resources, job listings, news and a calendar. It is intended as a supplement to the print newspaper.

The online discussion list archive at ERIC (gopher://ericir.syr.edu:70/11/Listservs) contains more than 160 discussion lists related to education. To subscribe to a list, send a message to "listserv*@location-of-list*" with the message "subscribe *LISTNAME yourname*." Don't forget to unsubscribe when you no longer wish to be on the list. (See Chapter 4 for more detailed instructions.) The American Educational Research Association at Arizona State University operates 12 discussion groups including Aera@asu.edu (American Educational Research Association List), Aera-a@asu.edu (Educational Administration Forum), Aera-b@asu.edu (Curriculum Studies Forum),

Aera-c@asu.edu (Learning and Instruction), Aera-d@asu.edu (Measurement and Research Methodology), and Aera-k@asu.edu (Teaching and Teacher Education).

Other interesting lists include Altlearn@sjuvm.stjohns.edu (Alternative approaches to learning), Chatback@sjuvm.stjohns.edu (Special education), Ecid-l@vm.cc.purdue.edu (Educational Computing and Instructional Development), Edad-l@wvnvm.wvnet.edu (Educational Administration), Edtech@msu.edu (Educational technology), Kidsphere@vms.cis.pitt.edu (International Kidlink discussion), Teacheft@wcupa.edu (Teaching effectiveness), and wwwedu.kudzu.cnidr.org (The World Wide Web in Education). Send subscription request to listproc@kudzu.cnidr.org.

## Chapter 13

Making the business grade

The needs and wants of people are met through businesses operating within some economic system that provides for exchanges of goods and services. The clothes you wear—if they come from natural fiber—started as an agricultural product that a farmer sold to a processor who cleaned up the raw fiber and sold it to a manufacturer who made cloth and sold it to a garmentmaker who created shirts, shorts and blouses and sold them to a distributor who sold them to a clothing store where you found them. The clothmaker bought dyes from someone else. The garmentmaker bought buttons, thread and zippers. Both had to buy machines to do their work. The distributor has a fleet of trucks, warehouses and salespeople.

The food you eat goes through a similar process involving farmers and ranchers, processors and distributors. If you picked up a burger or pizza on the run, you probably supported some fast-food franchise along the way. Then there's the apartment or dorm or house you live in—lumber, brick, Sheetrock, concrete, plumbing, wiring, tile, cabinets, counters, fixtures and then the craftsmen to put them all together.

So much for your material needs—food, clothing and shelter. Life would be pretty drab without a few of your wants, such as television, radio, music, automobiles, movies, and of course your stuffed animals, comics, cards, or whatever you collect. These are all wants, but important nonetheless. The very fabric of our lives—our wants, our needs, our jobs—are dependent upon business. Economies of the world are dependent upon business. You are in school at least in part because you hope to gain the knowledge and skills you need for some occupation or career.

Most students will take some kind of business or economics classes before they graduate. And beyond such formal study, it is difficult to escape the effects of these related disciplines. In this chapter you will learn some of the basic concepts behind and be introduced to some of the network resources in

- Accounting.
- Management.

- Marketing.
- Finance.
- Management Information Systems.
- Economics.

Business disciplines draw heavily on other fields. Accounting and finance rely on mathematical models and many simple arithmetic operations. Additionally, management and marketing employ social science methods and research. Management wants to keep human resources happy, productive and motivated. Marketing wants to communicate with consumers and to identify and meet (sometimes create) their needs. Economics, a social science in its own right, does all of these things. A good grounding in mathematics, sociology, psychology and communications will help the business student in the special applications of those fields to the needs of business.

Finding business information on the Internet

Students interested in or needing business information may find a wide range of business resources using keyword search engines and catalog browsing sites described on the inside cover of *The Online Student*. More thorough explanation of those tools and ways of developing search strategies is provided in Chapter 9.

Browsing and keyword searches should focus on terms like business, business administration, business management, and economics to find general resources. For information on more specific topics such as investments, marketing, accounting, or similar topics, you should focus on those terms.

As a starting point, students engaged in business inquiries could visit the sites described in this chapter. General business sites tend to house resources spanning several of the business fields and may provide documents giving a helpful overview of business in general.

General business sites

Business as an area of study encompasses several different disciplines. They range from the hard, mathematical practices of accounting to the more humanistic social science of motivating workers to produce more efficiently (management) and customers to buy (marketing). Economics tends to combine social science and sophisticated mathematical models as it seeks to explain systems for managing, maintaining and delivering goods and services.

Some general business resources on the Internet are listed here because they provide information about a range of companies rather than focus on one of the specialized business disciplines. Some of these sites provide links to business schools around the world.

Access Business Online requires a graphical Web browser. Using a card file interface, the site provides information about companies in two dozen market sectors. It is found at http://199.170.0.78/touch/home.htm.

Fig. 13-1: Nijenrode University (Netherlands) maintains a business server aimed primarily at the academic community.

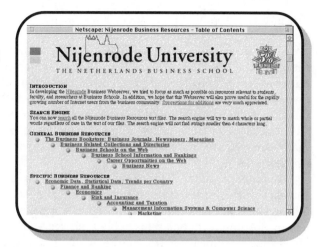

Michigan State University's Center for International Business Education and Research (MSU-CIBER) at http://ciber.bus.msu.edu/ includes extensive links to business resources including journals, research reports, statistics and other business sites.

Dartmouth University's Amos Tuck School of Business Administration maintains (at http://www.dartmouth.edu/pages/tuck/bschools.html) a collection of links to the Web sites of business schools worldwide. More than fifty links are listed, from the Babcock Graduate School of Management at Wake Forest University to the Vienna University of Economics. The site also provides indices to more extensive lists of schools.

Nijenrode University in the Netherlands maintains a business server with resources aimed at students, faculty and researchers at business schools. The site is accessible at http://www.nijenrode.nl/nbr/ (Fig. 13-1).

The Institute of Management and Administration, which publishes business and management information, has compiled hundreds of links to business and management resources on the Net, accessed at http://starbase.ingress.com/ioma/. Main departments at the site include Today's Business News, Competitive Intelligence & Strategy, Corporate Finance & Investment, Credit Management, Design & Construction, Financial Management, Accounting & Taxation; Human Resources & Benefits, Information Systems, Insurance & Risk, Internet Marketing, Legal Resources, Other Business Directories, Purchasing, Inventory & Supplier Management, Sales and Marketing, Small Business, and Usenet Newsgroups. All links are listed on one page.

At Harvard University, a Gopher server provides access to the catalog of all materials available from Harvard Business School Publishing. The catalog contains more than 6,000 items, including Harvard Business School case studies, teaching notes, background notes, case software, videos, Harvard Business School Press book titles and *Harvard Business Review* reprints.

The site is searchable at gopher://www.hbsp.harvard.edu/. There is also a Web version at http://bisonnet.harvard.edu/.

The Library of Congress Gopher provides links to many business resources at gopher://marvel.loc.gov:70/11/global/econ/biz. Another general business site goes by the title Internet Pearls Index at http://execpc.com:80/~wmhogg/bizlinks.html. The Pearls Index is especially strong in its links to business resources offered by colleges and universities.

Florida State University's Business Gopher (gopher://cob.fsu.edu:4070/) maintains links to many business information resources residing on Gopher servers.

A pair of popular business magazines publish electronic editions on the Internet. *Fortune* magazine online has links to special issues on the Fortune 500 and others. The site at http://pathfinder.com/@@*ShuVxGoAQMAQPtS/fortune/fortune.html has searchable archives and a database that lists the 500 by performance, profits, market value and location. *Business Week* at http://www.enews.com/magazines/bw/ also keeps searchable archives as well as current material.

For links to information dealing with government regulations on business, The Regulatory Affairs Information Home Page at http://www.nando.net/ads/ckbus/RAinfo/reglink1.htm is maintained by CK Business Resources. At the site, hundreds of resources are organized under a score of main categories.

The U.S. Securities and Exchange Commission's EDGAR database of information on American corporations is accessible at http://www.sec.gov/edgarhp.htm. The Electronic Data Gathering, Analysis, and Retrieval system (EDGAR) "performs automated collection, validation, indexing, acceptance, and forwarding of submissions by companies and others who are required by law to file forms with the (SEC)," according to the SEC.

The U.S. Academy of Management maintains a set of resources on business policy and strategy information at http://comsp.com.latrobe.edu.au:80/bps.html. Beyond the resources of its own organization, the site has links to many university and private sector resources on the topic.

Pronet Enterprises Ltd. of Vancouver, British Columbia, maintains an international directory of businesses with Internet "presences." The Pronet site at http://pronett.com/ offers searching by company name or browsing first by global region and then by industry.

The Thomas Register Of American Manufacturers Web site permits online searches to locate suppliers of products from more than 50,000 categories. The site is located at http://www.thomasregister.com:8000/.

Dun & Bradstreet Information Services maintains a Web server at http://www.dbisna.com/. For a fee the site will return a complete business background report on any of millions of U.S. companies. Other less specific reports are available without charge.

Deluxe Corporation maintains a list of business resources on the Internet covering a wide range of business disciplines and is accessible at http://204.157.36.3/./html/biz.sites.html.

To find e-mail discussion lists for business topics of all stripes you may search the Indiana University Mailing Lists Archive at http://www.ucssc.indiana.edu/mlarchive or the Tile.Net site (http://tile.net/lists/).

Accounting sites

Bookkeepers record what a company spends and receives. Accounts classify and interpret bookkeeping records with the goal of reporting whether the business is showing a profit or loss. Accounting also deals with the underlying principles and procedures for the practical application of accounting. Auditing entails independent examination of business accounts and related documents by people not involved with the preparation of the original documents.

Both auditing and bookkeeping are subdivisions of accounting. Accounting students, like those in other business disciplines, will find many resources on the Internet to help them in understanding their field of study. Some good starting points follow.

The Louisiana State University Virtual Library Webliography accounting resource at http://www.lib.lsu.edu/bus/account.html organizes its contents into seven major sections. They include Auditing, Big 6 (major accounting firms), Government, International Accounting Network, Journals and Scholarly Publications, Regulatory Bodies, and Taxes.

AccWeb at http://www.eskimo.com/~pretzl/ is aimed at accounting professionals. It includes classified advertising, a place for posting résumés, and links to other sites of interest to accountants.

A global approach to accounting is maintained by the International Accounting Network, composed of three sites rich in accounting resources. They

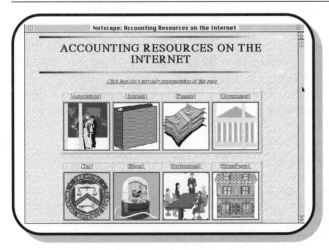

Fig. 13-2: The Rutgers Accounting Web provides the visitor with a series of icons representing different parts of the site.

include ANet at Southern Cross University in New South Wales, Australia, at http://www.scu.edu.au:80/ANetHomePage.html; the Summa Project at the University of Exeter, United Kingdom, at http://www.icaew.org.uk/; and the Rutgers Accounting Web at Rutgers University in New Jersey, at http://www.rutgers.edu/Accounting/raw/internet/int.htm. The Rutgers Accounting Web also hosts the American Accounting Association home page and has an extensive set of links to Internet accounting resources from http://www.scu.edu.au:80/anet/raw.html.

The Institute of Management Accountants maintains a set of Web resources at http://panoptic.csustan.edu/ima\imafront.htm.

James M. Kaplan and John Mayer maintain the Audit NetResource List at http://www.unf.edu/misc/jmayer/arl.html. The site's main feature is a very long, annotated list of network resources for auditors.

The Accountant's Hotlist of Internet Sites at http://www.k2e.com/~k2e/hotlist.html includes links to a number of research databases for accountants, to CPA firms and accounting services, and to relevant government agencies.

The University of San Diego's Accounting Society maintains a Web site with links to CPA firms, exam information, relevant government agencies, employment services, and other accounting information. Accessed at http://pwa.acusd.edu:80/~bay/, the site also boasts an e-mail directory for accountants.

The World Wide Web server for accounting and auditing information at the University of Massachusetts at Amherst was designed primarily as an information source for students in the accounting program at the university. Located at http://www.umass.edu/acctg/, the server provides links to sites containing accounting information.

Management

Management has to do with responsibility for the work performance of other people, who are the basic resource of business organizations. People in turn use material resources including money, facilities, technology, tools and raw materials to produce goods and services. Studies in management, therefore, become studies aimed at securing the highest level of performance from human and material resources.

The Management Archive (gopher://ursus.jun.alaska.edu/) contains working papers, teaching materials, conference announcements and the like on the subject of business management. The archives of discussion lists sponsored by the Academy of Management are maintained here, too.

Operations Management at Warwick Business School in the United Kingdom offers a collection of international links to Net resources in "the way organizations produce goods and services." The collection (http://www.warwick.ac.uk/~bsryd/om/om_index.html) is maintained by David Twigg and covers manufacturing, new product development, strategy and quality, among other topics.

HR Headquarters is a resource for human resource managers and others involved in hiring, training and managing a work force. The site is maintained by Personnel Journal. The heart of HR Headquarters is the Library, with scores of articles on human resource topics like Health Care, Career Development and Work Force Diversity. Other areas at the Headquarters include the Coffee Break, with cartoons and anecdotes, and the Conference Room, with several interactive discussion boards. The site at http://www.hrhq.com/ includes links to journal (library), which is searchable, forums for discussing problems and issues, and human resources news tips.

BenefitsLink (Fig. 13-3) provides a compendium of articles, directories, newsletters and shareware for both benefits administrators and individuals who want a better grasp on their benefits plan. The site at http://www.magicnet.net/benefits/ is maintained by Dave Baker, who also authors the *BenefitsLink Newsletter*. The site is simple in design, but the volume, variety and quality of links are extensive.

The United States Bureau of Labor Statistics maintains a server at http://www.bls.gov/ that contains data sets, research papers and a keyword search engine.

The Business School of the University of California at Berkeley provides Haas Week online and its archives at http://haas.berkeley.edu/~cbwweb/.

The management section of the Louisiana State University's Webliography is accessed at http://www.lib.lsu.edu/bus/managemt.html. Main content categories include Court Cases, Entrepreneurship, Journals and Scholarly Publications, Labor-Management, Organizations, Production Operations, and Working Papers.

The Society for Human Resource Management maintains a Web presence at http://www.shrm.org/, where there is news of the organization, a

Fig. 13-3: A list of articles available is one of the resources served at BenefitsLink.

reading room, and links to other sources of interest for human resource managers.

Marketing

The American Marketing Association has said, "Marketing is the process of planning and executing the conception, pricing, promotion, and distribution of ideas, goods, and services to create exchanges that satisfy individual and organizational objectives." That definition suggests some far-reaching interests maintained by marketers.

The process of satisfying "individual and organizational objectives" means that marketing folks address the wants and needs of people and groups. To do so involves a lot of research employing social science (especially psychology and sociology) principles and methods. "Distribution of ideas, goods, and services" entails serious study of transportation and communications. "Promotion" gets into communications disciplines, advertising and more. "Pricing" functions involve the concerns of financial managers as well as the social science assessment of "wants and needs" of people and groups. "Planning and executing the conception" of a company's products and services means that marketing comes into play at the very moment a product, good, or service is conceived, and marketers are concerned with strategic planning, analysis of markets and competition, and more.

In short, there is little business activity that is not subsumed by the marketing process. Traditionally, however, many think of marketing for the analysis of markets and matching the needs and wants of consumers with those of the company. A wealth of resources on the Internet is available to help a student desiring to strengthen an understanding of the marketing arm of business.

The Journal of International Marketing at http://ciber.bus.msu.edu/publicat/pubjim.htm is designed to serve both practitioners and educators. Its primary mission is to contribute to the advancement of international marketing practice and theory. JIM brings to the readership a selection of original articles, executive insights, and book reviews.

Direct Marketing World at http://mainsail.com/dmworld.htm includes information on mailing lists and databases, listings of direct marketing professionals, a virtual library and global calendar.

The Internet Marketing archives and resources is a compendium of postings to the Internet Marketing mailing list (600 postings/month), moderated by Glenn Fleishman of the Point of Presence Company. The majority of postings come from site maintainers, Internet consultants and marketers, making the archives lively and educational. Billed as "insider discussion of marketing and commerce on the Net," the site is accessed at http://www.popco.com/hyper/internet-marketing/.

Advertising trade magazines on the Net include *Advertising Age* at http://www.adage.com/ and the University of Texas' *Advertising World* magazine at http://www.utexas.edu/coc/adv/world/.

Fig. 13-4: The VALS site lets you complete a survey and then rates your likes and dislikes based on the VALS system.

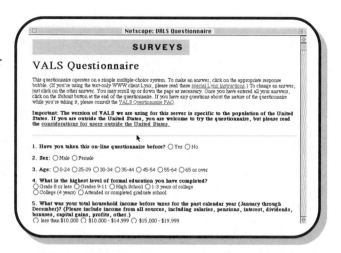

The Internet Advertising Resource Guide has links to select sources of information about advertising and marketing on the Internet. Maintained by Hairong Li of the Missouri School of Journalism at http://www.missouri.edu/internet-advertising-guide.html, the guide's main thrust is educational. As a result, Li says, "uniqueness, usefulness and depth of information are primary criteria for inclusion." Main sections of the guide include an Internet Marketing/Advertising Primer, Internet Marketing/Advertising Research & Teaching, Associations Web Pages, Advertising Departmental Web Pages (academic links), Doing Business on the Internet, and Exemplary Commercial Storefronts.

The American Demographics Inc. site at http://www.marketingtools.com/ is notable as the home for three magazines devoted to marketing strategies and consumer trends: *American Demographics*, *Marketing Tools*, and *Numbers News*. You need to be a subscriber to the printed version of the magazines to access some of the data and information on the server.

Other demographic and population resources are listed under Economics in this chapter.

Small & Home Based Business Links, http://www.ro.com/small_business/homebased.html, specializes in serving information to help run and market small or home-based businesses. Special attention is paid to news groups, marketing, search tools and links to other sites.

A psychographic consumer research program known as VALS (Values and Lifestyles), popular with many marketing people, has a home on the Web. The VALS site (Fig. 13-4) contains documents that explain the program and related research. The site at http://future.sri.com/ also permits visitors to participate in a VALS survey and then reports the primary and secondary VALS types that fit the survey taker. Information files at the site explain the types and suggest product, geographic and lifestyle preferences of people who fit the types.

Part of the Louisiana State University Virtual Library's Webliography, Internet Marketing Resources, is accessed at http://www.lib.lsu.edu/bus/ marketin.html. Major resource topics at the site include Advertising, Countries & Geography, Exporting, Foreign Policies, Journals and Scholarly Publications, Mutual Funds, National Trade Data Bank, News Organizations, Statistics, and Trade Conventions.

Finance

In simplest terms, the field of finance concerns itself with facts, principles and theories that address acquisition and use of money by businesses, individuals and governments. In a corporate setting, financial managers have as their main goal to maximize the value of the corporation's shares through practices consistent with the corporate social conscience. In any kind of business setting, those who manage company finances have the responsibility for devising plans that make the best use of limited company assets.

Because financial managers have stewardship over a company's assets, including money, they typically have to deal with investments, taxes, risk analysis, capital management, budgeting, the value of money, stocks, bonds, the raising of funds, debt, financial planning and forecasting, and a host of other things affecting company assets. The tools they work with include a complex set of formulas for analyzing asset values and projecting them in the future, principles for managing assets to get the greatest return, and a number of financial theories.

Students majoring in finance will not be disappointed in the rich libraries of information on the Internet treating their subject area.

The Investor Channel is a Canadian company that maintains information on publicly traded companies. Its Web site is accessed at http:// vanbc.wimsey.com/xr-cgi-bin/select?/128@/Magnet/mc/menu.html.

Mutual Funds Magazine, published by The Institute for Econometric Research, maintains an online presence at http://www.mfmag.com/. Magazine contents are available, plus database information on six thousand mutual fund portfolios.

RiskWeb at http://www.riskweb.com/ has as its primary purpose the serving of information to academics and professionals with significant research and/or professional interests in risk management and insurance. The site includes a fair number of documents and papers on risk, links to other risk and insurance servers in GopherSpace and on the World Wide Web, and links to other financially oriented Web services.

A searchable directory of more than 8,500 companies in the United States is one of the star attractions at Hoover's Online, http://www.hoovers.com/. The Hoover's MasterList answers search inquiries with financial reports and contact information, links to the reported company's Web site, current stock prices, and EDGAR filings. Included in the list is every public U.S. company traded on the New York Stock Exchange (NYSE), American Stock

Fig. 13-5: The Hoover's Online site contains a wealth of information about American business. It also offers a trivia contest for those so inclined.

Exchange (AMEX), and NASDAQ National Market (NASDAQ). Private U.S. companies (approximately 1,700) on the list include all companies on the Forbes list of the largest 400 private companies in the United States Foreign companies and U.S. subsidiaries of foreign companies listed number about 500.

The company plans for 1996 include adding 3,000 European and 1,250 Latin American companies. Other resources at Hoover's Online include BizBuzz weekly business news, a register of corporate Web sites, original feature articles, and a collection of business lists like Top 20 in CEO Compensation, and 20 Most Advertised Brands in the US.

Wall Street Research Net at http://www.wsrn.com/ contains more than 30,000 links chosen to help professional and private investors perform fundamental research on actively traded companies and mutual funds and to locate important economic data that moves markets.

Wall Street Journal Money and Investing Update at http://update.wsj.com/ features continually updated coverage of global markets and the top stories in business and finance worldwide, drawing on Dow Jones Company publications and news wires.

If you have a need to convert dollars to yen or pounds to deutschmarks, the Global Network Navigator/Koblas Currency Converter by David Koblas will do the trick. The converter is available at http://bin.gnn.com/cgi-bin/gnn/currency/. Select the desired currency and all other currencies will be converted relative to the one you selected.

The finance section of Louisiana State University's Virtual Library Webliography is found at http://www.lib.lsu.edu/bus/finance.html. Resources at the site are filed under Banking, Bankruptcy, Bonds, Commodities, Futures and Options, Economic and Corporate Research Reports, Encyclopedia, Federal Reserve Board, Financial Directories, Insurance, Mutual Funds,

Organizations, Public Laws, Securities and Exchange Commission, Stock Markets (U.S.), Stock Markets (International), and Uniform Commercial Code.

Media Logic maintains The Economics/Markets/Investments Index at http://www.mlinet.com/mle/. The site includes searchable indices of data, news, services, and other information of interest to investors and researchers.

StockMaster is the name of a server at Massachusetts Institute of Technology that provides recent stock market information, including previous day's closing prices and one-year graphs of historical prices. It is updated daily. The site's address is http://www.ai.mit.edu/stocks.html.

The Security APL Quote Server at http://www.secapl.com/cgi-bin/qs provides 15-minute delayed prices for most issues. The interactive site will graph the Standard and Poor's 500 with a five-minute bar chart, 12 months, five years, 10 years, or 25 years of performance.

Onramp Access, Inc. provides its Stocks and Commodities server at http://www.onr.com/stocks/investment.html. The site offers an extensive listing of Internet resources for investors.

The Chicago Mercantile Exchange at http://www.cme.com/ maintains a fair library of resources on trading in general as well as on subjects specific to the exchange's mission.

The American Stock Exchange holds forth at http://www.amex.com/. Trading information on 800 companies is available as well as market summaries and other related information.

Management information systems (MIS)

For a business to operate smoothly and to efficiently work toward its established goals all people and departments involved in the operation must have the right information at the right time. People must know what is expected of them, and decision makers must have useful information if they are to make well-advised decisions. This gives rise to the establishment of management information systems (MIS) in business.

The responsibility of MIS is to collect, organize and distribute relevant data in a manner that addresses the information needs of company managers. Data are comprised of raw facts such as numbers and other symbols that represent events, trends, people and concepts. When data are organized and interpreted in a meaningful way, they become information. Internet resources of value to MIS students include raw data sets, papers explaining how to manage the flow of information in a business or how to interpret data, and other resources. Descriptions of a few sites follow.

Business Researcher's Interests is a site maintained by Yogesh Malhotra, graduate student at the University of Pittsburgh. The site (http://www.pitt.edu/~malhotra/interest.html) provides a directory of more than one thousand links to information related to businesses. The site is sponsored by

Fig. 13-6: The welcome screen at ISWorld is a completely graphical interface.

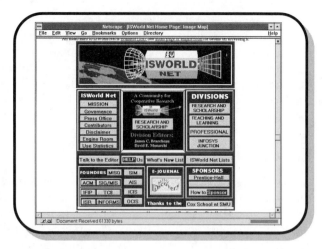

the Association for Information Systems, an international organization that seeks to identify, extend, unify and communicate knowledge in information technology, information systems and information management.

The Applied IS Information Gateway page contains a collection of Web sources from around the world that may be of interest to people in the Information Systems field of research. All entries have been submitted by readers. At http://www.cs.tcd.ie/www/dalgeo/aisg/is_inf.html/, the page is maintained by the Applied Information Systems Group (AISG) at Trinity College, University of Dublin, Ireland.

The ISWorld Net Home Page at http://www.isworld.org/isworld.html has as its mission to "provide information management scholars and practitioners with a single entry point to resources related to information systems technology and (to) promote the development of an international information infrastructure that will dramatically improve the world's ability to use information systems for creating, disseminating, and applying knowledge."

CIO Magazine, which describes itself as "the leading resource for those interested in the strategic application of information technology" maintains a Web server at http://www.cio.com/. This server contains new online materials, as well as excerpts from the print publication.

The David D. Lattanze Center for Executive Studies in Information Systems seeks to further the growth of executives by increasing their understanding of issues related to the management of information technology. The Lattanze Center at http://lattanze.loyola.edu/lattanze/ provides working papers, information about the program, news for its members, student résumés, and links to other related information on the Internet.

At least two journals on the topic are available online. *International Journal of Computational Intelligence and Organizations* publishes articles on theories, methods and applications of computational intelligence in organizations and is available at http://www.ecst.csuchico.edu/~ijcio/. The *PZZ–Hypertext Journal* provides information on advanced analysis and forecasting tools and on knowledge-processing systems for financial markets. The main topics are coming from statistics and economics, especially from financial computing, financial engineering, and financial data mining. The journal, based in Zurich, is available at http://www.ips.id.ethz.ch/PZZ/.

Economics

Economics is the study of the human activities of production, exchange and consumption of goods, services and wealth. The nature and intensity of these activities and their implications for individual and social welfare constitute the focus of economics and the policy prescriptions that economists make. The entire range of business activities, then, falls under the broad reach of economics. Economics scholars and business students, especially in the realms of finance and marketing, often work with the same kinds of raw data in their research.

As economists become involved in making public policy suggestions based on concerns for individual and social welfare they are firmly entrenched in enterprises that one normally associates with the social sciences. So in many ways it is difficult to isolate the study of economics from government and politics on one hand or from business on the other.

On the Internet you will frequently find business and economics material grouped together. And you will find the government to be one of the primary generators and consumers of economic and business data.

The primary objective of FinWeb is to list Internet resources providing substantive information concerning economics and finance-related topics. Located at http://www.finweb.com/, FinWeb serves up journals, working papers, links to other finance and economics WWW servers. The site's Miscellaneous category includes a section on jokes about economists and economics.

Sam Houston State University offers its Economics Gopher Server at gopher://Niord.SHSU.edu:70/11gopher_root%3A%5B_DATA. ECONOMICS%5D. Beyond a dozen folders (directories) of material provided and archived by SHSU, the SHSU Economics Gopher provides scores of links to other economic resources on Gopher and FTP servers, 12 screens (more than two hundred items) in all. This Gopher is probably the most extensive economics resource in GopherSpace.

The Business Cycle Indicators server (http://www.cris.com/~netlink/bci/bci.html) provides a set of 256 data series commonly known as the U.S. Business Cycle Indicators (Fig. 13-7). These indicators are used for tracking and predicting business activity in the United States. Some data are provided only on a quarterly basis, but most are monthly data, as published by the Bureau of Economic Analysis (U.S. Department of Commerce). Much of the

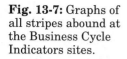 **Fig. 13-7:** Graphs of all stripes abound at the Business Cycle Indicators sites.

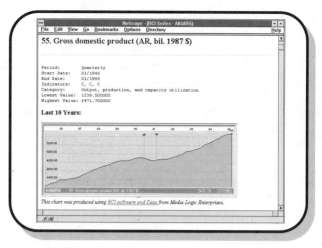

data is complete from 1948 to the present, making this site especially rich for students doing research in this area.

The BCI site is sponsored by Media Logic, and charts presented on these pages are generated by Media Logic's BCI software running under Microsoft Windows. The data are grouped into 16 categories. They are Composite Indexes; Labor Force, Employment, and Unemployment; Output, Production, and Capacity Utilization; Sales, Orders, and Deliveries; Fixed Capital Investment; Inventories and Inventory Investment; Prices; Profits and Cash Flow; Wages, Labor Costs, and Productivity; Personal Income and Consumer Attitudes; Saving; Money, Credit, Interest Rates, and Stock Prices; National Defense; Exports and Imports; International Comparisons; and Alternate Composite Indexes.

A large FAQ document with hot links titled Resources for Economists on the Internet may be accessed at http://econwpa.wustl.edu/EconFAQ/ EconFAQ.html.

Several sites maintained by the U.S. government are of particular interest for economics studies:
- The Census Bureau is accessible at http://www.census.gov as well as at gopher://gopher.census.gov.
- The Library of Congress Gopher economics resources at gopher:// marvel.loc.gov:70/11/global/econ/econ.
- The Department of Commerce at http://www.doc.gov/.
- The Department of Transportation at http://www.dot.gov/.
- The Department of Labor at http://www.dol.gov/.

Economics and Statistics Server from the Louisiana State University Virtual Library (http://www.lib.lsu.edu/bus/economic.html) provides information from the Federal Reserve Board, various journals and scholarly publications, links to relevant organizations, U.S. statistics, and a number of working papers. Federal Reserve Board information is also available at gopher://town.hall.org:70/11/other/fed.

A major collection of U.S. economic information is provided by the University of Michigan, together with a keyword search engine, at gopher://una.hh.lib.umich.edu/11/ebb.

The Economics Department of Washington University maintains an electronic archive devoted to the free distribution of working papers in economics. There are 22 subject areas to the archive accessible at http://econwpa.wustl.edu/.

Sites of international economic scope

The Financial Information Link Library at http://www.mbnet.mb.ca/~russell/ provides links to data and information from 27 nations arranged alphabetically.

Extensive links to financial data from many resources throughout the world are maintained at the Ohio State University Financial Data Finder, http://www.cob.ohio-state.edu:80/dept/fin/osudata.htm. Some data are directly downloadable from the site.

WebEc (http://www.helsinki.fi/WebEc/) is a volunteer classification effort to improve the availability of information in economics on the World Wide Web. Archives are searchable and it is also mirrored at http://netec.wustl.edu/WebEc/. WebEc is part of The NetEc Project, "a volunteer effort to improve the communication of research in economics via electronic media," which is available at http://netec.mcc.ac.uk/NetEc.html and http://netec.wustl.edu/NetEc.html.

A listing of economics resources on the Internet is maintained at the University of Waterloo and available at http://csclub.uwaterloo.ca/u/nckwan/fin/econ.html. It lists bulletin boards, Gopher sites and e-mail discussion lists with economic resources.

Trends in Developing Economies is a linked document from the World Bank maintained at http://www.ciesin.org/IC/wbank/tde-home.html.

The World Bank itself resides at http://www.worldbank.org/.

Demographics and population studies

The World Bank's Living Standards Measurement Study site reports surveys that are multitopic, household questionnaires which seek to measure household welfare and reveal household behavior in developing countries. The site is accessible at http://www.worldbank.org/html/research/prdph/lsms/lsmshome.html.

The Center for the Study of Population at Florida State University maintains a Gopher server that provides access to a growing volume of demography- and population-related information available on international computer networks. The address of the site is gopher://gopher.fsu.edu/11/FSU/Popctr. Resources available include

- Working paper titles, abstracts and ordering information for Florida State and for other population centers.
- Connections to Gopher sites containing downloadable population data, software and news bulletins.
- Connections to Gopher sites containing other types of information of interest to demographers (e.g., documentation for machine-readable data sets, lists of available data files, etc.).
- Contact information, such as e-mail addresses and phone numbers, for various organizations.
- The Electronic Employment Exchange for demographers, under which employers worldwide may post job notices or fellowship announcements, and demographers seeking jobs may post curriculum vitae or résumés.

Among the top demographic research facilities in the United States, the Population Research Center at the University of Texas at Austin is online at http://www.prc.utexas.edu:80/. Data and information available from the site reflect the many interests of faculty in sociology, economics, business administration, law, psychology, government, health and physical education, public affairs, human ecology, social work and history. Of particular value at the site are the library resources, working papers and abstracts, and the Immigration e-mail discussion list.

The Office of Social and Economic Data Analysis at the University of Missouri sustains a Web server focusing on social and economic information at http://www.oseda.missouri.edu:80/. The information, including thematic maps, is divided into Missouri and the rest of the United States segments. The site also provides links to other Web and Gopher sites, including social and economic sites around the world.

Like the Missouri server, the Louisiana Population Data Center at http://www.lapop.lsu.edu:80/ provides links to other sites as well.

With a focus on Africa, the Caribbean, Latin America, and the United States, the University of Pennsylvania Population Studies Center Gopher is accessible at gopher://lexis.pop.upenn.edu/.

The Population Studies Center at the University of Michigan maintains census and demographic materials and links to other sites at http://www.psc.lsa.umich.edu:80/.

The Australian National University Demography Program Archive offers resources at http://coombs.anu.edu.au:80/ResFacilities/ANUDemog Page.html.

Chapter 14

Making the sciences grade

Since the beginning of recorded time, people have studied the earth, the seas, the skies and themselves. The Greek philosopher Aristotle believed that the world was made up of four essential components: earth, air, fire and water. Some people believe the biblical prophets were, in fact, skilled astronomers, and many of their prophecies reflected their anticipation of comets passing close to the earth. The fundamental principles of geometry were described by the ancient Egyptians. The Chinese routinely employed advanced mathematical systems.

The study of what are called the natural sciences involves the systematic exploration of all aspects of the universe ranging from the question of the origins of the universe and life itself to the nature of the building blocks of matter and the forces that hold it together. The objective is to discover the fundamental principles and forces that govern the actions and interactions of the natural world and to apply those principles in appropriate ways. The application of scientific knowledge—technology—has helped create everything from wonder drugs for healing to military weapons of mass destruction.

Very roughly, the study of science is divided into two categories: the physical sciences, which look at inanimate elements, and life sciences, which claim living creatures as subject matter. The division, however, is not sharp. The areas of study in science overlap. The study of chemistry, for example, spans both the physical and life sciences (the division is often described in first- and second-year chemistry courses as inorganic and organic chemistry). And mathematics is a symbol system used to describe relationships in all areas of science.

In addition to subject matter, the study of science entails a method—the scientific method. Based on current knowledge and a theory about the way systems work, a hypothesis is developed about a specific process or result. An experiment is devised to test the hypothesis. Data is collected and analyzed and then conclusions are made. For the insights derived from the experiment to be considered valid, those conducting the experiment must use accepted methods, and the results must be able to be replicated by other scientists.

The scientific method, however, is more than just a technique. It is a philosophical perspective on the way to look at and understand the world. Science is concerned with objective knowledge—knowledge and information about which we can all agree regardless of religious, cultural or philosophical differences. The kind of objectivity associated with the scientific method is an important underpinning of industrial society.

In many colleges and universities, students will be required to take two to four courses in science and mathematics. Often, students will take at least one lab science—in which much of the experimentation that leads to knowledge can take place in a controlled, laboratory setting. The primary lab sciences are physics, biology and chemistry.

Many non-science majors like to take more field-oriented sciences in which knowledge is developed through the sophisticated observation of nature. Some major field-oriented sciences are astronomy, oceanography, earth and environmental sciences.

Finally, most students are required to take at least one course in mathematics. Mathematics is a symbol system and language that can effectively represent the kind of knowledge associated with science. Because computers are effective tools to perform mathematical calculations, some schools allow students to take a course in computer science to fulfill their science and math general educational requirements.

To some, science and math seem very difficult. After all, they involve a new, apparently complex way of understanding and representing the world. Precisely quantifying chemical reactions, for example, is not a routine activity for most people. To succeed in science, non-science-oriented people have to generate some degree of enthusiasm. In the United States, several major scientific institutions work hard to generate enthusiasm and support for science. Their presence and impact is felt across the disciplines.

General science sites

From the launch of the Mercury rocket in the early 1960s to the latest mission of the space shuttle, the space program spearheaded by NASA has been the United States' most visible science project. NASA has an extensive home page at http://www.nasa.gov. You can find news about the space program, access to more than three million citations of technical reports and research related to the space program, and links to 11 other NASA facilities around the country including a specialized Web site for space shuttle missions.

The NASA Dryden Flight Research Center (http://www.dfrf.nasa.gov/PhotoServer/photoServer.html) has digitized photos of many of the research aircraft flown by NASA astronauts and pilots and other interesting pictures.

Fig. 14-1: The National Academy of Sciences server offers vast resources, in part because of the multitude of constitutent organizations included within the academy.

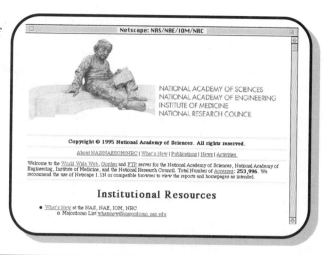

They offer a list of the most frequently downloaded photos each month as well as a Cool Photo of the Month.

The National Science Foundation (http://www.nsf.gov) is one of the major governmental funding agencies for scientific research in the United States. It both initiates and supports scientific and technical research and facilitates cooperation among researchers at every level of society. *Frontiers*, the NSF newsletter, offers interesting insights into scientific issues. Also, the Web site allows users to search research grant abstracts to determine who is working on what scientific problems.

The National Institutes of Health (http://www.nih.gov) and its constituent institutes such as the National Cancer Institute and the National Institute on Allergies and Infectious Diseases (which is the headquarters for the federal fight against AIDS) represent the focal point for the federal support of research into medicine and health sciences. The site offers extensive information about grant opportunities and awards, significant news and other information. It offers a link to the National Library of Medicine (http://www.nlm.nih.gov), which has taken the lead in the dissemination of medically related information. The National Library of Medicine also serves as the headquarters for the national High Performance Computing and Communications Initiative, a pioneering effort to develop the next generation of high performance computing across the scientific disciplines.

The mission of the National Oceanographic and Atmospheric Administration at http://www.noaa.gov is to promote global environmental stewardship in order to conserve and wisely manage the nation's marine and coastal resources. To that end, it describes, monitors and predicts changes in the earth's environment. Its Web site offers access to NOAA data centers including environmentally related images of the United States, weather maps and images of weather events such as Hurricane Emily bashing the outer banks of North Carolina, studies of solar terrestrial physics, information on marine biology from the National Marine Fisheries Service, sea surface temperatures from Coast Watch images, weather in space, and many other things. There is also a full accounting of NOAA in the news.

The National Academy of Science (http://www.nas.edu) is a private, nonprofit society of scholars dedicated to the advancement of scientific and technical knowledge and its use for the general welfare. The academy has several constituent organizations including the Institute of Medicine, the National Research Council and the National Academy of Engineering. In addition to the Web site, it operates a Gopher and an FTP server. NAS reports often have a dramatic impact on science and public policy.

The American Association for the Advancement of Science (AAAS) at http://www.aaas.org is a major interdisciplinary association of scientists. Its Web site includes resources for students and children, information about science policy and programs, online forums, and access to *Science,* the AAAS' flagship publication and a vehicle for publishing major research findings. Perhaps the most intriguing service, however, is Science's Next Wave, an electronic network to help appropriately trained people to navigate the complex landscape of science.

Physics

Physics consists of the study of matter, energy and motion. It explores phenomena like the laws of motion, the structure of space and time and the forces that hold matter together or, conversely, drive it apart.

Often the study of physics is divided into two areas—classical physics and modern physics. Classical physics includes topics such as mechanics, thermodynamics, sound, optics, electricity, magnetism and electromagnetic fields. But while the principles of classical physics seem to adequately describe larger systems and slower moving objects (those not close to the speed of light), they are not neatly applicable to atomic and subatomic interactions or for fast-moving objects.

Modern physics looks at motion, matter and energy in the atom and smaller systems. Modern physics is subdivided into quantum, or wave, mechanics that predicts the behavior of subatomic particles and relativistic mechanics that examines objects moving at speeds close to the speed of light. Most introductory physics courses will cover topics in both classical and modern physics.

One of the best starting points of information about physics is located at McGill University (http://www.physics.mcgill.ca/physics-services/physics_topical.html). A comprehensive index, it provides links to Web pages on topics such as general relativity, computational fluid dynamics, astrophysics, nonlinear dynamics and educational resources for physics research. There is also a link for theoretical physics. The index is international and includes resources from Israel to Sweden. You can also search the Physics Around the World Database for links to sites with information you may need.

The Harvard-Smithsonian Center for Astrophysics (CFA) at http://cfa-www.harvard.edu/cfa-home.html explores the basic physical processes that have determined the nature and evolution of the universe. It has divisions for atomic and molecular physics, high-energy astrophysics, solar and stellar physics and more. The CFA also operates three telescopes and houses the Astrophysical Journal Letters office, which provides bibliographic search services through the Web. *Sky and Telescope* magazine and educational resources are also available.

Physics and its subfields are the subjects of many Usenet Newsgroups. The Frequently Asked Questions (FAQ) postings from those groups can be found at http://www.cis.ohio-state.edu/hypertext/faq/usenet/physics-faq/top.html. Among the groups represented are General Physics, Classical Mechanics, Atomic Physics, General Relativity, Particle Physics, Quantum Mechanics, and Fluid Dynamics.

Another source for physics FAQs and answers to questions about physics in everyday life, such as why golf balls have dimples and which way will your bathtub drain, can be found at http://info.desy.de/user/projects/Physics/. It is part of the home page of a high-energy particle physics research center in Germany.

Physics teaching resources

Several online physics courses have been developed. One example is the stand-alone introductory mechanics workshop developed at the University of Illinois, Chicago (Fig. 14-2). It is intended as a supplement to the standard classroom offering. Available at http://sunhehi.phy.uic.edu/~clive/IP/instructions/browser_HTML3/00_toc.html, the modules include simulated experiments that correspond with the major topics in a standard course including the dimensions of motion, friction, potential energy and momentum.

Another good teaching resource is the Table of Nuclides at http://www.dne.bnl.gov/CoN/index.html. The table presents a chart of all known nuclides with the horizontal row representing individual elements; the vertical column representing nuclides with the same neutron numbers and red dots signaling known isotopes of the element. Clicking on regions of the chart or dot provides more in-depth information about the properties of the nuclide or atom.

Students can now monitor the progress of high-energy particle physics experiments around the world through the Web server at http://www-spires.slac.stanford.edu/find/explist.html. This document directs you to home pages of various high-energy physics experiments including those conducted in labs in Switzerland, Germany, and Japan as well as Stanford University, Cornell University and Fermilab in the United States.

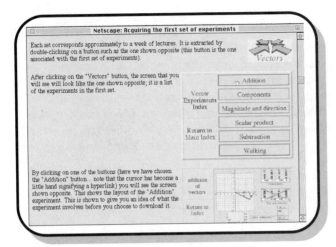

Fig. 14-2: One of many online physics courses is available through the University of Illinois, Chicago.

The home page of the *American Journal of Physics* is located at http://www.amherst.edu/~ajp. The journal celebrated its 60th birthday in 1995 and one of the more interesting sections of the page is its collection of memorable papers. Its first article was enigmatically titled Physics is Physics, whose author also wrote the classic textbook *Introduction to Physics*. In addition to memorable papers, the site lists the 13 most widely cited papers, according to the Institute for Scientific Information in Philadelphia.

Since the early 1990s, many physicists have not had to wait for papers to appear in a printed form. Since 1991, Los Alamos National Laboratory has operated an electronic preprint distribution and archive service. It is located at http://xxx.lanl.gov. Users subscribe to the service in their areas of interest. Currently there are 26 different options ranging from Algebraic Geometry to Quantum Physics. The high-energy particle physics laboratory in Switzerland also operates a preprint service at http://preprints.cern.ch. Topics include experimental physics, several subcategories of high-energy physics, nuclear theory and general relativity.

The American Institute of Physics (AIP) is a not-for-profit membership corporation chartered for the purpose of promoting the advancement and diffusion of the knowledge of physics and its application to human welfare. It is a primary publisher of physics information, including eight archived journals. Its home page at http://www.aip.org/aip/wwwinfo.html provides links to member and affiliated societies and institutes including the American Association of Physicists in Medicine and the American Geophysical Union.

Formed in 1899 and dedicated to the advancement and diffusion of information in physics, the American Physical Society consists of more than 41,000 physicists worldwide. It publishes some of the world's most respected physics research journals, organizes scientific meetings and conducts educational and public affairs programs. Its home page is at http://aps.org.

The American Association of Physics Teachers promotes quality physics education in America and around the world. The association publishes the *American Journal of Physics and Physics Teachers*. It also produces and distributes educational resources and runs educational events such as the Physics Bowl. Finally, the association organizes conferences on topics of interest for physics teachers at the undergraduate and graduate level. Its home page is at http://www.physics.arizona.edu/~robson/AAPT.html.

Discussion lists of interest to physicists include

- phys-l@uwf.cc.uwf.edu (for teachers of college physics courses).
- phys-stu@uwf.cc.uwf.edu (physics students).
- physnews@aip.org (digest of physics news).
- astro-ph@babbage.sissa.it (astrophysics).

Biology

Biology is the study of life ranging from the molecular interactions within the cells of living creatures to the organization and classification of different organisms such as plants and animals.

What is a living creature? That is a complex question. But among the fundamental characteristics of living things that distinguish them from non-living matter is a specific organization, a range of chemical reactions, the ability to maintain an appropriate internal environment despite changes in the external environment, movement, reproduction, growth, responsiveness and adaptation to change.

One of the fundamental concepts of biology is cell theory—the idea that the cell is the basic unit of living things. While there are one-cell organisms, in complex multicellular life such as human beings the functioning of the entire organism consists of the coordinated activities and organization of the individual cells.

Introductory biology classes survey the range of activities that generally characterize life. They will look at the chemical basis of life by studying molecular and cellular biology and biochemistry; they analyze the energy involved in life processes and the chemical reactions associated with that energy; they review the way different kinds of life can be classified and categorized; they study evolution and the development of life, reproduction and genetics; and they can touch on ecology and environment, the conditions and interactions of living and non-living creatures.

Most classes look at those issues for plants, animals and humans. To a large degree, research in biology and related fields such as anatomy and physiology and biochemistry provides the basis of contemporary medicine. And with the development of biotechnology and breakthroughs in our understanding of the way genetics and DNA function, biology is one of the hottest areas in science.

Some starting places for biology resources

An excellent starting point for biological resources on the Internet can be found at http://golgi.harvard.edu. It provides links to a wide range of biological databases including those for specific organisms, a variety of different genome projects, the Protein Data Bank that contains information about proteins that have been characterized, and links to other resources. For example, students can find links to The Tree of Life: A Phylogenetic Navigator for the Internet, and Bacterial Species Nomenclature. Moreover, the same server hosts the Virtual Library for Biosciences at http://golgi.harvard.edu/htbin/biopages. The Virtual Library is divided into topics ranging from agriculture to virology to whale watching.

Another site with links to many databases with biological information, access to electronic publications for biology, and a primer on molecular genetics is found at The Johns Hopkins University Bioinformatics Web Server at http://www.gdb.org/hopkins.html. You can also find an interface to the protein and DNA sequence comparison server at Oak Ridge National Laboratory.

The Biodiversity and Biological Collections Web server at http://muse.bio.cornell.edu is oriented toward systemists and organismic biologists. It contains information about biological collections, taxonomic authority files, and reports by standards bodies. It houses the archives for the e-mail lists MUSE-L and CICHLID-L and has access to online journals.

The Biotechnology Information Center at http://www.inform.umd.edu:8080/EdRes/Topic/AgrEnv/Biotech/ is one of ten information centers of the National Agricultural Library of the U.S. Department of Agriculture. It provides links to bibliographies and resource guides on a range of biotech topics as well as biotechnology educational resources and biotechnology newsletters. A typical report is "Biotechnology for the 21st Century: New Horizons," published by the National Science and Technology Council.

The purpose of CSUBIOWEB is to consolidate biological teaching and research resources and to create and distribute multimedia teaching resources in biology. At http://arnica.csustan.edu/, CSUBIOWEB collects submissions from biologists and other interested people.

Network resources for the classroom

A starting point for classroom resources to be used in life science class is located at http://www-sci.lib.uci.edu/SEP/life.html. The people maintaining the site have located more than 2,000 Web resources. Some of the classifications of interest to life sciences include Living Things: Origin and Molecules and Cells: Energetics to Heredity and Ecology.

The Biotech Server at Indiana University (http://biotech.chem.indiana.edu) is a hybrid biology/chemistry educational and research resource aimed at the broad community from high school students to

Fig. 14-3: This 3-D image of insulin is among the biomolecules portrayed at a University of Missouri server.

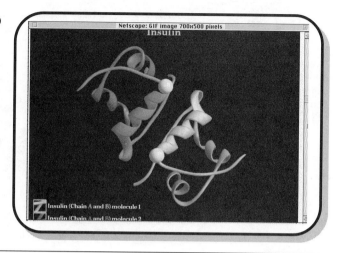

academic researchers. Among the resources available are the Dictionary of Biotechnology Terms, Nucleic Acid Sequence Database, a Protein Sequence database, and sections on virology, particularly HIV and AIDS and other topics. Biotech project members have developed a series of educational guides to help people integrate Internet tools into their work. Some of the more interesting pointers include one to The Chemist's Art Gallery, which has full motion images of protein binding and other chemical processes of interest to chemists and biologists. There is also a tutorial on cell biology.

A picture is often worth a thousand words. Links to three-dimensional images of biomolecules can be found at http://www.missouri.edu/~c621913/links.html. These images are so popular that their servers are often inaccessible during the normal workday. Some of the images are of insulin (Fig. 14-3), B-DNA and a variety of proteins.

BIOSCI consists of the Bionet Usenet Newsgroups and parallel e-mail lists used by biologists worldwide. It is located at http://www.bio.net. The groups are intended to facilitate communication among professional biologists. While others are free to listen in, the participants do not expect to answer basic questions.

The goal of Cell and Molecular Biology Online serves as a resource to the academic biological community. At http://challenge.tiac.net/users/pmgannon, it is particularly geared to cell and molecular biologists.

The Visible Human Project is an ambitious attempt to create a complete, anatomically detailed, three-dimensional representation of the male and female human body using CAT, MRI and cryosection images at one-millimeter intervals. An introduction to the project and sample images can be found at http://www.nlm.nih.gov/extramural_research.dir/visible_human.html. Related projects and additional images can be found at the Center for Human

Fig. 14-4: The University of Queensland's Nanoworld is dedicated to the understanding of the tinier elements of life.

Simulation at the University of Colorado (http://www.hsc.colorado.edu:80/chs/vhm.html) and the M.D. Anderson Cancer Center at the University of Texas (http://rpisun1.mda.uth.tmc.edu/se/anatomy) among other locations.

The Nanoworld Home Page (Fig. 14-4) at http://www.uq.oz.au/nanoworld/nanohome.html is dedicated to understanding the structure and composition of matter from the atomic to cellular and macromolecular scales. It has an impressive picture gallery of different biological material such as blood cells, bone marrow and chloroplasts.

The Frequently Asked Question posting for evolutionary biology is located at http://rumba.ics.uci.edu:8080/origins/faqs-evolution.html. Intended for the participants of the Usenet Newsgroup talk.origins, it provides a good overview of evolution.

Additional insight into the work of Charles Darwin and other scientific pioneers in evolution can be found at http://ucmp1.berkeley.edu/exhibittext/evolution.html. The site provides an excellent historical look at evolution and its usefulness.

An index to bibliographies about entomology on the Internet is located at http://www.ent.iastate.edu/List/Bibliographies.html. You can read about everything from ants to screwworms. There are links to the Hawaiian Biological Survey and a large Gopher site at the University of Notre Dame. A collection of favorite readings about entomology is located at http://www.colostate.edu/Depts/Entomology/readings.html. It is an idiosyncratic book list of some of the best books on the natural history of insects and the experiences of scientists who work with them.

The International Organization for Plant Information was created in 1991 to consider the establishment of a Global Plant Species Information System. Its Web site at http://life.anu.edu.au/biodiversity/iopi/iopi.html includes demonstrations of hypermedia taxonomic information and access to the Australian Plant Name Index. There are links to other Web servers of interest to botanists.

The American Society for Biochemistry and Molecular Biology has nearly 10,000 members, most of whom teach and conduct research at universities and colleges. Its Web server at http://highwire.stanford.edu/asbmb/asbmb.html provides access to the online version of its *Journal of Biological Chemistry* as well as minireviews and links to areas of interest to biochemists. The society is on the campus network of the Federation of American Societies for Experimental Biology (FASEB).

Abstracts of articles scheduled for publication in the journals of The American Physiological Society (another constituent of FASEB) can be found at http://www.uth.tmc.edu:80/apstracts/1995/. The publications include specialized versions of the *American Journal of Physiology*, the *Journal of Applied Physiology* and *Physiological Reviews*.

The American Institute of Biological Sciences at gopher://aibs.org is a component of the National Academy of Sciences. It is a federation of more than 45 scientific societies and laboratories and has a total membership of more than 80,000 biologists, students and others concerned with the life sciences.

Bioline Publications is an electronic publishing service for bioscientists at http://www.bdt.org.br/bioline/. Abstracts and summaries of articles as well as listings of contents in journals, newsletters and reports in the fields of microbiology, biotechnology, biodiversity and bioinformatics are available. New material is announced through the Bioline-L e-mail list. To receive full text and graphics, you must register with the service.

Discussion lists of interest to biologists include
- bioguide@yalevm.cis.yale.edu (biology resources).
- molbio-l@mizzou1.missouri.edu (molecular biology).
- biotech%umdd.bitnet@listserv.net (biotechnology).
- biomed-l@vm1.nodak.edu (medicine and medical technology).
- gentalk@usa.net (genetics and biotechnology).
- humevo@gwuvm.gwu.edu (human evolutionary research).

Chemistry

Chemistry is the general study of matter. All matter is defined by two characteristics—it has mass, that is, it weighs something, and it has volume, that is, it takes up space. A simple glance around you indicates that matter comes in many shapes and forms.

One of the most simple classification systems used divides matter into three categories—gas, liquid and solid. Another classification scheme categorizes matter according to its constituent parts. It can either be a pure substance or a mixture. A pure substance has a consistent composition and always has the same properties regardless of its origins. Mixtures are made of different constituent parts. Their properties differ when the proportions of the component parts are changed. Pure substances can be further subdivided into elements and compounds. Compounds can be changed into substantially different materials under certain sets of circumstances. Elements defy efforts to change them.

Chemistry investigates and analyzes the changes in the basic nature and composition of pure substances when they undergo certain processes. The original substance may be transformed into a new one or react with a third substance in a different way. The changes different substances undergo when subjected to different processes are called chemical properties.

Chemistry is often divided into two major areas. Physical or inorganic chemistry looks at the chemistry of nonliving matter. Organic or biochemistry looks at the chemical transformation in living organisms.

Chemistry, of course, has broad application in the world. It is an integral process in everything from discovering new wonder drugs in medicine to cleaning up the environment.

Internet starting points for chemistry

There are several excellent starting points for chemistry resources on the Internet. In addition to having many of the standard categories to be expected from a starting point, the pages maintained by Thomas C.O. Haver at the University of Maryland at http://www.inform.umd.edu:8080/UMS+State/UMD-Projects/MCTP/Technology/Chemistry.html have a very strong section about online chemical conferences, including pointers to the software needed to participate and a listing of upcoming online events.

The Analytical Chemistry Springboard at http://www.anachem.umu.se/jumpstation.htm is an ambitious attempt to collect most of the pertinent information about chemical analysis found on the Web. It has pointers to resources to most significant analytical techniques from atomic spectroscopy to x-ray spectroscopy. It also provides an extensive range of general chemistry resources including online journals, links to news groups and listserv discussion groups, nonprofit organizations, software repositories and more.

An extensive listing of software for chemistry is maintained at http://nmr400a.mols.susx.ac.uk/~steven. The site contains short descriptions of software written for the major computing operating environments including Windows and Windows NT, Macintosh OS and Unix.

The Clearinghouse for Chemical Information Instructional Materials is a joint project of the American Chemical Society and the Special Libraries Association. Its Gopher server at gopher://lib-gopher.lib.indiana.edu:7050/11/cciim archives items that have been developed by chemists and chemistry and science librarians to instruct people in the use of chemical information sources. Many of the papers are available in ASCII format. Those not in ASCII can be ordered.

Chemistry teaching resources

A comprehensive site for resources for chemistry education can be found at http://www.anachem.umu.se/eks/pointers.htm. The site has pointers to dozens of courses offered using Internet resources ranging from A Brief Review of Quantum Chemistry to Computational Chemistry and Organic Synthesis. Moreover, there are links to software repositories, news groups, mailing lists and other relevant information. Finally, there are pointers to molecular models, visualizations, images and databases.

The Chemistry Hypermedia Project at Virginia Tech University at http://www.chem.vt.edu:80/chem-ed/CHP/overview.html develops tutorials to supplement undergraduate chemistry education. The documents contain hypermedia links to remedial material describing chemical principals. For analytical chemistry, some of the topics currently covered include an Introduction to Analytical Chemistry, Analytical Chemistry Basics, and an Encyclopedia of Instrumental Methods. The organic chemistry section includes still and motion videos of molecular model representations and snapshots of an interactive multimedia project about atomic structures. The group is also converting its multimedia project Visualization of Fundamental Concepts in Chemistry into a Web format.

Global Instructional Chemistry is pioneering the concepts of the distributed teaching of chemistry. Located at http://www.ch.ic.ac.uk/GIC, the team is building case histories to illustrate chemistry in action. The histories will include active molecules that users will be able to rotate, measure and otherwise manipulate. Some of the contents currently online include Organic Reaction Mechanisms, Analyzing 2D NMR Spectra using Hyperactive Molecules, Principles of Protein Structure, and Molecular Animations.

Molecular modeling involves the use of computational methods for simulating and predicting the structures and properties of molecules. The National Institutes of Health has developed an introductory course in molecular modeling available at http://www.nih.gov/molecular_modeling. The course units include establishing goals, defining models, methods for modeling and analysis, and an overview of hardware and software necessary and available.

The Equilibrium Dialysis Experiment is often discussed in textbooks for upper-level college and first-year medical school courses in immunology. It is performed to study the chemical properties of antibody molecules. An interactive computer simulation of the experiment is available at http://131.183.61.190/eqDial/Intro.

Chemistry reference materials

WebElements is a periodic table database containing information about the elements on the periodic chart (Fig. 14-5). It is available at http://

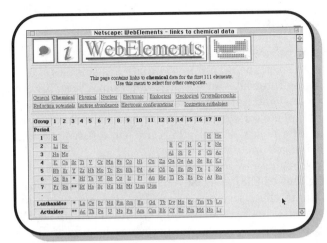

Fig. 14-5: The WebElements site contains a database about elements, with a periodic table interface.

www.shef.ac.uk/uni/academic/A-C/chem/web-elements/web-elements-home.html. The site also has interactive calculators for isotope patterns and element percentages as well as information about a range of different chemical and physical properties including crystallographic information.

An interactive weights and measures calculator and converter is located at http://eardc.swt.edu/cgi-bin/ucon/ucon.pl. It is operated by the Edwards Aquifer Research and Data Center. The Computational Chemistry Archives at Ohio State University at http://ccl.osc.edu/ccl/cca.html is a comprehensive source of information about computational chemistry. Not only does it house the archives of the computational chemistry e-mail discussion list, it has pointers to sets of data for use in computational chemistry programs; documents describing methods, standards and approaches associated with computational chemistry; periodicals of interest; and computational chemistry software. There is also a search engine to help you find the information you want.

The Chemical Heritage Foundation provides a comprehensive list of pointers to resources on the Web about the history of chemistry as well as access to its online collections. There are online oral histories with top scientists, including biographical information and images. The site is located at http://beckman1.sas.upenn.edu.

The American Chemical Society consists of nearly 150,000 members at all degree levels. Its web site at http://www.acs.org provides insight into the concerns of professional chemists. You can find subscription information about the more than 25 journals the Society publishes including *Chemical & Engineering News, Biochemistry,* and the *Journal of Physical Chemistry.* There is also a link to the home page of the Chemical Abstract Service, a service of the ACS and a major database of information about chemical structures. A schedule of ACS-sponsored events and other programs is also available.

The Royal Society of Chemistry at http://chemistry.rsc.org/rsc is the British equivalent of ACS. Open to the public, the RSC library and information center is the largest center in the United Kingdom devoted to chemistry and related subject areas. The Web page also has a searchable index for chemistry information.

The *Journal of Molecular Modeling* claims to be the first fully electronic journal in chemistry. At http://www.organik.uni-erlangen.de/info/JMOLMOD/jmolinfo.html, articles, which cover both applications and methods development, are archived in a database for two years and then stored on CD ROM as well. Recent articles include Folding of Globular Proteins by Energy Minimization and Monte Carlo Simulations with Hydrophobic Surface Area Potentials and A Conjugate Gradient Algorithm with a Trust Region for Molecular Geometry Optimization.

Discussion groups of interest to chemists include
- Cheme-l@ psuvm.psu.edu (chemical engineering).
- Chemlab-l@beaver.bemidji.msus.edu (people interested in chemistry labs).
- Chminf-l@iubvm.ucs.indiana.edu (information sources to answer questions).
- CCL@ccl.osc.edu (computational chemistry list). Send subscription to chemistry-request@ccl.osc.edu.
- Watoc@ic.ac.uk (World Association of Theoretical Chemists).

Astronomy

More than 30,000 years ago, Cro Magnon people made engravings that may depict the phases of the moon. These calendars are considered the oldest astronomical documents and predate writing by nearly 25,000 years. Clearly, astronomy, the study of the universe and its different forms of energy and matter, is a fundamental science, stimulated by people's curiosity about the world in which they live.

Astronomy is divided into several different branches according to the objects of study and the methods used. Working outward, astronomers study the Earth (particularly the atmosphere), the moon, the planets, the sun, the stars, the galaxies and all the objects of the universe. Working inward, astronomers study the atoms, molecules, elementary particles and dust that make up the seemingly endless space between stars.

Astronomical research is conducted in different broad areas. Spherical astronomy is concerned with the places of the celestial bodies in the sky; celestial mechanics studies the movements of bodies in the universe; astrophysics applies the findings of modern physics to the heavens. Data is often gathered through the measurement of wavelengths. Among the different wavelengths used are radio, infrared, optical, ultraviolet, x-ray, and gamma rays.

The NASA Astrophysics Data System at http://adswww.harvard.edu provides a wealth of information for astronomers in an electronic format. Its main emphasis is on an abstract service that provides access to more than 700,000 abstracts in astronomy and astrophysics, space instrumentation, physics and geophysics. ADS also provides pointers to astronomical data catalogs and archives.

The Earth Observation Guide and Directory Service of the European Space Agency at http://gds.esrin.esa.it:80/ describes Earth observation data, systems and applications. Its section on remote sensing offers sets of images collected by instruments carried on satellites in space which are gathering information about activity on earth.

The Usenet space and astronomy FAQ is archived at http://hcs.harvard.edu:80/~stahr/info/faq.html. It has 13 sections. There are also pointers to FAQs for physics and for amateur telescope enthusiasts.

The AstroWeb Consortium is a collection of information gathered by members at seven institutions around the world. Located at http://fits.cv.nrao.edu/www/astroweb.html, it serves as the basis for the Virtual Library pages for astronomy.

Images from space

The Hubble Space Telescope (HST) has sent back spectacular images to Earth. The home page for the Space Telescope Science Institute, which operates HST, is at http://www.stsci.edu. In addition to its Greatest Hits image gallery, which displays some of the most dramatic images HST has produced, the site has links to information of general interest to educators and students. Hubble observations are also available in motion video and animation formats.

A huge listing of links to astronomical images is available at http://msowww.anu.edu.au/anton/astro_pictures.html (Fig. 14-6). Among the linked sites are NASA Ames SPACE archive, the Astronomical Images Archive, a range of images from the Comet Shoemaker-Levy, images from the Magellan spacecraft and more.

Another great resource for planetary and lunar images is located at http://ic-www.arc.nasa.gov/ic/projects/bayes-group/Atlas. In addition to links to other sites, each image, which was selected for visual appeal or to illustrate an interesting feature, includes educational summaries. The site has images returned by the Voyager mission to outer planets, the Space Shuttle, the Magellan mission to Venus and others.

The NSSDC Photo Gallery at http://nssdc.gsfc.nasa.gov/photo_gallery/about_photogallery.html provides access to many of NASA's most popular images. They are generally organized by object or phenomenon. Only some of the images have captions.

Fig. 14-6: A wealth of images from space, such as this from the Astronomical Data Archive, may be obtained from servers on the Internet.

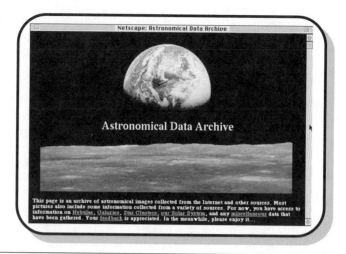

The Lake Afton Public Observatory in Wichita, Kansas, sponsors an Ask The Astronomer section on its home page at http://twsuvm.uc.twsu.edu:80/~obswww/o20.html. You can submit the questions by e-mail. The page also has links to astronomical resources for teachers.

The Planetary Society was founded by Carl Sagan and other internationally known astronomers in 1980 to encourage the exploration of the solar system and the search for extraterrestrial life. It now has over 100,000 members. Its home page at http://planetary.org/tps is an excellent source of news about space exploration. There is also a link that allows people to participate in NASA online activities.

The National Undergraduate Research Observatory is a consortium of primarily undergraduate institutes that have joined together to provide hands-on training and research experiences for undergraduate students. It shares about 60 percent of the observing time of the Lowell Observatory's 31-inch telescope. Its home page is at http://nuro.phy.nau.edu. An image gallery displays some of the observations that have been made using the telescope.

Some discussion lists of interest to students of astronomy include
- Hastro-L@wvn.wvnet.edu (History of Astronomy).
- Astro@gitvm1.gatech.edu (General Astronomy sponsored by the Atlanta Astronomy Club).
- Sednews@tamvm1.tamu.edu (Students for the Exploration and Development of Space).
- spacesci@uga.cc.uga.edu (Planetary and space-based science).

Earth and environmental sciences

Since the publication of Rachel Carson's *Silent Spring*, the environment has been the renewed locus of interdisciplinary scientific research. Earth and environmental sciences use many of the tools, techniques, strategies and insights of the other major scientific disciplines as they look at the development of the earth and atmosphere and try to determine how major systems interact and influence each other. Some of the disciplines included in earth and environmental sciences are geology, meteorology, oceanography, ecology and seismology.

Because the issues involved in earth and environmental sciences are central to the preservation of human life on this planet, earth and environmental sciences have become the purview of major government agencies such as the U.S. Environmental Protection Agency. And since the environmental processes do not respect national borders, there are many cooperative international efforts at data collection and education.

The Web server for the U.S. Environmental Protection Agency is located at http://www.epa.gov. The EPA has established a comprehensive service giving people insight into its activities, the issues facing the environment and the results of its efforts. There are links to data sets and software developed by EPA scientists, software and test methods, news items and other Internet links. The EPA's National Center for Environmental Publications and Information at http://www.epa.gov/epahome/NCEPI-Welcome.html is a repository for technical, scientific and public-oriented publications. The documents are provided free of charge to the public.

The Consortium for International Earth Science Information Network (CIESIN) was established in 1989 to study global climate change. Located at http://www.ciesin.org, it specializes in integrating and providing access to physical, natural and socioeconomic information across scientific disciplines and in building a technical infrastructure for global environmental change for research scientists. In addition to serving as an introduction to its own projects, the CIESIN home page provides gateways to a range of other sources on the Internet.

An excellent starting point for resources in geology and seismology can be found at http://www.ts.umu.se/~widmark/lwgeolog.html. This site has links to other Web pages in a dozen categories, including museums, societies and software, in addition to different disciplines such as seismology, volcanology and geochemistry. There is also information about nine appropriate Usenet Newsgroups. Altogether there are more than 700 links.

The National Resources Research Information Pages at http://sfbox.vt.edu:10021/Y/yfleung/nrrips.html serves as a guide for students, researchers and practitioners in natural resources. It has links to relevant databases and literature archives as well as a section on outdoor recreation research. A typical online document is A Biological Survey for the Nation published by the National Research Council. Linked periodicals include the *Biological Conservation Newsletter* (Smithsonian Institution), *EarthLink* (EPA) and the *Journal of Soil and Water Conservation*.

The Environmental Library, a project of the EnviroLink Network, is meant to be a clearinghouse of environmental information on the Internet.

Fig. 14-7: The Geological Survey of Canada sponsors an Earth Science Site of the Week, providing access to a number of outstanding sites in the field.

It contains archives of environmentally oriented discussion groups, links to governmental agencies around the world, a primer on key environmental issues and a directory of organizations. It is located at http://envirolink.org/envirowebs.html.

The Executive Environmental Report at http://www.bpinews.com/bpinews provides an excellent news service about issues of interest to people involved in environmental issues. There are also links to environmentally related companies.

The Atlantic division of the Geological Survey of Canada sponsors an Earth Science Site of the Week (Fig. 14-7) at http://agcwww.bio.ns.ca/misc/geores/sotw/sotw.html. It also includes an index to and a search mechanism for sites that have been featured in the past.

The Institute of Geophysics and Planetary Physics at UCLA is the founding branch of a multicampus research unit that has pioneered the application of physics and chemistry to earth science. Located at http://www.igpp.ucla.edu, the institute is now exploring the application of paleontology and microbiology to the study of the origin and evolution of life, visualization to the understanding of the Earth's space environment and global change studies.

For more than 90 years, the Scripps Institution of Oceanography (http://sio.ucsd.edu) has been one of the nation's premier centers of oceanography. The Web page provides links to data collections as well as an index for Oceanographic and Earth Science Institutions. An interesting project under development is called the Center for Coastal Studies Data Zoo, which will centralize the data for a range of California coastal data collection projects.

NOAA's National Geophysical Data Center at http://www.ngdc.noaa.gov/ngdc.html manages environmental data in solar terrestrial physics, solid earth geophysics, marine geology, glaciology (the study of ice and snow) and other areas. NOAA's National Environmental Satellite, Data and Information Service home page at http://ns.noaa.gov/NESDIS/NESDIS_Home.html is also a comprehensive source of environmental and earth science data. The site also has excellent images of hurricane data.

The American Geological Institute is a federation of 28 geoscientific and professional organizations. Its GeoRef service provides access to what is claimed to be the most comprehensive database of geoscience literature in the world. It is located at http://agi.umd.edu/agi/agi.html.

The U.S. Geological Survey is the United States' largest earth science research and information agency. Its home page at http://www.usgs.gov has links to educational resources, environmental research and news about the USGS.

An excellent source for educational materials for environmental and earth sciences can be found at http://www-sci.lib.uci.edu/SEP/earth.html. Some of the subcategories there include Measurement and Scientific Investigation, Atmosphere and Weather, Oceans and Dynamics, and Water and Its Effects.

An excellent site for the study of the weather is Weather World at http://www.atmos.uiuc.edu/wxworld/html/top.html. Developed by the Atmospheric Sciences Department at the University of Illinois, Urbana-Champaign, it is a comprehensive collection of weather information, including satellite images, maps, charts and text. The department's Weather Visualizer can be found at http://storm.atmos.uiuc.edu/covis/visualizer/covisualizer.text.html. It gives users the opportunity to customize weather maps and images and to learn about weather process.

Discussion lists of interest to environmental and earth scientists include

- envst-l@brownvm.brown.edu (undergraduate and graduate studies).
- biosph-l@ubvm.cc.buffalo.edu (anything relating to the biosphere).
- env-link+@andrew.cmu.edu (send request to env-link+forms@andrew.cmu.edu). Free information about news of interest to environmental scientists.

Mathematics and statistics

Mathematics is a way of representing data and activity in the world that is used across the sciences and other areas of life. Basic mathematics is essential to functioning in modern society.

Introductory college math can be broadly divided into three areas—precalculus, calculus and statistics. Precalculus includes arithmetic, algebra, and geometry, which teach students rules for reasoning and manipulating with symbols. Algebra involves the manipulation of systems of linear equations. Geometry looks at the analysis of shapes.

Unlike algebra, which is primarily concerned with static systems—solving for a particular variable—calculus is the study of how change in one variable affects another variable. As such, calculus is a method for exploring what are called dynamic systems such as instantaneous rates of change.

Statistics is a set of mathematical tools used to describe and understand data. Information is collected and then analyzed statistically to better determine the significance of the information gathered.

A mathematics starting point

An excellent starting point for mathematics on the Internet is Mathematics on the Web sponsored by the American Mathematical Society at http://www.ams.org/mathweb. It has guides to mathematical literature, bibliographic servers for abstracts, reviews and databases, and sources for all sorts of specialized looks at mathematics. The American Mathematical Society itself (http://www.ams.org) was founded in 1888 and has more than 30,000 members. Its mission is to promote mathematical research, increase the awareness of its value in society and to foster excellence in mathematical education. The Web page has a preprint server for mathematical journal articles and a link to MathSciNet, providing access to mathematical literature from 1940 on.

The Mathematical Association of America is the largest professional society of college and university mathematics teachers in the world. At http://www.maa.org, the MAA is focused on improving mathematical education, professional development for mathematical scientists, enhancing student activity in the mathematical sciences and influencing public policy.

The *Mathematics Archives* at http://archives.math.utk.edu is intended to provide organized Internet access to mathematical resources. Its primary strength is on the collection of educational software. It has also assembled an extensive list of links to electronic journals, preprint services, publishers of mathematical textbooks and software and journals. There are sections devoted to electronic news groups and discussion lists as well as material intended for undergraduate education.

Planet Earth Mathematics Page at http://canyon.ucsd.edu/infoville/goldmine/Mathematics/mathematics.html (Fig. 14-8) is also a comprehensive resource for mathematical materials accessible via the Internet as is CSC TopMath at http://www.csc.fi/cgi-bin/math-top. CSC TopMath collects hyperlinks to information services about mathematics submitted by mathematicians on the Internet.

Project NExT is a program for new or recent Ph.D.s in mathematical sciences who wish to improve their teaching skills. Its Web server at http://archives.math.utk.edu/~toddwill/projnext.html provides resources and classroom material sorted by method and by subject. Among the subjects covered are precalculus, calculus, linear and abstract algebra and differential equations.

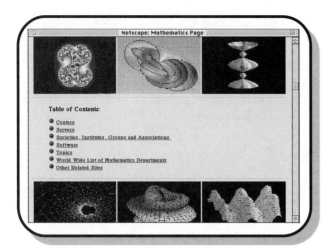

Fig. 14-8: The Planet Earth Mathematics Page is a comprehensive resource for mathematical materials available on the Net.

The University of Minnesota's Geometry Center at http://www.geom. umn.edu is a unified mathematical computing environment to support math and computer science research, mathematical visualization and math education from kindergarten through college. It has a gallery of interactive geometry in which famous geometric problems are visualized. It also has interactive applications that Web users can manipulate, a reference archive and a multimedia archive with hypertext papers, preprints and other materials.

Calculus@Internet is an interactive Web server that integrates a common laboratory sequence with different computer-aided algebra packages such as Theorist from Waterloo Maple and Mathematica from Wolfram Research. Found at http://calculus.sjdccd.cc.ca.us/cai-home.html, some of the units covered include precalculus, differential calculus, integral calculus and differential equations.

Problem Solving in the 21st Century at http://www2.hawaii.edu/ suremath/home.html presents a comprehensive approach to problem solving including problem solving in algebra and physics. There is a link to the Journal of Modern Problem Solving and an explanation behind this new approach to mathematics at the college level.

Graphics in the calculus classroom reflects work in the graphical presentation of numerical and computational analysis. It can be found at http://www.math.psu.edu/dna/graphics.html.

The Interdisciplinary Course in Chemistry, Physics and Mathematics is a 15-unit course that integrates synthesized material from all three disciplines. At http://dept.physics.upenn.edu/courses/gladney/mathphys/ Contents.html, some sample units include Describing How Things Change, and Conserving Equations.

Steven Finch of the research and development team at Mathsoft, a publisher of mathematical software, has posted his favorite mathematical constants at http://www.mathsoft.com/cgi-shl/perl.exe?constant.pl.

The history of mathematics is the focus at http://www-groups.dcs.st-andrews.ac.uk:80/~history. The archive contains the biographies of more than 1,000 mathematicians. About 200 of the biographies are reasonably detailed and contain pictures of the subjects. Articles about the development of some mathematical ideas have been cross-linked to the biographies.

A Web site devoted to Albert Einstein can be found at http://www.sas.upenn.edu/~smfriedm/einstein.html. Sections includes several accounts of his life, quotes, pictures, organizations which bear his name and discussions of his ideas.

The Department of Mathematics at Furman University has a mathematical quotation server at http://math.furman.edu/~mwoodard/mquot.html. A typical quote—"Technical skill is mastery of complexity while creativity is mastery of simplicity." E. Christopher Zeeman. The site can be searched by keyword.

An excellent starting point for Internet resources in statistics can be found at the Virtual Library for statistics at http://www.stat.ufl.edu/vlib/statistics.html. It has links to statistics programs around the world, statistical archives, links to vendors and to software FAQs.

The American Statistical Association, founded in 1839, has 19,000 members serving the industrial, governmental and academic sectors. It publishes six journals, conducts scientific conferences and is active in developing educational resources. Its home page is at http://www.amstat.org.

The UCLA Statistics Home Page at http://www.stat.ucla.edu offers preprints of articles by UCLA faculty, an introductory course in statistics and biographical information about famous statisticians such as Carl Friedrich Gauss.

Statlib is a system for distributing statistical software, data sets and other information located at http://lib.stat.cmu.edu. You can find many statistical algorithms, material from the statistical computing section of the American Statistical Association and information from the Core Mathematical Library of the National Institute of Standards and Technology, which has Fortran source code for many statistical and numerical procedures.

Discussion lists of interest to mathematicians include
- nyjmth-a@chsibm.albany.edu (New York Journal of Mathematics).
- jcmst-l@vm.cc.purdue.edu (Journal of Computers in Mathematics and Science Teaching).
- stat-l@vm1.mcgill.ca (statistics discussions).

Computer science

As the use of computers has become more pervasive, many colleges and universities now allow introductory courses in computer science to be used to meet general education requirements. Introductory computer science can be divided into four areas—hardware architecture, or the way computer hardware is structured; software architecture and programming, or how to develop programs to get hardware to perform specific tasks; software applications, or how to use commercial or ready-made software such as word processors, spreadsheets and databases; and information systems, which look at the ways computer users can effectively store, retrieve and manipulate information to meet their goals.

Of course the Internet and the World Wide Web themselves are basically huge computer applications developed by computer scientists. Consequently, there is a massive amount of information for computing available—literally thousands of Web sites, and hundreds of discussion lists and news groups ranging from the social uses of computers to advanced problems in parallel processing. Virtually every software and hardware company of any size has its own Web site. Hundreds of computer science departments are online.

For many, the National Center for Supercomputing Applications (http://www.ncsa.uiuc.edu/General/NCSAHome.html) has served as the U.S. headquarters for the Internet. An NSF-funded supercomputer center, the Web browser Mosaic was developed at NCSA. Scientists at the center have developed a broad array of software—including updates of Mosaic, Telnet programs and other Internet tools—for Windows, Macintosh and Unix operating systems. The software directory is at http://www.ncsa.uiuc.edu/SDG/Software/SDGSoftDir.html. The site also has a multimedia collection containing descriptions of more than 10,000 scientific projects that have used the resources of the NSF supercomputing centers.

Another interesting NSF supercomputer center is the Cornell Theory Center at http://www.tc.cornell.edu/. The center has pioneered the use of virtual workshops, workshops that are available to the public through the Web and offer self-paced instructional material about the application of supercomputing technology to computational science. During these courses, registrants have access to CTC consultants and computational time while receiving instructional material online. Virtual workshops are only one of several educational initiatives from the center. Another intriguing offer explores scientific graphics and visualization.

For many years the NSF supercomputing centers formed the backbone of the Internet and facilitated the emergence of virtual communities. The four centers have joined together in some sense in the Metacenter at http://pscinfo.psc.edu/MetaCenter/. The Metacenter is intended to combine the strengths of the constituent supercomputing centers to foster a computational infrastructure for high-performance computing. Its goal is to facilitate collaboration through heterogeneous networks.

A collection of bibliographies in computer science can be found at http://www.pilgrim.umass.edu/pub/misc/bibliographies/index.html and mirrored at http://glimpse.cs.arizona.edu:1994/bib/. The collection consists of 650 locally stored bibliographies with about 390,000 references, primarily to journal articles, conference papers and technical reports. About 12,000 references contain URLs to online versions of the paper and there are 1,100 links to other bibliographic information.

The Artificial Intelligence Laboratory at MIT (http://www.ai.mit.edu/) is a repository of information about artificial intelligence, a provocative branch of computer science. The site includes the archives for relevant mailing lists and news groups, bibliographies, AI FAQs, conferences, bibliographies and the personal home pages of AI researchers. The entire site is searchable.

An excellent starting point for educational material in computer science can be found at http://www.netlib.org/nhse/cs_edu.html. The site includes course materials, tutorials, short courses, books and articles on a wide range of relevant topics.

The Computational Science Educational Project sponsored by the U.S. Department of Education at http://csep1.phy.ornl.gov/csep.html is intended to supply materials to prepare students for research and studies in computational science and computational engineering. A copyrighted electronic textbook is provided with sections surveying available computer tools, computational methods and case studies of the application of computing to specific problems and techniques. The course incorporates public domain software tutorials as well.

A free online directory of computer terms is available at http://wombat.doc.ic.ac.uk and mirrored at http://wagner.Princeton.EDU/foldoc/. It is a searchable directory of acronyms, jargon, programming languages, tools architecture, operating systems and anything else that has to do with computing. It contains 8,611 definitions. Entries are cross-referenced to each other as well as to related resources on the Internet.

Carl and Gary's Visual Basic home page at http://www.apexsc.com/vb/ would like to be the definitive source of information about Microsoft's Visual Basic programming language. There is a section for beginners, news and information, pointers to Usenet Newsgroup archives, and a list of other sites with information about Visual Basic. The VB Info Booth at http://www.buffnet.net/~millard/vblinks.htm is the source for all three FAQs for the comp.lang.basic.visual.* hierarchy in Usenet.

Ziff Davis, recently purchased by Softbank of Japan, is a multibillion-dollar publisher of computer magazines including *PC Magazine, Computer Life, PC Week, Mac Week* and *Computer Shopper.* You can access the magazines at http://www.zdnet.com/home/filters/magrack.html.

The Virtual Museum of Computing includes an eclectic collection of links about the history of computing and online computer exhibitions. Located at http://www.comlab.ox.ac.uk/archive/other/museums/computing.html, it contains sections about the pioneers of computing, a brief history of algebra and computing and material on the work of Charles Babbage as well as links to news groups.

The Ada Project at Yale University http://www.cs.yale.edu/HTML/YALE/CS/HyPlans/tap/tap.html serves as a clearinghouse for information and resources relating to women in computing. It includes information on conferences, projects, discussion groups and grants as well as profiles of notable women in computing and a substantive bibliography of references.

The Internet Computer Index at http://ici.proper.com/ offers an Internet search engine organized by computer platform. It allows people to search for a specific software program for specific computer platforms.

Chapter

15

Chapter

After class: A different grade

College shouldn't be all work and no fun. After class there should be time to relax, enjoy time with friends, listen to music, chill and have a life. And when you graduate, it's time to find a job and join the rat race. Yes, the Internet can help you do that as well. In this chapter you have a brief introduction to all of these activities—and more. The assumption is that with just a little nudging in the right direction, you should be able to use your instincts to find a little network fun here and there.

First, there is a common expression you might already have picked up if you've done much cruising on the Net—*cool sites*. Cool sites lists abound on the network. Of course what may seem cool to your neighbor may be a bore to you. But nonetheless, somebody who has gone to the trouble of compiling and publishing a list of sites he or she thinks are worth visiting for their own sakes probably is worth following to a few sites—until you decide your interests lie elsewhere.

A few cool sites lists are network institutions. One of these is maintained by the authors of Netscape, at http://home.netscape.com/home/whats-cool.html. This site is updated on a regular basis. Another is Glenn Davis' Cool Site of the Day at http://cool.infi.net/. The site contains links to past sites deemed cool by Glenn. Bob Allison keeps a similar site called The Spider's Pick of the Day at http://gagme.wwa.com/~boba/pick.html. A variant on the cool site list is the hot list, and one of these is called Digital Main Street at http://www.main.com/dms/interesting-sites.html. Fred Langa's HotSpot! is another variant at http://www.winmag.com/flanga/hotspots.htm.

Entertainment: music, TV, films and such

If you're looking for entertainment, there's plenty of it on the Internet. You can find television program listings, music, movie and music reviews, and more. Here are a few starting places.

Fig 15-1: Virtual Radio serves digital recordings of popular bands and provides links to the bands' Web pages where they exist.

For music lovers, MTV has a slick Web site at http://www.mtv.com/. You can access MTV news, listings and clips of the top 20 videos of the week, reviews and animations of some of MTV's best-known shows such as "Beavis and Butthead." The graphics are about what could be expected from MTV.

An edgier site for music is http://www.sonicnet.com/, which has links to shows, videos and features such as The Losers' Guide to New York. The strength of the site is its live chat rooms in which people can interact real time with artists like Jim Thirwell of Foetus and hip-hop artist Coolio.

Many bands are setting up their own home pages. For example, The Grateful Dead have a Web site at http://grateful.dead.net. In fact, Virtual Radio at http://www.microserve.net/vradio/ has music samples from many bands and links to their Web sites where appropriate.

To listen to music in real time over the Internet, you may want to download RealAudio at http://www.realaudio.com/. The software allows your browser to play audio on demand without waiting for long file transfers. The site also has feed from National Public Radio and other sources.

Magazine readers should check out Time Warner's Pathfinder service at http://pathfinder.com/. Not only is there access to online versions of all Time Warner magazines including *Sports Illustrated*, *People*, *Time*, *Money*, *Life*, *Fortune* and others, there is also a daily news update, links to many technology magazines, an interesting arts and entertainment section and lots of other goodies.

A must-stop site for movie lovers is the Internet Movie Database at http://www.msstate.edu/Movies/. It is an international volunteer effort to provide free and timely information about movies. It currently covers 54,000 movies and has more than 750,000 entries. Users can search the database by title, star, director, cast, crew, year, quote, plot description or a host of other criteria. The database is updated weekly, quite authoritative and fun to use.

Cinemedia (http://www.afionline.org/CINEMEDIA/CineMedia.home. html) bills itself as the Internet's largest film and media directory. Sponsored by the American Film Institute (AFI), Cinemedia's main divisions include radio, cinema, new media and television. There are also the Resource Room (reference/software), an extensive online magazine rack, and AFI Online. AFI Online provides information about careers in film, workshops, training sessions, and other things involving AFI.

Mr. Showbiz (http://web3.starwave.com/showbiz/) has movie news and reviews, articles about stars, chat and sound-off areas including a Celebrity Lounge where you can visit with various TV and movie stars, and a writers' zone that includes an Ask Mr. Showbiz section. There are also TV, music, theater, and book reviews and a chance to vote for your box office favorites. Other articles about the entertainment world wind their ways through this site.

A new "network" for television

The CBS Television Home Page (http://www.cbs.com/) has links to "The Late Show with David Letterman," including his Top Ten lists and some of his jokes. Network programming guides, CBS Sports, and even a CBS eye screen saver are served. Similarly, NBC maintains the NBC httv site at http://www.nbc.com/. Available are NBC news, sports, links to NBC affiliate sites (with local news) and special NBC online ventures. Of special interest is NBC's HyperChannels, the developing home of several new content areas and channels. The HyperChannels include Peacock Park, a cyberspace amusement park. The park's Souvenir Stand includes free copies of the NBC screen saver.

Fig. 15-2: David Letterman's Top Ten List is part of the CBS site.

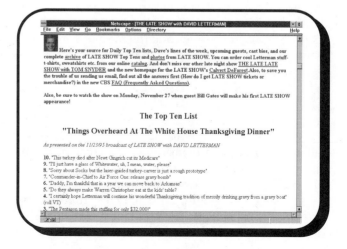

The focus of the ABC Primetime site (http://www.abctelevision.com/) deals primarily with programming on the network. The Web offerings describe special series and upcoming programs. Fox Broadcasting (http://www.eden.com/users/my-html/fox.html) site describes sports, specials, and Fox scheduling and also provides links to the Fox cable network site. The Fox home site is http://www.foxnetwork.com/.

Independent television sites worth investigating include TVNet at http://tvnet.com/TVnet.html; Web O Vision, with links to a wide range of media sites at http://www.webovision.com/cgibin/var/media/index.html; and InfoSearch Broadcasting Links (links to more than 500 broadcasting related sites) at http://www.xmission.com/~insearch/links.html.

The Discovery Channel Online holds forth at http://www.discovery.com/. The online version features originally produced interactive stories with film, music, photography and illustrations. The offerings are updated daily.

Some network games

Do you want to play a quick card game with someone across the state? How about an online chess tournament? Or perhaps you'd like to get secret codes and gaming tips for your video system. All of these are part of the fare served up daily on the Internet.

Want a game of chess? The SportSite GameMaster at http://www.sportsite.com/chess serves up cross-network games. The site also provides a discussion group for visitors to find partners, discuss strategies, or to suggest changes to the game interface.

If you'd like to play cards, http://www.waste.org/~oxymoron/cards/ is the home for a site called Card Games on the Web. Or, you can play Connect Four at http://csugrad.cs.vt.edu/htbin/Connect4.perl; Boggle at http://mundil.cs.mu.oz.au:8004/~dnich/boggle_intro.html; Battleship or tic-tac-toe at http://csugrad.cs.vt.edu/~jfink/gameroom.html.

If your interests incline toward video games, the Video Gaming Hypermag may be to your liking. Accessed at http://www.vgh.com/, it contains tips for beating video games or getting the most out of them. Content is in the form of interactive text, pictures, sounds and movie clips.

Recreation and sports

For sports fans, all the latest scores are available from ESPN at http://espnet.sportszone.com/. Although the objective of this site is to get people to subscribe for $4.95 a month, there is enough free information to make it interesting. If you wish to go online with an NFL star, you can try the NFL on CBS Radio at http://www.cbsradio.com/.

Other commercial sports sites include Sportsline at http://www.sportsline.com/; the Professional Football Server at www.netgen.com/sis/NFL/NFL.html; the Sports Server maintained by Nando.Net, http://

152.52.2.143/SportServer/; the Infohub recreation page at http://www.infohub.com/TRAVEL/ADVENTURE/recreation.html; SGMA Sportlink at http://www.sportsite.com/mac/allshop/sgma/html/sgma_hp.html; and the GNN Sports server at http://gnn.com/gnn/meta/sports/index.html.

MIT keeps a major collection of sports links at http://www.tns.lcs.mit.edu/cgi-bin/sports.

Snoweb (http://www.skiweb.com/) is written for skiers and snowboarders, by skiers and snowboarders.

Virtual relationships

Relationships are an important element of college life. Many people meet each other online by participating in discussion lists (Chapter 3) or news groups (Chapter 7) concerning common interests. Some meet through IRC channels or in MUDs or MOOs (Chapter 8).

And there are also several dating services on the Web, including Blind Date at http://www.america.net/~carbone/blind_date.html and the Computerized Matchmaking Online at http://www.calweb.com/~swifty/match.html. A similar site is called the Singles Web at http://www.ios.com/~hyson/singles/welcome.html. You should first explore these sites to see if you are comfortable using them before posting any personal information.

Perhaps the ultimate in college pen pals is found at http://www.taponline.com/. There is a series of chat boards including one that uses low-cost video conferencing software called CU SEE-ME available over the Internet from Cornell University. Video conferencing allows you to see people in their dorm rooms and interact with them. If you can hook a low-cost video camera to your computer, your image can be transmitted in real time to other folks online as well.

Virtual relationships are nice but so are the flesh-and-blood variety. People who like to look nice when they go out and are interested in fashion can stay up to date through FashionNet at http://www.fashion.net/. With sections for both the industry and the public, Fashion Net has been designed to be a global meeting point. There are links to a wide array of fashion magazines available online, among other services.

Food and grog

The drink of choice for most college students is beer. The Real Beer Page at http://realbeer.com/rbp/ provides a virtual brew tour of microbreweries as well as links to a lot of information about beer and microbreweries. Currently there are links to specialized beer publications, information about beer festivals and beer-oriented gift catalogs.

Hawaii's Best Espresso Company (http://hoohana.aloha.net/~bec/) catalogs exotic coffees with descriptions and pictures. If you like what you find, the online order form automatically calculates the cost.

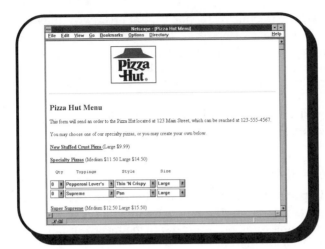

Fig. 15-3: Pizza Hut won't deliver just anywhere yet, but even if you are not in their delivery area, they will let you practice ordering a pizza.

The publishers of *Gourmet* and *Bon Apetit* have created a site replete with recipes, food articles, snappy graphics and wit. Under the title Epicurious, it may be found at http://www.epicurious.com/.

The Electronic Gourmet Guide at http://www.2way.com/food/egg/ is an e-zine devoted to food and cooking. The cooking site has recipes, feature articles, columns, and even a trivia game. On the same server is American Wine on the Web at http://www.2way.com:80/food/wine/.

Want to order a pizza? Try http://www.pizzahut.com/, the home of Pizza Hut. You can choose your crust and toppings online. If you live in the right part of California, Pizza Hut will actually deliver. But even for those who do not live in the right area, the server allows you to build a pizza as a demonstration.

Health matters

The single life can be dangerous these days if you are not responsible. Drinking to excess is dangerous and having a designated driver is important. Sexual practices can also impact your health and well-being. The University of Iowa offers short, concise descriptions of primary sexually transmitted diseases at http://indy.radiology.uiowa.edu:80/Patients/IowaHealthBook/STDs/STDs.html.

For much more extensive information about STDs as well as links to other medically oriented pages, you should look at the home page of The Johns Hopkins University School of Medicine STD Research Group at http://www.jhustd.org/pub/jhustd/. The information there is intended for patient information and education. There are links to the Safer Sex Page, information about contraception and diagnostic and treatment guidelines.

If you still have health-related questions, you can Go Ask Alice, a service sponsored by Columbia University Health Services at http://www.

Fig. 15-4: From the pages of City.Net you can call up images of subway systems and link to a server in France that will actually plot a trip and report times required.

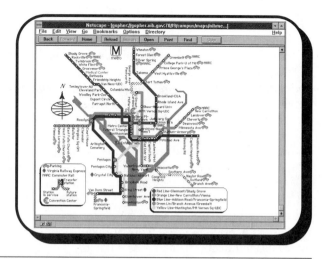

cc.columbia.edu/cu/healthwise/. Each week Alice answers about 10 to 12 questions about health. A typical question involves the efficacy of foam and spermicide as forms of birth control. If you have a pressing health problem or concern, however, do not rely on the Internet. Go to a doctor.

Travel

Many students like to study and travel abroad. The National Registration Center for Study Abroad evaluates foreign language immersion centers and universities and has information online about the top 100 to 200. You can access the site at http://www.execpc.com/~nrcsa/.

Studyabroad.com provides listings of study abroad programs from 625 institutions from 110 countries. The site at http://www.studyabroad.com/ can be searched by country or program and has other fun elements as well.

If you want to stay in the United States but find out more about programs at other colleges, you can investigate CollegeNet at http://www.unival.com/cn/collegenet.html. The site allows you to browse institutions by different criteria, identifying schools that meet your needs.

College students planning to travel outside the United States can find a wealth of information at http://asa.ugl.lib.umich.edu/chdocs/travel/travel-guide.html. This site was created by students at the University of Michigan for people planning trips with the emphasis on economy. Major sections include links to relevant news groups and mailing lists; a section that allows you to learn more about your destination (be it Tahiti or Trenton, New Jersey); and information about how to get there, where to stay, what to wear and what to eat. For the true armchair traveler, there are links to Internet-based travelogues.

The International Student Travel Confederation was founded in 1949 to protect the welfare of the student traveler. It has chapters in countries from

Algeria to Venezuela and can help members obtain discounts at a wide range of locations. Its Web site is at http://www.istc.org/.

People planning to go abroad may wish to first bone up on their knowledge of the United States so they will be prepared to answer questions on their travels. An interesting site is the home page of the United States Information Service of the United States Information Agency at http://www.usia.gov/usis.html. It is like having access to a part of the State Department or at least to a well-informed U.S. embassy somewhere. You can also find information about academic and youth exchange programs and an archive of speeches, news reports and documents ranging back three years.

An outstanding site for general information about cities all over the world is City.Net at http://www.city.net/. City.Net has links to the Subway Navigator, which serves up maps and computes travel times on subway systems in three dozen major cities. The Subway Navigator is accessed at http://metro.jussieu.fr:10001/bin/cities/english.

PC Travel offers links to airline schedules, provides announcements regarding special fares, and facilitates making of flight reservations. The site is accessed at http://www.pctravel.com/.

Finding a job

Before you graduate you should be looking for a job. A number of Internet sites provide servers that allow you to search for jobs. Others permit posting of résumés. If you want to do a search yourself, you should consider such keywords as employment, job, and career for your search terms. Another strategy is to find the Web pages of specific employers. They frequently have sections describing job and career opportunities at the business.

One site worth visiting is The Business Job Finder at Ohio State University, http://www.cob.ohio-state.edu/dept/fin/osujobs.htm. Maintained at the Fisher College of Business, the site caters especially to college students looking for that first real job.

The Fieldwork and Employment Centers page of The Catapult resides at http://www.wm.edu/catapult/jobsall.html. The site offers job listings organized by a number of different methods. JobHunt, at http://rescomp.stanford.edu/jobs/, includes online job listings, résumé banks, reference materials and other metalists. This is a great site for finding many resources.

JobWeb at http://www.jobweb.org/ is sponsored by the National Association of Colleges and Employers. It features job search articles and tips, job listings, and company information for college students, recent graduates and alumni. There are also significant resources for college career services and employment professionals, including career and employment information, training, and services sponsored by the National Association of Colleges and Employers, formerly the College Placement Council. The association is supported by more than 1,600 colleges and universities and many thousands of

Fig. 15-5: From the Comic Strip Page of United Media you can browse a fair stable of comic strips originally prepared for newspapers.

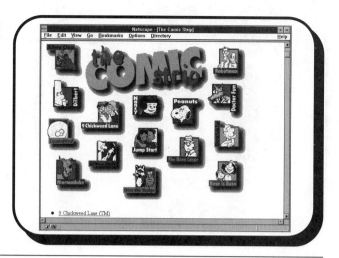

professional employment managers from more than 1,300 organizations throughout the United States.

A major Web site dedicated exclusively to making direct connections between job candidates and employers is maintained by Heart CyberFairs at http://www.career.com/. You can read job announcements and browse job listings by category or by employer. You can also do keyword searches. Another major site, CareerMosaic at http://www.careermosaic.com/, is one of the pioneers of the Internet career sites. A jobs database allows job searching.

From Acorn Career Counseling and Résumé Writing you can get counseling on how to build your résumé—including demonstrations on the most common résumé weaknesses and how to fix them. The site is accessible at http://www1.mhv.net/~acorn/Acorn.html.

The *Chicago Tribune* maintains a site called Career Finder that focuses on employment opportunities in the Midwest. Accessed at http://www.chicago.tribune.com/, the site lists job opportunities, company profiles, feature articles about jobs and job hunting, and more.

Several Gopher sites provide help in the job search. They include: Online Career Center, gopher://occ.com:70/11/occ; Internet Employment Network, gopher://garnet.msen.com:70/11/vendor/napa; and MedSearch America, gopher://garnet.msen.com:70/11/vendor/medsearch.

Hanging out

So much of the Web is good for sheer entertainment value. It can be interesting and rewarding just to surf the Net for a few hours now and then. The possibilities are almost limitless.

Even though the trial of O.J. Simpson ended, the Web site of Court TV at http://www.courttv.com/ is worth visiting again and again. It has updates of

Fig. 15-6: The Pigs in Space sequence from the Muppets is part of the display at The Fabulous Miss Piggy Page.

the famous, infamous and simply interesting trials underway. You can also get a live feed from the cable show itself.

Your interests may lead you to enjoy The Rainforest Action Network at http://www.ran.org/ran/. If you have a browser (such as Netscape) capable of interpreting HTML 3 code and you'd like to visit a different kind of site, try the Offworld Metaplex at http://offworld.wwa.com/.

Worth visiting is chibamoo—the sprawl, a public-access Web server and multimedia MOO. The sprawl is a "collaborative hyperarchical integrated media environment" (chime). The sprawl (http://sensemedia.net/sprawl) is a virtual community where all users have the ability to extend the cyberscape in an unrestricted manner, creating a huge and sprawling virtual reality.

For a taste of the bizarre try Cockroach World at http://www.nj.com/yucky/roaches/.

If you have any interest in cars, The All Things Automotive Directory resides at http://www.webcom.com/~autodir/.

You can browse through some of your favorite comic strips at http://www.unitedmedia.com/comics/.

No after-hours tour of the Net is complete without a visit to The Fabulous Miss Piggy Page, http://www-leland.stanford.edu/~rosesage/Piggy.html.

Glossary

alias — (n.) An e-mail address given as a substitute for a longer, less intuitive address. For example, a college may issue a student the address z4j28@pegasus.acs.ttu.edu. Through an alias utility, the student may get mail addressed simply to McCoy@ttu.edu.

Anonymous FTP — (n.) A process allowing anyone with an FTP (File Transfer Protocol) client to access FTP servers and to get files from that server. Under Anonymous FTP, one typically logs in using the ID "anonymous" and one's e-mail address as the password.

Archie — (n.) A program that searches for files publicly accessible at Anonymous FTP sites.

ASCII — (n.) An acronym for American Standard Code for Information Interchange, ASCII (or ascii) commonly refers to the set of characters used to represent text on paper. Distinguished from binary (q.v.), or computer instruction code, text is sometimes used as a synonym. Most word processors allow you to save files in text or ASCII format. E-mail, by its nature is communication carried in ASCII format. Files that contain only text characters are called ASCII files.

binary — (n., adj.) Computer code, distinguished from text or ASCII. Binary files contain instructions that tell computers and computer peripherals such as printers how to do their work.

Boolean — (adj.) Applied to logic used in searching for information. Boolean logic uses terms such as "AND," "OR" and "NOT" to limit the results of information searches. A search for "defense AND policy NOT nuclear" would produce a list of files and directories containing both defense and policy in them but would eliminate from the list any such files or directories that contain the word nuclear in the title.

client — (n.) Name given to a computer or software program that negotiates with another computer (called a server) the delivery of files and information to the first computer.

code — (n.) Programming instructions that tell computers (and computer peripherals) what to do. (v.) To write computer programs.

cyberspace — (n.) The collective environments or places created by computer networks. Term coined by William Gibson in the book *Neuromancer*.

database — (n.) A body of facts generally focused on a predefined topic, and gathered together in some computer. Organized into meaningful patterns, data (facts) in a database become information.

DNS — (n.) Domain Name Server. A computer that uses a distributed database to translate network address names (like pegasus.acs .ttu.edu) into numeric Internet Protocol addresses (like 129.118.2.52) and vice versa.

domain — (n.) A naming system given to Internet nodes, or subnetworks connected to the Internet. All computers belonging to the subnetwork share the same domain name when they are linked to the Internet. A university typically has several large computers and many lesser computers under one domain. For example, ttu.edu is the domain for Texas Tech University. Host computers sharing that domain include Unix machines named Pegasus and Unicorn and a VAX cluster under the generic name TTACS.

download — (v.) To retrieve a file from a server or any other computer.

e-mail — (n.) Electronic mail. Text messages sent across computer networks to digital mailboxes where they are retrieved and read at the leisure of the recipient.

ethernet — (n.) A type of local area network (LAN) in which computers containing network cards are linked by cabling to other computers with similar cards.

e-zine — (n.) Electronic magazine. Refers to the content and the site of an online magazine product.

FAQ — (n.) Acronym for Frequently Asked Questions, commonly pronounced "fak." A text file that addresses common concerns about a given subject or topic.

file — (n.) A discreet, complete set of digital information containing such things as a text document, program instructions, graphics images, or database resources. (v.) To cause information to be placed in computer storage.

firewall — (n.) A network security barrier designed to protect a local network from being accessed by unauthorized persons via the Internet. Typically, firewalls disable some of the Internet's packet-sharing features to make outside access more difficult.

FTP — (n.) Acronym for File Transfer Protocol, FTP is a set of instructions for moving files across the network from one computer to another. Sometimes employed as if it were a verb (FTP'ed FTP'ing): "I FTP'ed that program from Sunsite."

GIF — (n.) A graphics file specification popularized on the CompuServe network. GIF is an acronym for Graphics Interchange Format. Widely used on the World Wide Web.

Gopher — (n.) An Internet program that organizes information into menu hierarchies. Gopher puts a uniform interface on network navigation, providing links to varied network resources scattered throughout the world and providing access to search tools for finding that information. Created at the University of Minnesota, where the school mascot is the Golden Gopher. (v.) To use a Gopher client to access network resources.

Gopher hole — (n.) Nickname given to a Gopher site and the collection of resources accessible from the site. Also called a burrow.

GopherSpace — (n.) Aggregate of all resources available worldwide through Gopher servers. The cyberspace places occupied by Gopher servers and their resources.

home page — (n.) Applied to http documents on the World Wide Web. Originally used to describe the page first loaded by a World Wide Web client program (browser) when it starts up. Has come to refer to the top page (welcome, or index page) of Web sites and to personal pages placed on Web servers by many individuals.

host — (n.) A computer (system) offering network access, disk storage space and client software to its account holders. Typically, the host is the computer where a person's electronic mail is received, stored and processed. See also "client" and "site."

HTML — (n.) HyperText Markup Language, an ASCII-based scripting language used to create documents served on the World Wide Web.

HTTP — (n.) HyperText Transfer Protocol, the network data communications specification used on the World Wide Web.

hypertext — (n.) A means of linking information.

list — (n.) In e-mail, all the people subscribed to a discussion group.

Listproc — (n.) A program for managing an e-mail discussion list. Very much like ListServ software.

ListServ — (n.) Software for managing an e-mail discussion list. ListServ takes messages sent to a list and reflects those messages out to all who are subscribed. ListServ is also used to designate the machine on which the software resides.

lurk — (v.) To read, without posting, messages to a news group or an e-mail discussion list. Recommended behavior for people new to a list or group.

mirror — (n.) A computer site that provides the same resources as another distant one. Set up to redirect network traffic away from especially popular, busy sites.

newbie — (n.) Term applied to a person new to a network or any of its online communities.

news group — (n.) A discussion forum within the Usenet news system.

node — (n.) Term applied to a host computer (or computer system) for a subnetwork (LAN or WAN). The node is assigned a domain name and all other computers that are part of the system share that domain name.

packet — (n.) A discrete block of data carried over a network. The packet contains all or part of a text message (or a binary file), the addresses of the originating and destination computers, message assembly instructions, and error control information.

PC — (n.) Personal Computer. In this book it may mean a Macintosh or an IBM compatible or any other machine that is yours to work with and on which you may run programs of your choosing.

PPP — (n.) Point to Point Protocol. A set of communications parameters that allows a computer to use TCP/IP over a standard-voice telephone line and a high-speed modem. PPP gives to the computer the functionality of one directly connected to the Internet through a network card and cable.

program — (n.) A set of instructions written in binary code, telling a computer how to perform certain tasks. (v.) The act of writing such instructions.

protocol — (n.) A set of rules and procedures by which computers communicate.

server — (n.) A machine on which resides software designed to deliver information across a network in a manner specifically recognized by a client. Also describes the software that delivers the information.

SIG — (n.) Acronym for Special Interest Group, a virtual community of people who meet online to exchange information on a clearly defined topic of interest.

SLIP — (n.) Acronym for Serial Line Internet Protocol. A set of communications parameters that allows a computer to use TCP/IP over a standard-voice telephone line and a high-speed modem. SLIP gives to the computer the functionality of one directly connected to the Internet through a network card and cable.

string — (n.) A series of characters tied together without interruption. A unique sequence of characters used to locate specific text is called a search string.

sysop — (n.) The systems operator, usually the owner of a computer bulletin board. Sometimes used to identify the person who moderates a SIG on a larger system such as CompuServe or America Online.

system prompt — (n.) A character or string of characters that tell the computer user in a command line environment that the machine is waiting for a new command and that all non-system programs have terminated. In DOS, the system prompt is typically a "C:>"; in UNIX it often is "%"; in VMS it frequently is "$".

TCP/IP — (n.) Acronym for Transmission Control Protocol/Internet Protocol, the set of communications rules by which computers connected to the Internet talk to each other.

terminal — (n.) A computer workstation composed of a monitor (VDT) for viewing computer output and a keyboard for talking to the computer or network. One of the most universally accepted terminals is the DEC VT 100. Most personal computer communications programs allow the computer to emulate terminals such as VT 100s so that the network host or server can understand what you type at your computer.

username — (n.) A name generally assigned to an account holder by a system administrator. The username is associated with a password in providing access to network computing resources.

virtual — (adj.) Having the quality of existing in effect but not in reality. Network news groups are said to be *virtual communities* because they bring together many people who are united by common interests and goals.

virtual community — (n.) A term used to describe the collective presence of people who come together in an online setting to chat or exchange information on a topic of mutual interest. Used by Howard Rheingold as a title to a book about life on computer networks.

Index